Baking Country Breads and Pastries

Rosemary Wadey

Baking Country Breads and Pastries

David & Charles

Newton Abbot   London   North Pomfret (Vt)

Line drawings by Denys Baker

Colour photographs by John Lee

British Library Cataloguing in Publication Data
Wadey, Rosemary
    Baking country breads and pastries.
    1. Bread
    2. Pastry
    I. Title
    641.8'15   TX769

        ISBN 0 7153 7860 0

Printed in Great Britain
by
Redwood Burn Ltd., Trowbridge & Esher
for David & Charles (Publishers) Limited
Brunel House Newton Abbot Devon

Published in the United States of America
by David & Charles Inc
North Pomfret Vermont 05053 USA

Contents

6 Pastry Making   119

7 Savoury Pies & Pastries   131

8 Sweet Pastries   157

What Could Go Wrong?   181

Index   185

Introduction

British food is uncomplicated and satisfying, many of the traditional recipes having been passed down through the generations to the present day with only subtle changes. The food is basically substantial, with such traditional dishes as Steak and Kidney Pudding, Cornish Pasties and the various home-baked breads, scones and teacakes created to satisfy healthy appetites resulting from working in the fresh air – and a climate frequently damp and chilly.

Traditional foods have developed in different parts of the country, regions formed mainly by geography and the employment of the inhabitants. In the Highlands of Scotland, for example, the barren landscape made it difficult to produce crops of a high yield and sufficient food for animals; industry was not developed there, and clan rivalry caused its own problems. An abundance of fish and game was there for the taking, but the inclination to catch it was small because of the poor condition of the people. There was plenty of whisky – and oatmeal, which stored well over a long period and became the mainstay of the local diet. The Highlanders (except for the clan chiefs, who lived royally in comparison) did not make the most of what they had and their physique suffered. The Lowlanders, on the other hand, had plenty of good land suitable for growing fruit and vegetables and grazing cattle and other animals, and consequently they lived well. They could afford the ingredients needed for baking the scones, breads and buns for which they are world-famous. In fact today, the Scots are still thought to have that 'special touch' necessary for baking light-textured pastries and teatime fare.

Wales, up to the time of the Industrial Revolution, was also isolated, though not to the degree that afflicted the Scottish Highlands, and there were no clan problems. The mountains provided grazing for sheep, most farms or habitations had a small plot of land, and there was plenty of natural food in the form of fish and game; although there was poverty in places, the people did not starve. With the development of the South Wales coal mines came more employment and as a result people were eager to buy the local produce. As with all Celtic areas, the griddle or bakestone (as it is called in Wales) was a feature of much of the cooking, and all types of scones and breads were cooked on it over an open fire, often using recipes for types of pancakes or using oatmeal which was probably the most popular cereal. The leek, emblem of Wales, features widely in the native recipes, as do lamb, salmon and trout, all of which are produced locally and excellent they are!

The Irish had a milder climate than the Highlanders and certain crops could flourish in spite of boggy, acid soil. Plots of land were usually small because of the Irish system of land tenure, which encouraged landlords continually to divide up the holdings and thus collect more rent. However, potatoes flourished well enough, needing only a small amount of space to yield a reasonable return, and were therefore the mainstay of Irish cooking, together with buttermilk, cabbage and bacon. The traditional recipes for scones, bread, potato dishes and others have largely survived; many of the former are still baked on the griddle over an open peat fire, the smell of which permeates the food, giving it its own particular delicious taste.

England has its own regions, but not so markedly for, although the countryside changes

7

from North to South, communications have been better and the people on the whole more prosperous. In the North, the griddle is still used for the famous griddle cakes and scones – some recipes are similar to the Scottish and Welsh ones – and the more inexpensive foods have remained popular, often being cooked quickly in one pot on the range to produce a substantial meal to fortify hardworking husbands and children against biting cold and harsh winds. The Singing Hinny or other griddle scones and cakes appear frequently on the traditional high-tea table, still warm and oozing with butter, just begging to be eaten. The West Country has its specialities too, often including local clotted cream or fish; apples are traditionally popular there, probably because cider-apples were grown in quantity and the tart apple-pulp discarded after the cider pressing could be incorporated into all sorts of savoury recipes – such as the Pork and Apple or Squab Pies. Saffron was grown and used in Cornwall to flavour and colour cakes and buns; pilchards caught locally were baked whole with their heads protruding from a pastry crust for Stargazey Pie; and scalded cream was lavishly spread on scones and yeasted 'splits' as part of a traditional tea.

London saw most of the class differences, and has long had to bring in most of its food from elsewhere, so recipes developed to suit all tastes. The muffin-man and crumpet-seller would walk the streets selling their wares, as did the pieman. The Old Chelsea Bun House in Pimlico produced buns for people from all walks of life, from royalty downwards. Eel and pie shops were very much part of Cockney London.

As travel became easier it was discovered that recipes thought to be peculiar to a specific area were being followed, more or less, under different names elsewhere; how this happened has been a matter of great interest.

Our Daily Bread

Bread is a part of mankind's way of life. Each country produces its own particular type of bread, most often using grain grown locally or the most easily available variety of flour.

Britain has always grown a certain amount of grain suitable for milling for bread flour, but a substantial proportion has been imported. During the eighteenth century and earlier, wheat was not commonly grown except in the South of England, and a high proportion of that was exported to Europe; it was in any case too expensive for the general public to buy. The main cereals grown throughout the country were rye, barley and oats, which were consequently used for bread-making but made loaves very different from those most popular today. The large quantities of grain imported for bread flour have obviously influenced the breads baked and the flavours which have come to be preferred, both in the past and now.

Home baking is a fascinating subject and has become increasingly popular over the last few years, particularly with the reaction against factory-made bread, the beginning of the health food era – and all the specialised shops it created – and the need to be self-sufficient during bakery workers' strikes. People who were at first rather apprehensive about making bread for themselves have found it is a perfectly practical thing to do, and now many of us bake bread either once a week or every other week, storing enough in a deep-freeze to keep the family supplied until the next baking day arrives – and thoroughly enjoying both the job and the bread! Some people find the process of kneading removes tensions and gives time to think out problems, leaving one relaxed and ready to face the week afresh.

Pastries, Pies and Pasties

The art of pastry making has been passed from mother to daughter for centuries, particularly in country areas. But not everyone has a good light touch or produces a really good pastry. The 'feel' of a correctly made pastry must be learnt, for the proportion of water added will make or mar: it will be difficult to roll out if too dry, too short or too sticky. Fingertips only should be used for rubbing in, and pastry – even the flaked pastries – needs the minimum amount of careful handling. However, once this art has been mastered its uses are unlimited.

Pies of one sort or another have been baked for centuries; indeed raised pies were always a feature of Elizabethan banquets and today they are still baked for their splendid appearance as well as their taste. Many types of fruit are enhanced by the addition of a pastry crust, be it flaky or shortcrust, and in times gone by a pastry crust, with sweet or savoury filling, acted as a 'filler' when ingredients were expensive or difficult to obtain. Pasties were created to provide a substantial and easily carried packed lunch: an interesting filling enclosed in pastry not only made good eating, but could be simply wrapped in the traditional red-and-white-spotted handkerchief and carried in the pocket.

The old saying that 'the way to a man's heart is through his stomach' rings true even these days; for who can resist a succulent Steak and Kidney Pie, traditional Apple Pie, sticky Treacle Tart or extravagantly filled Cream Slice – not many, I believe. And for those who insist that British cooking is plain and sometimes uninteresting, I hope this book will show that the country breads and teatime fare, the sweet and savoury pastries, are as good as any cooking in the world.

Yeast Cookery

Some people have a mild fear of yeast cookery and all it entails; but it is really very simple and easy once you remember that yeast is a living plant and requires understanding and care. Unlike the other raising agents it is alive and needs gentle warmth, food and liquid. Given these conditions, the yeast grows rapidly giving off a harmless and tasteless gas called carbon dioxide. This causes bubbles which in turn make the dough rise, and these trapped bubbles are then baked into the bread to give the characteristic light airiness to the loaf. The yeast also produces alcohol during rising and it is this which when driven off during baking, gives a delicious smell, and also the special taste of freshly baked bread.

Yeast is a traditional raising agent, universally used until about a hundred years ago when the chemical raising agents were introduced and became popular. However, it is very versatile and can be used for a wide range of recipes apart from the basic breads, rolls and buns. For instance, puddings, batters and pastry can also be made with yeast and the variety of fruited or spiced buns, cakes and tealoaves is unlimited. Yeast is a good source of the B vitamins which are an essential part of all diets.

Basic Rules

Yeast

There are two types of yeast which can be used for bread-making and both are readily available. Do not use brewer's yeast as this is not suitable for bread-making.

Fresh yeast is the yeast most often used by bakers and is sometimes also called compressed or moist yeast. It is putty coloured, smooth textured and moist, and will cut easily with a knife; it should smell fresh and slightly fruity like wine. If the yeast is crumbly, dark or spotty, it is stale and not suitable for use. Fresh yeast is available in health food shops and some baker's shops, but is becoming more difficult to obtain in some areas. It will stay fresh for up to 2–3 weeks if properly stored in a loosely tied polythene bag in the refrigerator; or for 4–5 days in a cool place. It will also freeze for about 6 months if wrapped first in cling film or polythene and then foil; package it in usable amounts, such as 15g (½oz) or 25g (1oz), for once thawed it needs to be used quickly. Fresh yeast is simply blended with the warm liquid and added to the dry ingredients.

Dried yeast consists of small granules of compacted yeast and is sold in tins or packets. It will keep for up to 6 months after opening, if put in an airtight container. Instructions for activating the yeast and quantities required are given on the tin or packet. It should either be reconstituted in warm liquid with a little sugar added and be left in a warm place until the granules have dissolved and the liquid froths up – this usually takes 10–20 minutes; or it can be mixed into a flour, sugar and milk and/or water batter which should also be left in a warm place until it froths up, but will take 20–30 minutes – this method is more often used for richer doughs. If the liquid does not froth up properly then the yeast must

be stale and should be discarded, for it will not give the required rise to the dough. It is widely available from chemists, supermarkets, grocers, health food shops, etc.

The quantities of yeast required vary with different types of dough, but if using dried yeast and the recipe states only a quantity for fresh, then use half as much. For example, 25g (1oz) fresh yeast = 15g (½oz) or 1 tablespoon dried yeast plus 1 teaspoon sugar (caster, or as you prefer). For plain bread doughs, ie without extra fat added, allow: 15g (½oz) fresh or 1½ teaspoons dried yeast and 1 teaspoon sugar to 450–675g (1–1½lb) white flour; and 25g (1oz) fresh or 1 tablespoon dried yeast and 1 teaspoon sugar to 1·4kg (3lb) flour.

Wholemeal flour requires, on average, a higher proportion of yeast, say double the quantities given above. Enriched recipes which contain extra fat, sugar, eggs and/or fruit retard the growth of the yeast and therefore extra is required (see the individual recipes).

Flour

A strong, plain flour, called bread flour by bakers, should be used to achieve the best results. It has a higher gluten content than ordinary plain household flour, allowing more absorption of liquid and thus giving a greater volume and lighter bread. A soft or household flour absorbs more fat but less liquid, giving a smaller volume and a closer, shorter texture; however, this type of flour is sometimes used for rich, fancy breads. Special bread flours are now widely available in white, 100 per cent wholewheat, and wheatmeal from many supermarkets, and can also be obtained along with other speciality bread flours from health food shops. The speciality flours such as compost-grown, granary meal, rye, etc, can all be used in bread-making – either alone or mixed with white flour – to give variety to bread, but they are more expensive than the basic flours. Salt is added to flour to give flavour to all yeasted food, and bread baked without sufficient salt is tasteless. Too much salt, however, can kill the yeast.

Liquid

Where possible the liquid should be added all at once to the dry ingredients – even if this is done gradually to make sure the correct consistency is obtained – so that the dough is mixed evenly. Extra flour can be added easily if the dough is too sticky, but adding extra liquid usually causes lumps and unevenness which are difficult to remove. The liquid is usually water, milk or a mixture of the two, but beaten eggs and melted fat sometimes count for part of the liquid content. The liquid, or part of it, is used to dissolve the yeast and is then added to the dry ingredients with any that remains. Milk adds extra food value and strengthens the dough, and the fat content in the milk gives the bread better keeping qualities. It also gives a closer crumb and softer-textured crust. Approximately 300ml (½pint) liquid is required for each 450g (1lb) strong flour.

Fat

A small amount of fat added to plain mixtures helps to keep the bread moist, but is not essential. It is usually rubbed into the dry ingredients, and is normally lard but can also be butter or margarine. With richer mixtures, more fat is required; it is often melted or sometimes softened and added with the other liquid ingredients, but it can be rubbed in. It can also be put on to the rolled-out dough in flakes or spread in a softened form – the dough is then folded up and rolled out several times, as with puff and flaky pastry, to incorporate it evenly. This method gives extra crispness and lightness by trapping the air in two ways as is necessary in Croissants and Yeasted Pastries. Oil can be used in place of fat in some recipes.

Warmth

All yeast mixtures need warmth at least at some stage. For the best results the bowl, flour and liquid should all be warmed before starting. Liquids must be warm (between 37–43°C/98–110°F) for if too cool the yeast will take a very long time to activate; too much heat, or liquid that is too hot, will quickly kill the yeast. Rising dough should be put in a *warm* place not a hot one. The exceptions are the flaked doughs such as Croissants and Yeasted (Danish) Pastries which require chilling between the rolling and folding processes but, once shaped, need warmth for proving prior to baking.

Kneading

All doughs must be kneaded after mixing to strengthen and develop the gluten in order to give a good rise and even texture to the baked loaf. Knead by folding the dough towards you, then push it down and away, using the palms of your hands. Give the dough a quarter turn and continue the kneading process, developing a rocking action. Continue for about 10 minutes until the dough feels firm and elastic and is no longer sticky. It should be kneaded on a lightly floured surface using as little extra flour as possible. A large electric mixer can be used if the maker's instructions recommend it for kneading, but if there is no mention of dough then you will probably break the machine if you try to use it. Use a dough hook and switch on at the slowest speed for 3–4 minutes; follow the instructions for the maximum amount the mixer can handle as overloading will damage the machine.

Rising

All yeast doughs must rise at least once before baking. After kneading, the dough should be shaped into a ball and put into a large oiled polythene bag which is loosely tied at the neck, or a lightly greased sauce-pan, casserole, bowl or plastic storage container, etc. There must be enough space for the dough to at least double in size. The dough must be kept covered to prevent a skin forming; a damp cloth or sheet of oiled polythene are best for covering. Some rich and soft doughs are simply beaten and left to rise in a covered bowl.

Rising times vary with temperature, but the dough needs time to rise to double its size and should spring back when lightly pressed with a floured finger. There are several ways of rising the dough and although a slower rise gives the best volume and results, choose whichever fits in best with your daily routine. If using a refrigerator rise, remember that the dough must be allowed to return to room temperature before shaping – this usually takes about an hour. On average, allow: ¾–1 hour in a warm place; 2 hours at room temperature; up to 12 hours in a cold room or larder; or up to 24 hours in the refrigerator.

Surplus dough can be stored in a closed polythene bag or container for up to 2 days in the refrigerator.

Knocking Back

This process is simply a short second kneading of the dough to knock out the air bubbles and make it smooth and even, ready for shaping. It should only take about 1–2 minutes. Do not knead in any more flour than is necessary at this stage for it will spoil the colour of the crust of the baked loaf.

Shaping and Proving

The dough is now ready for shaping. Follow the recipe instructions for whatever type of bread, rolls, cake, etc, you are making. The shaped dough then requires a second rising (or proving as it is called). Put the loaf tins, cake tins or baking sheets into large oiled polythene bags or lay a sheet of oiled poly-thene loosely over them to prevent a skin forming; put in a warm place until the dough has doubled in size again and springs back when lightly pressed with a floured finger. Remove the polythene before baking.

Baking

Loaves, rolls or cakes can be glazed before baking or left plain; beaten egg, milk, salted water or a dredging of flour each give different finishes. They should be baked in the centre of the oven which should be moderately hot to very hot (190–230°C/375–450°F, Gas Mark 5–8) with the plain doughs requiring the hottest temperature and the richer ones a cooler oven. A cooked loaf should shrink slightly from the sides of the tin and the base should sound hollow when tapped with the knuckles. Turn out and cool on wire racks. A pan of hot water in the bottom of the oven helps give the steamy atmosphere found in commercial bakers' ovens and often bakes a better loaf, but is by no means essential.

Freezing

Many breads, rolls, buns, yeast cakes, etc, will freeze satisfactorily. They should be cooled quickly, wrapped tightly in foil or heavyweight polythene and frozen at once. Storage times vary from 1–2 months for very rich or spicy recipes, to up to 6 months for plainer varieties. See recipes for suggested storage times. Thaw out completely before use.

Freezing Raw Bread Dough
Unrisen dough This can be frozen after kneading. Form into a ball, place in a greased polythene bag and freeze immediately. Store plain doughs for up to 2 months, enriched doughs for up to 5 weeks. To thaw, tie bag loosely to allow for rising and leave for 5–6 hours at room temperature, or overnight in the refrigerator. Knock back and continue as usual.

Risen dough After knocking back shape the firm dough into a ball, place in a greased polythene bag and freeze immediately. Store for up to 4 weeks for brown and white doughs. Thaw as for unrisen dough.

Important
Follow either the metric quantities or the imperial quantities in the recipes – *never mix them*. Each recipe has been tested and balanced using each type of measurement.

Family Breads

Home-baked bread always has that rather special taste and tantalising smell, particularly when it emerges from the oven hot and crusty. The baker's skill is age-old, dating back as far as can be remembered, for people all over the world have always baked some type of bread. Methods and skills have been passed down through the generations and some of today's master bakers can trace their trade way back through their families. But you don't need to be a master baker to achieve a skill in bread baking; indeed you simply need a little time, patience, practice and the basic know-how, and very quickly the bread-baking 'bug' will be caught.

There are a few simple rules as already described, and provided these are adhered to, baking your own bread will soon become an enjoyable habit and the trips to a baker's shop less and less frequent. Remember that yeast is a living plant, unlike other raising agents, and it needs food, moisture and gentle warmth to work; the first two being provided by the flour and liquid necessary for the bread, with the warmth coming from the temperature of the liquid and the room where the rising is done. Time is necessary for mixing and kneading but the dough can then be put to rise at different temperatures for varying lengths of time to suit yourself and fit in with your everyday routine, and whilst rising it can be almost forgotten. Only when doubled in size does it require further attention, prior to the proving and baking.

These 'Family Breads' recipes cover the basic everyday types of bread you might need to make (the fancy or sweet teatime favourites appear in other sections of the book). They include white and wholemeal breads; an enriched dough which has a much closer texture and soft crust; milk bread with extra fat added to help keep the loaf moist for longer; brown country bread made from a mixture of white flour for lightness and brown flour for extra flavour; and short-time breads which cut out the long first rising, replacing it with a short rest and the addition of ascorbic acid which together produce the same results as the normal procedure but in much less time. Some of the doughs are used later on as the basis of richer and fruited dough recipes.

Basic White Bread

675g (1½lb) strong white flour

2 level teaspoons salt

15g (½oz) lard

15g (½oz) fresh yeast, or
  1½ level teaspoons dried yeast and 1 level teaspoon caster sugar

450ml (¾pt) warm water (43°C/110°F)

Grease either one 900g (2lb) loaf tin or two 450g (1lb) tins, or two to three baking sheets (for making rolls). Sift the flour and salt into a bowl and rub in the lard. Blend the fresh yeast with the water; for dried yeast, dissolve the sugar in the water, sprinkle the yeast on top and leave in a warm place until frothy – about 10 minutes.

Add the yeast liquid to the dry ingredients all at once and mix to form a firm dough, using a palette knife or fork. Add a little extra flour if necessary, until the dough leaves the sides of the bowl clean.

Kneading: the dough should be firm but not too stiff. Turn on to a lightly floured surface and knead thoroughly until the dough is smooth and elastic and no longer sticky. To do this, hold the dough in front of you, fold it towards you, and punch it down and away using the palms of your hands, then give it a quarter-turn; fold it towards you again, and continue in this way for about 10 minutes. Shape the dough into a ball. The dough can be mixed and kneaded in a large electric mixer fitted with a dough hook – allow 3–4 minutes on the slowest

BASIC WHITE BREAD

1 Sift in the flour, salt and rub in lard

add yeast liquid

2 Knead dough with the palms, punching it down and away. Put into a lightly oiled polythene bag

3 Knocking back. Remove from oiled bag. Flatten with knuckles to knock out any air bubbles

avoid adding too much extra flour

4 Knead and stretch dough to same width as tin

then fold over three times, turn over

then in an oiled poly-thene bag

and place in tin

speed and check with the manufacturer's instructions on suggested maximum load.

Rising: put the dough into a large lightly oiled polythene bag and tie loosely at the top; this will prevent a skin forming on the dough. Put it to rise until it has doubled in size and springs back when lightly pressed with a floured finger.

Quick rise – 45–60 minutes in a warm place.
Slower rise – about 2 hours at room temperature.
Overnight rise – up to 12 hours in a cold larder.
Refrigerator rise – up to 24 hours in the refrigerator.
A slow rise is said to give the best results but use whichever fits in best with your routine. Remember that refrigerated dough needs to be left to 'come to' again at room temperature for about an hour.

Knocking Back: remove the dough from the bag to a very lightly floured surface and flatten with the knuckles to knock out the air bubbles, then knead for about 2 minutes until smooth and even again. Too much extra flour kneaded in at this stage will spoil the texture and colour of the crust of the baked bread. Knocking back the dough can be done in a large electric mixer fitted with a dough hook, when it will take 1–2 minutes.

Shaping and Proving: for a large loaf, knead and stretch the dough to make an oblong shape the same width as the tin and three times as long; then fold it into three and turn it over so that the join is underneath. Tuck in the ends, smooth the top and place it in the large greased loaf tin. For two 450g (1lb) loaves, divide the dough in half and shape each piece as for the large loaf. For rolls, divide the dough into 50g (2oz) pieces, shape as described on page 34 and place well apart on greased baking sheets. Put the tins or baking sheets inside large oiled polythene bags and put to rise again (prove) in a warm place for 45–60 minutes or until the dough reaches the tops of the tins. Rolls should double in size in about 20 minutes.

Baking: remove the tins or baking sheets from the polythene and bake in a very hot oven (230°C/450°F, Gas Mark 8), allowing 35–40 minutes for the large loaf, about 30 minutes for smaller loaves and 15–20 minutes for rolls. Loaves should be well risen, golden brown and just beginning to shrink slightly from the edges of the tin; their bases should sound hollow when tapped.

Glazes
1. Beaten egg – either beat a whole egg with 2 teaspoons water or just the egg yolk with 1 teaspoon water.
2. Salted water – dissolve 1 tablespoon salt in 6 tablespoons water and use when cold.
3. Use milk or top of the milk.

Shaping Loaves

Basic white bread dough and other risen plain bread doughs can be shaped in numerous ways before baking; some shapes need tins whilst others are put straight on to greased baking sheets. Even the traditional sandwich loaf can have a variety of cuts on top and different glazes (see above) to add interest. All the loaves baked without tins give the crusty outside favoured by many people.

Coburg

Shape half the recipe quantity of risen basic dough into a round ball. This is done by rolling the dough in a circular movement with the palm of your hand and gradually easing the pressure to give a smooth round ball – it takes practice to perfect. Place on a greased baking sheet and if liked, brush all

Types of loaf: (left to right) *Coburg; Farmhouse; Bloomer;* (foreground) *Crinkled or Ribbed*

over with milk or beaten egg. Using a sharp knife, cut a cross on top of the loaf taking it from side to side. Place in a large oiled polythene bag or cover with oiled polythene and put to prove in a warm place until doubled in size. Remove polythene, brush again with milk or egg and bake in a very hot oven (230°C/450°F, Gas Mark 8) for 30–40 minutes until golden brown. Cool on a wire rack.

A coburg loaf can also be baked in a sandwich tin, in which case it is called a pan coburg; the top part of the loaf with the cross on it spreads out during cooking, making it look rather like a cauliflower or the top of a hot soufflé.

Cob

The plain round loaf so often bought because of its crustiness is easy to bake yourself. It originated as a round brown loaf but now can be made from either brown or white dough. It can be left unglazed or be brushed with milk, beaten egg or salted water for different finishes to the crust. Cracked wheat, oatmeal or crushed corn-flakes are often sprinkled on brown cobs whilst the white counterparts can be sprinkled with poppy or sesame seeds. Use half the recipe quantity of risen basic white dough for each loaf and shape, prove and bake as for a coburg loaf. Although cuts are not usual, some people prefer to score the top once or twice just before baking.

College

Eliza Acton called this checkerboard-topped bread a college loaf but it is sometimes known as a porcupine. Shape half the recipe quantity of risen basic white dough as for a coburg loaf, place on a greased baking sheet, flatten slightly and glaze if liked. With a sharp knife make fairly deep cuts across the top of the loaf at 2·5cm (1in) intervals, then give the loaf a quarter turn and make another series of cuts at right angles to the first ones to give a checkerboard effect. Put to prove, when the checkerboard effect will open out, and then bake as for a coburg loaf. This gives a very crusty and unusual topping to the loaf.

Cottage

This is a crusty, traditional round loaf which is often used as the baker's own emblem. Use one recipe quantity of risen basic white dough for a large loaf or divide in half to make two smaller ones. Remove one-third of the dough for the topknot, then shape both pieces into round balls as for coburg loaves. Place the larger piece on a greased baking sheet and flatten it slightly with the palm of your hand. Damp the base of the topknot and position it centrally on top of the large ball of dough; secure it by pushing your first finger and thumb right through the centre of the loaf to the base, taking care to keep the topknot central. Brush with beaten egg or salted water, cover loosely with oiled polythene and put to prove in a warm place until doubled in size. Remove polythene and bake in a very hot oven (230°C/450°F, Gas Mark 8) for 30–40 minutes.

For a fancy notched cottage loaf, after shaping make slashes all round the lower part of the loaf and then round the topknot. Prove and bake as above.

Bloomer

This is sometimes known in the bakery as a London bloomer. It is a long fat baton-shaped loaf with diagonal slashes along the top. It is usually crusty and can be sprinkled with poppy or sesame seeds. Use one recipe quantity of risen basic white dough for a large loaf or divide in half for smaller ones. Shape each piece into an even thickness baton by rolling the dough backwards and forwards with the palms of both hands. Tuck the ends underneath and place on a greased baking sheet. If liked, brush with milk, beaten egg or salted water, then cover with oiled polythene and put to prove until doubled in size. Remove polythene, cut diagonal slashes all along the top of the loaf with a very sharp knife and bake in a very hot oven (230°C/450°F, Gas Mark 8) for 30–40 minutes, depending on size. Cool on a wire rack.

Bloomer loaves can also be 'batch' baked by putting the pieces of shaped dough close to each other on a baking sheet; during proving and baking they join up. Baked loaves are pulled apart to reveal soft crustless sides but still have the favoured crusty top.

Plait

This attractive method of shaping dough is suitable for basic doughs or enriched doughs and can be used for varying sized loaves. The loaf can be baked plain or glazed with milk, beaten egg or salted water and sprinkled with poppy or sesame seeds for variety. Divide the required amount of risen bread dough into 3 equal pieces and, with the palms of the hands, roll them into fairly thin, even sausage shapes of equal length. (For thicker plaits roll the dough into thick sausage shapes.) Place the 3 pieces of dough next to each other straight in front of you. Beginning in the centre, plait the pieces evenly towards you, pinching the ends together. Carefully turn the plait completely over and away from you so that the unplaited strands face you. Complete the plaiting, secure the ends by pinching together and place the loaf on a greased baking sheet. Prove and then bake in a very hot oven (230°C/450°F, Gas

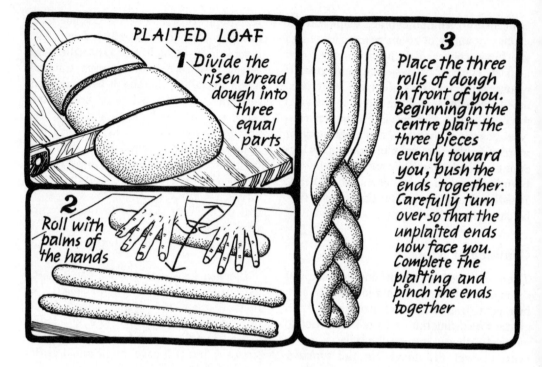

PLAITED LOAF

1 Divide the risen bread dough into three equal parts

2 Roll with palms of the hands

3 Place the three rolls of dough in front of you. Beginning in the centre plait the three pieces evenly toward you, push the ends together. Carefully turn over so that the unplaited ends now face you. Complete the plaiting and pinch the ends together

Mark 8) for 20–35 minutes, depending on size.

Crescent

This is an attractive loaf but it takes a little practice to get it really even. Use half the recipe quantity of risen white bread dough and roll it out on a floured surface to an oval shape. Leave to rest for 5 minutes, then beginning at a wide edge, roll the dough up tightly to form a sausage, taking care to keep the middle very tight or the sausage will 'bulge'. Bend into a crescent shape and put on to a greased baking sheet. Prove and then bake as for plaited bread for about 25 minutes.

Split Tin

This is the normal tin loaf, shaped and put into the tin and baked as described under Basic White Bread (see page 22). However, for variety and increased crustiness, the top of the loaf is often slashed so that during

proving and baking the inside dough rises up and produces a secondary crust. Whereas with crusty bread the cuts are usually made after the proving and immediately prior to baking, the split tin loaves are usually cut about 10 minutes after the loaf has been put into the tin and before it has risen very much, thus the cut spreads as the dough continues to rise.

Batch Tin

Similar to split tin loaves with the same cuts on top but several are shaped and put into a large, wide, deep tin, fairly close together so that they join up during proving and baking and when cold are pulled apart to reveal soft crustless sides.

Farmhouse

Traditionally, this was a loaf made in a wider and shallower tin than the tin or sandwich loaf and was not made with white dough as is usual today. At the end of the last century 'farmhouse' bread was specially made from a light brown wheatmeal flour which was believed to be nutritious – at least in comparison with the whiter-than-white bread which was becoming more and more popular, even though it caused worries about its lack of 'natural properties'. Nowadays it is usually a white loaf and is more often than not cut along the top as for a split tin, or deeply slashed as for a bloomer. Farmhouse bread is also batch baked, using a shallower and even wider tin than for the batch tin loaves.

Crinkled or Ribbed

These are baked in a special double cylindrical mould and the resulting loaf has ridges marked all round it which can be used as guides for cutting thin slices of bread. Basic white dough can be used but it is more usual to bake Milk Bread in this mould. Put enough risen dough in one half of the greased mould to fill it to about two-thirds full. Put to prove until just over the top of the tin, then close the tin, secure and bake in a hot oven (220°C/425°F, Gas Mark 7) for about 30–40 minutes. Remove from tin and return to the oven for a few minutes to crisp up.

Wholemeal Bread

This bread can be made with any of the plain brown bread flours, from wholemeal or wholewheat to the stone-ground and compost-grown varieties. Some of the rougher flours give a coarser-textured loaf with a little less volume. The dough must not be too firm and dry for kneading.

675g (1½lb) wholemeal, wholewheat
  or other plain brown flour
1½ level teaspoons salt
1 level tablespoon caster sugar

25g (1oz) lard
25g (1oz) fresh yeast, or
  1 level tablespoon dried yeast and 1 level
  teaspoon sugar
450ml (¾pt) warm water (43°C/110°F)

Put the flour into a bowl, mix in the salt and sugar and rub in the lard. Blend the fresh yeast with the warm liquid; for dried yeast, dissolve the sugar in the liquid, sprinkle the yeast on top and leave in a warm place until frothy – about 10 minutes. Add to the dry ingredients and mix to form a pliable dough which leaves the sides of the bowl clean. If too dry, add a little more warm water. Turn on to a lightly floured surface and knead until smooth, even, and no longer sticky. Shape into a ball, place in an oiled polythene bag and put to rise until doubled in size – about an hour, or longer in cooler conditions. Remove from the bag, knock back and knead until smooth.

Shape to fit one greased 900g (2lb) loaf tin or two 450g (1lb) tins, or bake in any of the shapes described on pages 23–26, or shape into a jointed baton (see below). For extra crispness, brush the loaves with salted water. Cover with oiled polythene, put to prove in a warm place until the dough almost reaches the top of the tin or doubles in size. Remove polythene and bake in a very hot oven (230°C/450°F, Gas Mark 8) for 30–40 minutes for loaves in a tin and a little less for those without tins, or until the base sounds hollow when tapped.

Note This dough can also be made into rolls (see page 34 for shaping).

Jointed Baton

Using half the risen dough, remove 50g (2oz) and divide the remainder into 65–75g (2½–3oz) pieces. Roll each piece into a thick sausage shape with blunt ends and put on to a baking sheet in a line with each piece touching its neighbour to form a loaf. Halve

Types of loaf: (left to right) *Cottage; Baton; Tin*

the reserved dough and roll each piece into a thin sausage a little longer than the loaf. Twist these two strands together and lay them along the centre top of the loaf, tucking the ends underneath. Put to prove and bake as above.

Suitable to freeze for up to 6 months.

Flowerpot Bread

The traditional old terracotta flowerpots make very good bread moulds and give a good crisp crust to the bread, as well as an interesting shape. Although quite difficult to obtain now, if you are lucky enough to find some, they should, for preference, measure about 14cm (5½in) in diameter by 11·5cm (4½in) deep. They need to be specially prepared before using for the first time by being brushed inside and out with oil and then baked (still empty) in a hot oven for about 20 minutes. Repeat this process two or three times to prevent the

bread sticking during baking; the pots will then need very little greasing at all – the loaves simply slip out. The lightly greased pot can also have cracked wheat or oatmeal scattered over the base and sides before adding the dough, so that the baked loaf has an interesting and crunchy crust. The recipe here is for a quick (one rise) bread which has a very close texture, but is so speedy to make; however, an ordinary brown bread dough or granary dough can also be used.

225g (8oz) brown flour
225g (8oz) strong white flour
2 level teaspoons salt
2 level teaspoons sugar
15g (½oz) lard
15g (½oz) fresh yeast, or
    2 level teaspoons dried yeast and 1 level teaspoon sugar
300ml (½pt) warm water (43°C/110°F)
cracked wheat or oatmeal (optional)

Flowerpot Bread

Mix together the flours, salt and sugar and rub in the lard. Dissolve the fresh yeast in the water; for dried yeast, dissolve the 1 teaspoon sugar in the water, sprinkle the yeast on top and leave for about 10 minutes or until frothy. Add the yeast liquid to the dry ingredients and mix to a fairly firm dough. Turn on to a lightly floured surface and knead until smooth and even – about 10 minutes by hand or 3–4 minutes in a large electric mixer fitted with a dough hook. Divide the dough in half and shape to fit the flowerpots so that they are about half full. Brush the tops with salted water and sprinkle with cracked wheat or oatmeal then cover lightly with oiled polythene. Put to rise in a warm place for 1–1½ hours or until doubled in size. The dough should spring back when lightly pressed with a floured finger. Remove the polythene and bake in a very hot oven (230°C/450°F, Gas Mark 8) for about 30–40 minutes. Turn out and cool on a wire rack. The dough can also be shaped into 1 or 2 cobs (see page 24) or shaped to fit two 450g (1lb) loaf tins, in which case reduce the cooking temperature after 15 minutes to fairly hot (200°C/400°F, Gas Mark 6) and continue for 20–30 minutes.

Note Use all brown flour if preferred. The loaves are best made smaller than usual as they do not keep fresh for as long as the normal bread dough with two risings.

Suitable to freeze for up to 3 months.

Farmhouse Brown Bread

This makes a coarser, closer-textured loaf than the Wholemeal Bread recipe, but probably has the best flavour of all. The quantities can be doubled up to make larger loaves.

675g (1½lb) 100 per cent stone-ground wholemeal or wholewheat flour
2 level teaspoons salt
15g (½oz) butter or lard
15g (½oz) fresh yeast, or
  1½ level teaspoons dried yeast and 1 level teaspoon sugar
450ml (¾pt) warm water (43°C/110°F)

Grease two 450g (1lb) loaf tins or one 900g (2lb) tin. Put the flour and salt into a bowl and rub in the fat. Blend the fresh yeast with the liquid; for dried yeast, dissolve the sugar in the liquid, sprinkle the yeast on top and leave in a warm place until frothy – about 10 minutes. Add to the flour and mix to form a soft dough. Turn on to a floured surface and knead until smooth and even – about 10 minutes by hand or 3–4 minutes if using a large electric mixer fitted with a dough hook. Shape into a ball, place in an oiled polythene bag and put to rise in a warm place until doubled in size. Remove dough, knock back and knead until smooth, then shape to fit the tins. Cover with oiled polythene and put to prove in a warm place until the dough has doubled in size or reaches just over the tops of the tins. Remove polythene and bake in a very hot oven (230°C/450°F, Gas Mark 8) for 20 minutes; reduce to hot (220°C/425°F, Gas Mark 7) and continue for a further 20–25 minutes for a large loaf and about 15 minutes for smaller ones.

Suitable to freeze for up to 6 months.

Crown Loaf

This loaf is made with an enriched white dough which has a much higher proportion of fat and an egg included. It is made by the batter method and is an especially good bread to make when using dried yeast, for the reconstituting of the yeast can be done during the batter fermentation, not as a separate process. The texture is shorter and closer than plain white dough because of the extra ingredients. A crown loaf is easily made and attractive, but the dough can be used for most other shapes of bread as well, baking with or without a tin, and also for making rolls.

450g (1lb) strong white flour
1 level teaspoon caster sugar
25g (1oz) fresh yeast, or
  1 level tablespoon dried yeast
250ml (8fl oz) warm milk (43°C/110°F)
1 level teaspoon salt
50g (2oz) butter or margarine
1 egg, beaten

Glaze
1 egg, beaten
1 level teaspoon caster sugar
1 tablespoon water
poppy or sesame seeds (optional)

Grease one 23cm (9in) or two 15cm (6in) round sandwich tins. Put 125g (5oz) flour into a bowl with the sugar, yeast (fresh or dried) and milk. Leave in a warm place for about 20 minutes or until frothy. Sift the remaining flour and salt into a bowl and rub in the fat until the mixture resembles fine breadcrumbs. Add the yeast batter and beaten egg and mix to form a fairly soft dough. Turn on to a lightly floured surface and knead until smooth and even and no longer sticky – about 10 minutes by hand or 3–4 minutes in a large electric mixer fitted with a dough hook. Shape the dough into a

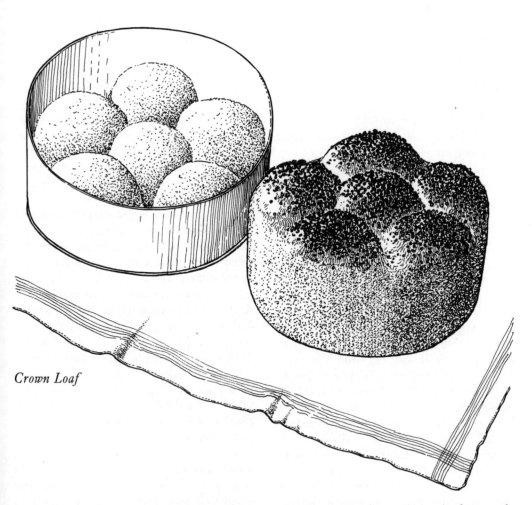

Crown Loaf

ball and place in a lightly oiled polythene bag. Put to rise in a warm place for about an hour or until doubled in size. Remove dough, knock back and knead until smooth – about 2 minutes. Divide the dough into 12 even-sized pieces and roll each into a ball. For a large crown, place a circle of dough balls around the edge of the large tin with three or four in the centre, whilst for the small tins, arrange five around the outside with one in the centre of each tin. Make the glaze by beating the egg, sugar and water together and brush all over the loaves. Sprinkle with poppy or sesame seeds, if liked. Place in a large oiled polythene bag and put to prove in a warm place until doubled in size and puffy. Remove polythene and bake in a moderately hot oven (190°C/375°F, Gas Mark 5) for 50–60 minutes for the large loaf and 30–40 minutes for the smaller ones, or until a good golden brown and the base of the loaf sounds hollow when tapped. Cool on a wire rack.

Suitable to freeze for up to 6 months.

Milk Bread

This bread when made with all milk gives a soft close-textured loaf with a softer crust than usual. It can also be made using half milk and half water, but so long as there is a good proportion of milk, the texture will always be entirely different from a loaf made with water only. The added fat plus the milk fat help to keep the loaf moist for longer than usual.

15g (½oz) fresh yeast, or
    1½ level teaspoons dried yeast and 1 level teaspoon sugar
about 450ml (¾pt) warm milk or milk and water, mixed (43°C/110°F)
675g (1½lb) strong white flour
2 level teaspoons salt
50g (2oz) lard or margarine

Blend the fresh yeast with the liquid; for dried yeast, dissolve the sugar in the liquid, sprinkle the yeast over the surface and leave in a warm place until frothy – about 10 minutes. Sift the flour and salt into a bowl and then rub in the fat. Add the yeast liquid and mix to form a fairly soft dough. Turn on to a lightly floured surface and knead until smooth and elastic – about 10 minutes by hand or 3–4 minutes in a large electric mixer fitted with a dough hook. Shape into a ball and place in a lightly oiled polythene bag. Tie the top loosely and put to rise in a warm place for about an hour or until doubled in size. Remove from the bag, knock back and knead until smooth. The dough is now ready to shape into a loaf or rolls (see pages 23 and 34). Bake milk bread, after proving, in a hot oven (220°C/425°F, Gas Mark 7) for 30–40 minutes for loaves and 15–20 minutes for rolls.

Suitable to freeze for up to 6 months.

Brown Country Bread

A small proportion of a coarse brown flour gives colour and flavour to this light-textured brown loaf. It can be baked in a tin or made into rolls.

450g (1lb) strong white flour
1 level teaspoon salt
225g (8oz) wholewheat flour, or
    any coarse granary or brown flour
25g (1oz) lard
25g (1oz) fresh yeast, or
    1 level tablespoon dried yeast and 1 level teaspoon caster sugar
450ml (¾pt) warm water (43°C/110°F)

Sift the white flour and salt into a bowl, mix in the brown flour and rub in the lard. Blend the fresh yeast with the water; for dried yeast, dissolve the sugar in the water, sprinkle the yeast on top and put in a warm place for about 10 minutes, or until frothy. Add the yeast liquid to the dry ingredients and mix to form a fairly firm dough. Turn on to a lightly floured surface and knead until smooth and even and no longer sticky. This should take about 10 minutes by hand or 3–4 minutes if using a large electric mixer fitted with a dough hook. Shape into a ball, place in a lightly oiled polythene bag and put to rise in a warm place until doubled in size – about an hour. Remove from the bag, knock back and knead until smooth – about 2 minutes. Divide the dough in half and shape each piece into an oval ball. Place on greased baking sheets and cut a deep slash

1 *White tin loaf;* 2 *Granary cob;* 3 *Crown loaf;* 4 *Savoury herb bread;* 5 *Poppy seed knots (white rolls);* 6 *Vienna loaf;* 7 *Cottage loaf rolls;* 8 *Small brown split tin*

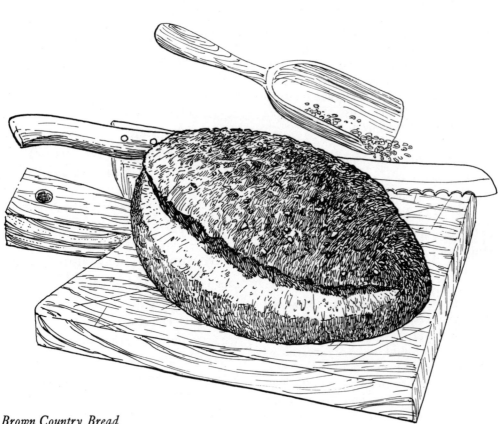

Brown Country Bread

1 *Bath buns;* 2 *Brown cottage loaf;* 3 *London buns;* 4 *Rich floury scones;* 5 *Yorkshire teacake;* 6 *Apple and Orange teabread and Malted teabread*

across the top of each loaf, off centre. Cover loosely with oiled polythene and put to prove in a warm place until doubled in size. Remove polythene, dredge lightly with flour and bake in a very hot oven (230°C/ 450°F, Gas Mark 8) for about 30 minutes or until the base sounds hollow when tapped. Cool on a wire rack.

Suitable to freeze for up to 6 months.

Short-time White Bread

There is a method of bread-making which cuts out the initial rising stage, replacing it with a 5–10 minute resting period. It does, however, require the addition of ascorbic acid (vitamin C) – available from larger chemists in 25mg, 50mg and 100mg tablet form – which is crushed and added to the yeast liquid. This type of bread-making requires fresh yeast for quick success; dried yeast takes much longer to use, thus spoiling the speediness of the bread.

675g (1½lb) strong white flour

2 level teaspoons salt

1 level teaspoon sugar

25g (1oz) lard or margarine

25g (1oz) fresh yeast

425ml (14fl oz) warm water (43°C/110°F)

25mg tablet ascorbic acid, crushed

Sift the flour, salt and sugar into a bowl and rub in the fat. Blend the fresh yeast with the water, then add the ascorbic acid, making sure it dissolves. Add to the dry ingredients and mix to form a firm dough, adding more flour if necessary, until the sides of the bowl are clean. Turn on to a floured surface and knead the dough until it is smooth and elastic and no longer sticky – about 10 minutes by hand or 3–4 minutes in a large electric mixer fitted with a dough hook. Shape into a ball, place in an oiled polythene bag and leave to rest for 5 minutes. Remove from the bag, knead lightly and the dough is ready for shaping. Either shape to fit one greased 900g (2lb) loaf tin or two 450g (1lb) tins, or use to make 18–20 plain round or shaped rolls (see this page). Cover with oiled polythene and put to rise in a warm place for 45–60 minutes for loaves and up to 30 minutes for rolls, or until the dough springs back when lightly pressed with a floured finger. Remove polythene and either leave plain, dust with flour or brush with beaten egg or milk before baking in a very hot oven (230°C/450°F, Gas Mark 8) for 30–35 minutes for a large loaf, 25–30 minutes for smaller ones and 15–20 minutes for rolls. They are ready when the base sounds hollow when tapped. Cool on a wire rack.

Short-time Wholemeal Bread

675g (1½lb) wholemeal flour

2 level teaspoons salt

2 level teaspoons caster sugar

25g (1oz) lard or margarine

25g (1oz) fresh yeast

450ml (¾pt) warm water (43°C/110°F)

25mg tablet ascorbic acid, crushed

Make in the same way as short-time white bread (p 33).

Short-time Enriched White Bread

450g (1lb) strong white flour

1 level teaspoon salt

1 level teaspoon caster sugar

50g (2oz) butter or margarine

25g (1oz) fresh yeast

200ml (8fl oz) warm milk, or milk and water mixed (43°C/110°F)

25mg tablet ascorbic acid, crushed

1 egg, beaten

Make as for short-time white bread but add the beaten egg with the yeast liquid. Leave to rest for 10 minutes instead of 5 minutes and knead for 1–2 minutes to knock out the air bubbles. Make into loaves, plaits or rolls.

Shaping Rolls

All of the plain doughs can be shaped into rolls of one sort or another and many of the richer or fruited doughs are suitable for making into simple round or finger-shaped buns. The size of the roll is your choice but it needs to fit its purpose; the amount of dough used can vary from 50–100g (2–4oz) with the smaller amount making an average-sized roll. Once shaped, place the rolls on greased baking sheets, fairly well apart,

cover loosely with oiled polythene and put to prove in a warm place until doubled in size and puffy. This should take 15–30 minutes, with the shorter time for plainer doughs. Remove the polythene and either leave as they are or brush with egg glaze, milk or salted water before baking in a very hot oven (230°C/450°F, Gas Mark 8) for 10–20 minutes depending on size, until well risen and browned. Poppy or sesame seeds can also be sprinkled over rolls just before baking. Richly fruited rolls or buns are better cooked in a moderately hot oven (190°C/375°F, Gas Mark 5). Cool rolls on a wire rack.

Round

Shape the pieces of dough – of the required size – by rolling round and round on a lightly floured surface with the palm of your hand, pressing down hard at first and

gradually releasing the pressure until the ball is shaped. They can also be shaped by folding the edges of the piece of dough into the centre until smooth, even and round; turn over to keep the smooth side of the roll upwards. The tops can be slashed, if liked. Put on to greased baking sheets, prove and bake as above.

Coils

Shape each piece of dough into a long thin sausage. Then, beginning in the centre, roll the sausage round and round to give a coil, tucking the end of the dough underneath. Prove and bake as above.

Finger

Roll the pieces of dough into finger shapes with the palms of the hands. They can be placed well apart on the greased baking

35

sheets to give crusty rolls, or nearly touching so that during proving and baking, they join up to give soft-sided rolls when they have cooled and are pulled apart. Score the tops diagonally, if liked. Prove and bake as above.

Cloverleaves

Divide each piece of dough into three and roll each of these into a small ball. Place on the greased baking sheet in a cloverleaf pattern so that all 3 pieces of dough touch, ie two at the base and one centrally above them. They may be slashed or left plain. Prove and bake as above.

Knots

Roll each piece of dough into a long even sausage shape with the palms of the hands and then quickly tie into a simple knot. With practice more sophisticated knots can be shaped. Place on a greased baking sheet, prove and bake as above.

Cottage

Break off one-third of each piece of dough then shape both pieces into balls. Place the large ball on the greased baking sheet, damp the topknot and place centrally on top. Secure by pressing your first finger right through the topknot to the baking sheet. Prove and bake as above.

Plaits

Divide each piece of dough into 3 even-sized pieces and roll them into thin sausages. Join the 3 strands at one end, plait evenly towards you and secure the other ends. This method is easier for plaiting rolls than the method given for plaiting loaves on page 25. Place on greased baking sheets, prove and bake as above.

Twists

Divide each piece of dough into 2 even-sized pieces and roll into sausage shapes. Twist these 2 pieces together and secure each end. Put on to greased baking sheets either straight or in curves or 'S' shapes. Prove and bake as above.

Note Rolls freeze well for 4–6 months but they are often better refreshed in a hot oven for a few minutes, once thawed.

Fancy Breads

After the basic breads come the fancy breads. These are not the richly fruited buns or tea-breads, but the more interesting doughs and flavourings which can be used in bread baking. Some of these are (or can be) made from basic risen dough of one sort or another whilst others are made from particular types of flour or meal such as granary or rye.

Different areas of the country have their own specialities, some of which are now almost forgotten or at least unknown in other regions. Take Kent Huffkins, which are large rolls turned over during baking to produce a soft crust to the top and base; or the baps of Scotland, being soft and floury flat rolls mainly served at breakfast in their own region, but widely used for packed lunches and picnics elsewhere; or Potato Bread which was often baked when there were grain shortages since mashed potato added to the flour helped eke it out as well as making a very moist and long-keeping loaf; while Rice Bread kept moist for a very long time with the addition of almost mushy cooked rice – an essential factor years ago when bread was baked in large batches but there were no freezers to preserve the freshness.

Many regions also had their own breads but often these were only slight variations on a basic loaf, perhaps mixed in a different way or, more often, baked in other shapes or sizes from the normal.

Many flavours can be added to bread for variety: try onion, herb or cheese for savoury loaves, or the better known Currant Bread, the lesser known Caraway Bread, or Orange Bread which utilises the discarded shells of the fruit.

The recipes here show a selection of these breads, some of which are old favourites, some less well known and perhaps a few completely new to you; your own experiments with flavours and shaping can give even more variety. Most of the breads freeze satisfactorily, but check with each recipe for the recommended storage time.

Large and Small Baps

Floury Baps

The bap is known as the breakfast roll of Scotland, where it is often called a morning roll. Baps are soft flat rolls of varying shapes – from round to oval, to three-cornered, to sometimes almost square. It appears that the small oval ones are the most common with the flattish bap loaf usually made round. They are never glazed but are sometimes brushed with milk before being dredged with flour. They are traditionally served straight from the oven, still warm, but are just as good served cold, and will toast well when stale.

It is said that baps should be eaten as they are, or split, buttered and reassembled, but never pulled apart as with many other types of roll.

15g (½oz) fresh yeast, or
  1½ level teaspoons dried yeast and 1 level
  teaspoon caster sugar
150ml (¼pt) warm milk (43°C/110°F)
450g (1lb) strong white flour
1 level teaspoon salt
50g (2oz) lard
150ml (¼pt) warm water (43°C/100°F)

Blend the fresh yeast with the warm milk; for dried yeast, dissolve the sugar in the milk, then sprinkle the yeast over the surface and put in a warm place for about 10 minutes or until frothy. Sift the flour and salt into a bowl and rub in the lard. Stir in the yeast liquid and water, and mix to form a fairly soft dough. Turn on to a lightly floured surface and knead until smooth and elastic – about 10 minutes by hand or 3–4 minutes in a large electric mixer fitted with a dough hook. Shape the dough into a ball, put into a lightly oiled polythene bag and secure the top. Put to rise in a warm place until doubled in size – this should take about an hour. Turn out on to a lightly floured surface and knead until smooth. To make 2 large baps, divide the dough in half, shape each piece into a ball, then roll out to a circle 2–2·5cm (¾–1in) thick using a well floured rolling pin. Place on greased and floured baking sheets and dredge the tops with flour.

For small baps, divide all the dough into 10–12 pieces, shape each into a ball, then roll out to an oval shape about 1cm (½in) thick. Place on greased and floured baking sheets and dredge with flour. Cover all baps lightly with oiled polythene and put to prove in a warm place until doubled in size – about 20–45 minutes depending on size. Remove polythene and press the centres of all the baps with 3 or 4 fingers to prevent blisters forming during baking, or prick with a fork, 2 or 3 times in the centre. Bake in a fairly hot oven (200°C/400°F, Gas Mark 6) for 15–20 minutes for the rolls and 20–30 minutes for the larger baps, or until a pale golden brown. Cool on a wire rack.

Makes 2 large baps or 10–12 small bap rolls, or 1 large bap and 5–6 rolls.

Note 100g (4oz) white flour can be replaced with wholemeal flour; and in place of dredging with flour, the baps can be lightly brushed with milk and sprinkled with poppy or sesame seeds.

Suitable to freeze for up to 6 months.

Kent Huffkins

These delicious large rolls with a soft crust all round – from being baked first one side and then the other – originated in Kent, and are ideal for man-sized picnics or lunch-boxes. They can be split and filled; split twice and filled with two different savoury fillings; or simply served with a hunk of cheese and pickles.

675g (1½lb) strong white flour
1½ level teaspoons salt
1 level teaspoon caster sugar
50g (2oz) lard
15g (½oz) fresh yeast, or
  1½ level teaspoons dried yeast and 1 level teaspoon sugar
about 450ml (¾pt) warm milk and water, mixed (43°C/110°F)

Sift the flour, salt and sugar into a bowl and rub in the lard. Blend the fresh yeast with the warm liquid; for dried yeast, dissolve the sugar in the liquid, sprinkle the yeast on top and leave in a warm place until frothy – about 10 minutes. Add to the dry ingredients and mix to a fairly soft dough. Turn on to a lightly floured surface and knead until smooth and even – about 10 minutes by hand or 3–4 minutes in a large electric mixer fitted with a dough hook. Shape into a ball, place in an oiled polythene bag and put to rise in a warm place until doubled in size – about an hour. Remove from the bag, knock back and knead until smooth, then divide into 8 even-sized pieces. Roll these out to circles about 2·5cm (1in) thick and place on greased baking sheets. Cover with oiled polythene and put to prove until doubled in size. Remove polythene and bake in a very hot oven (230°C/450°F, Gas Mark 8) for 10 minutes. Carefully turn the huffkins over and continue baking for a further 10 minutes or until an even, light golden brown. Turn on to a wire rack covered with a clean cloth, wrap up loosely and leave until cold. This prevents the steam escaping and gives a soft and tender crust.

Makes 8.

Suitable to freeze for up to 4 months.

Oatmeal Twists

The slightly nutty flavour of oatmeal gives an unusual taste to this soft-textured bread. Oatmeal was used long ago to make rather heavy bread often with only a small proportion of a brown or white flour. I think it better to use just a small proportion of oatmeal – either fine ground for a smooth loaf or medium ground for a coarser texture.

400g (14oz) strong white flour
1 level teaspoon salt
1 level teaspoon caster sugar
25g (1oz) lard
100g (4oz) oatmeal, fine or medium
15g ($\frac{1}{2}$oz) fresh yeast, or
   1$\frac{1}{2}$ level teaspoons dried yeast and 1 level teaspoon sugar
150ml ($\frac{1}{4}$pt) warm milk (43°C/110°F)
150ml ($\frac{1}{4}$pt) warm water (43°C/110°F)
milk to glaze
oatmeal (optional)

Sift the flour, salt and sugar into a bowl, rub in the lard and then mix in the oatmeal. Blend the fresh yeast with the warm milk; for dried yeast, dissolve the sugar in the milk, sprinkle the yeast on top and leave in a warm place until frothy – about 10 minutes. Add the yeast liquid and warm water to the dry ingredients and mix to a fairly soft dough. Turn on to a lightly floured surface and knead until smooth and even – about 10 minutes by hand or 3–4 minutes using a large electric mixer fitted with a dough hook. Shape into a ball, place in an oiled polythene bag and put to rise in a warm place for about an hour or until doubled in size. Remove from the bag and knead lightly until smooth, then either divide the dough into 75g (3oz) pieces for rolls or into 2 equal pieces for loaves. To make twists, divide each piece of dough in half and roll each of these out to a thin sausage about 20cm (8in) long for rolls and

35cm (14in) for loaves. Secure the ends of 2 dough sausages and twist, pressing the other ends together. Place on a greased baking sheet, cover with oiled polythene and put to prove until doubled in size – 15–30 minutes depending on size. Remove cover, brush with milk and sprinkle the tops with oatmeal if liked. Bake in a very hot oven (230°C/450°F, Gas Mark 8) for 15–20 minutes for rolls and 20–25 minutes for larger twists. Cool on wire racks.

Makes 10 rolls or 2 large twists.

Suitable to freeze for up to 6 months.

Bridge Rolls

These are made from a rich bread dough shaped into varying sized finger rolls and are the traditional rolls used for parties, buffets, etc. They are either split and filled or cut in half and served as open rolls with savoury or sweet toppings. The ends are slightly tapered to give a good shape and the rolls are baked fairly close together to give partly soft sides.

15g ($\frac{1}{2}$oz) fresh yeast, or
   1$\frac{1}{2}$ level teaspoons dried yeast and 1 level teaspoon sugar
200ml (8fl oz) warm milk (43°C/110°F)
450g (1lb) strong or plain white flour
1 level teaspoon salt
75g (3oz) butter or margarine
1 egg, beaten
beaten egg to glaze (optional)

Blend the fresh yeast with the warm milk; for dried yeast, dissolve the sugar in the milk, sprinkle the yeast on top and leave in a warm place for about 10 minutes or until frothy. Sift the flour and salt into a bowl and rub in the fat. Add the yeast liquid and beaten egg and mix to form a fairly soft dough, adding a little extra flour if neces-

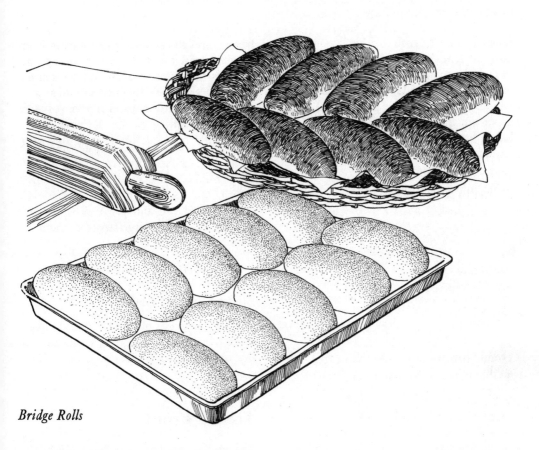

Bridge Rolls

sary, until the dough leaves the sides of the bowl clean. Turn on to a floured surface and knead until smooth, even and elastic. Allow about 10 minutes by hand or 3–4 minutes in a large electric mixer fitted with a dough hook. Shape into a ball and put into a lightly oiled polythene bag. Put to rise in a warm place until doubled in size and the dough springs back when lightly pressed with a floured finger. Turn out on to a floured surface, knock back and knead until smooth again. Divide into the required-sized pieces: 25g (1oz), 40g (1½oz) or 50g (2oz), or larger or smaller if so preferred. Each piece is shaped into a long finger roll with slightly tapering ends by rolling backwards and forwards with the palm of one hand or two (depending on the size of the roll) until the required thickness, length and shape is achieved. Place on greased baking sheets in rows so that the sides are about 1cm (½in) apart. They will then rise and join up during baking. If firm sides are preferred, then place them further apart. Cover with a sheet of oiled polythene and put to prove in a warm place for about 20 minutes or until doubled in size. Remove polythene, glaze with beaten egg (if liked) and bake in a hot oven (220°C/425°F, Gas Mark 7) for 10–20 minutes, depending on size, until golden brown. Slide them on to a wire rack still joined together and leave until cold. Pull apart as required.

Suitable to freeze for up to 6 months.

Currant Bread

A favourite with all, this loaf is easy to bake and when stale the left-overs can be toasted.

It is a typical English loaf but is not really associated with any particular region although the spices and fruit proportions vary in some areas; the Welsh equivalent is the famous Bara Brith (see page 88). The use of brown sugar makes the colour of the baked loaf a pale coffee brown, but caster sugar may be used if preferred.

450g (1lb) strong white flour

1 level teaspoon salt

25g (1oz) butter, margarine or lard

25g (1oz) soft brown sugar

100g (4oz) currants

25g (1oz) mixed peel (optional)

25g (1oz) fresh yeast, or
   1 level tablespoon dried yeast and 1 level teaspoon sugar

150ml (¼pt) warm milk (43°C/110°F)

6 tablespoons warm water (43°C/110°F)

2 tablespoons clear honey or water

clear honey or syrup to glaze

Grease two 450g (1lb) loaf tins. Sift the flour and salt into a bowl. Rub in the fat, then mix in the sugar, currants and peel. Blend the fresh yeast with the warm milk; for dried yeast, dissolve the sugar in the milk, sprinkle the yeast on top and leave in a warm place until frothy – about 10 minutes. Add the yeast liquid, water and honey to the dry ingredients and mix to form a fairly firm dough. Turn on to a lightly floured surface and knead until smooth and even. This should take about 10 minutes by hand or 3–4 minutes if using a large electric mixer fitted with a dough hook. Shape into a ball, place in a lightly oiled polythene bag and put to rise in a warm place for 1–1½ hours or until doubled in size. Turn out and knead until smooth.

Divide the dough in half and shape each piece to fit the tins. Place in oiled polythene bags and put to prove in a warm place until the dough reaches the tops of the tins.

Remove polythene and bake in a hot oven (220°C/425°F, Gas Mark 7) for 30–40 minutes until the base of the loaf sounds hollow when tapped. Turn on to a wire rack and brush the tops of the loaves with honey or syrup.

Note For a larger loaf, shape all the dough to fit a 900g (2lb) loaf tin and bake for 45–50 minutes. For currant buns, divide the dough into 50g (2oz) portions, shape each into a round ball and place well apart on greased baking sheets. Bake for about 15 minutes.

Suitable to freeze for up to 4 months.

Spicy Currant Bread

Add 1 teaspoon of either mixed spice, cinnamon, nutmeg, ginger or allspice to the dry ingredients, if liked.

Treacle Bread

Treacle is usually associated with rye breads, but it can also be used to give a good flavour to other bread doughs. The texture will be much lighter than a rye loaf and the process of making much shorter, for it does not need the starter (or sour) dough. For a close-textured wholemeal treacle loaf use all brown flour but for a lighter loaf, alter the proportions to a quarter brown flour with the rest being strong white flour.

2 level tablespoons black treacle

50g (2oz) butter or margarine

300ml (½pt) boiling water

25g (1oz) fresh yeast, or
   1 level tablespoon dried yeast and 1 level teaspoon caster sugar

450g (1lb) wholemeal flour or half wholemeal and half strong white flour

1 level teaspoon salt

100g (4oz) chopped walnuts or sultanas (optional)

Grease two 450g (1lb) loaf tins. Put the treacle and fat into a basin, pour on most of the boiling water and mix until dissolved; leave until lukewarm. Blend the fresh yeast with the treacle liquid; for dried yeast, add the sugar, sprinkle the yeast on top and leave in a warm place until frothy – about 10 minutes. Sift the flour and salt into a bowl and add the nuts or sultanas, if used. Add the yeast and treacle liquid and mix to form a rather soft dough, adding more warm water if necessary. Beat well with your hand or a wooden spoon, then cover with a damp cloth and put to rise in a warm place for about an hour or until doubled in size.

Remove cover, turn on to a floured surface and knead until smooth. Divide in half and shape each piece to fit a loaf tin. Cover with oiled polythene and put to prove in a warm place until the dough reaches the tops of the tins. Remove polythene and bake in a hot oven (220°C/425°F, Gas Mark 7) for about 30 minutes. Turn out and cool on a wire rack.

Note For a sweeter loaf, add 25g (1oz) sugar to the dry ingredients.

Suitable to freeze for up to 4 months.

Granary Bread

This type of bread requires a special granary meal which is made of malted wheat, rye flour and whole or cracked wheat grains to give the texture and that well known 'crunch'. It is an easy bread dough to make, giving good volume and texture, and has exceptionally good keeping qualities, staying fresh much longer than most other breads. A proportion of white flour prevents an overstrong taste of malt but is not essential. It also makes good rolls.

450g (1lb) granary meal
225g (8oz) strong white flour
1½ level teaspoons salt
1 level teaspoon caster sugar
25g (1oz) lard
25g (1oz) fresh yeast, or
   1 level tablespoon dried yeast and 1 level teaspoon sugar
about 450ml (¾pt) warm water (43°C/110°F)

Put the granary meal into a bowl, sift in the white flour, salt and sugar, and then rub in the lard. Blend the fresh yeast with the water; for dried yeast, dissolve the sugar in the water, sprinkle the yeast on top and leave in a warm place until frothy – about 10 minutes. Add the yeast liquid to the dry ingredients and mix to a fairly firm dough. Turn on to a lightly floured surface and knead until smooth and even – about 10 minutes by hand or 3–4 minutes in a large electric mixer fitted with a dough hook. Shape into a ball, place in an oiled polythene bag and put to rise in a warm place until the dough has doubled in size and springs back when lightly pressed with a floured finger – about an hour, or longer in cooler conditions.

Remove from the bag and knead for 2 minutes or until smooth, then divide the dough in half. Either shape into batons or small bloomers, cobs (see page 24–5), or to fit two greased 450g (1lb) loaf tins. Cover loosely with oiled polythene and put to prove in a warm place until the dough has doubled in size or reached the tops of the tins. The tops can be slashed with a very sharp knife, if liked. Bake in a very hot oven (230°C/450°F, Gas Mark 8) for about 30 minutes or until the base sounds hollow when tapped. Turn on to a wire rack to cool.

Note For a coarser-textured loaf, use all granary mix in place of the proportion of white flour.

Suitable to freeze for up to 6 months.

Croissants

For those who travel abroad, particularly to the Continent, these classic, mouth-watering, crisp and flaky delicacies served at breakfast will recall many a happy holiday. They can be made at home if you have time, for it is a long process with no short cuts. The secret of good croissants is to have both the dough and the butter firm so that they will form definite layers; the lightness is a combination of the trapping of air in the rolling and folding process and the yeast fermentation. It is essential to use butter for the correct flavour and croissants must be served fresh. The dough can be frozen either before shaping or after baking.

25g (1oz) fresh yeast, or
    1 level tablespoon dried yeast and 1 level teaspoon sugar
about 200ml (7fl oz) warm water (43°C/110°F)
450g (1lb) strong plain flour
2 level teaspoons salt
25g (1oz) butter or lard
1 egg, beaten
175g (6oz) firm butter

Egg Glaze
1 egg, beaten
½ level teaspoon caster sugar
1 tablespoon water

Blend the fresh yeast with the warm water; for dried yeast, dissolve the sugar in the water, sprinkle the yeast on top and leave in a warm place until frothy – about 10 minutes. Sift the flour and salt into a bowl and rub in the 25g (1oz) butter or lard. Add the yeast liquid and egg and mix to form a pliable dough. Turn on to a floured surface and knead very thoroughly until smooth, even and elastic; this should take 10–15 minutes by hand or 4–5 minutes in a large electric mixer fitted with a dough hook.

Roll out the dough to a rectangle about 50 × 20cm (20 × 8in) and about 0·5cm (¼in) thick, taking care to keep the edges straight and corners square. Divide the butter into three and use one portion to dot evenly over the top two-thirds of the dough leaving a small margin clear all round. Fold the plain third of dough up over the buttered piece of dough and the top third downwards over the other two. Seal the edges lightly with the rolling pin, put into a polythene bag and chill for 15 minutes. Remove and give the dough a quarter turn so the fold is to the right. Roll out again to a long strip 3 times as long as it is wide. Repeat the dotting of the top two-thirds with another portion of butter, the folding and resting, until all butter is used, keeping the dough to a neat shape at all times. Then repeat the rolling, folding and resting process 3 more times (without adding any fat). Replace in the bag and chill for at least an hour. The dough is now ready to shape and bake, but it can be left in the refrigerator for 24 hours or be frozen for up to 4 months at this stage. Allow frozen dough to thaw out properly before proceeding.

Roll out the dough on a lightly floured surface to a rectangle about 55 × 33cm (22 × 13in). Cover with oiled polythene and leave to rest for 10 minutes. Trim to a rectangle 53 × 30cm (21 × 12in) and divide in half lengthwise. Cut each piece into 6 triangles 15cm (6in) high and 15cm (6in) at the base. Beat the egg glaze ingredients together and use to brush all over the dough. Roll each triangle up loosely starting at the wide base up to the point. Bend into crescent shapes, keeping the tip underneath, and place on greased baking sheets. Glaze again and cover with oiled polythene. Put to rise at room temperature for about 30 minutes or until puffy. Remove cover and glaze again before baking in a hot oven (220°C/425°F, Gas Mark 7) for 15–20 minutes until crisp and golden brown. Croissants are best served warm.

Makes 12.

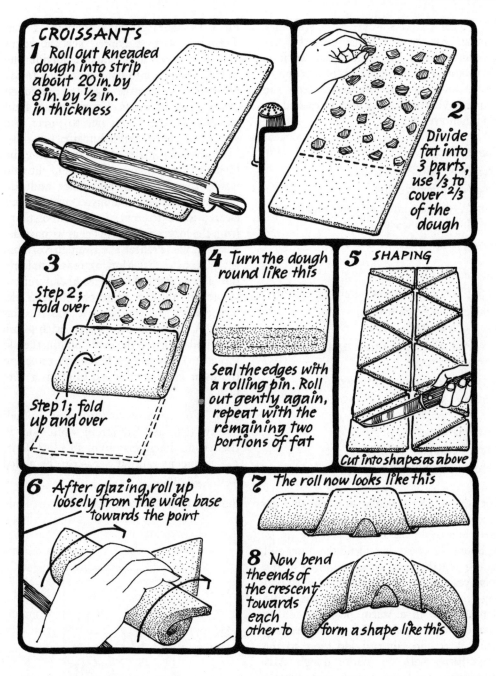

CROISSANTS

1 Roll out kneaded dough into strip about 20 in. by 8 in. by ½ in. in thickness

2 Divide fat into 3 parts, use ⅓ to cover ⅔ of the dough

3 Step 2; fold over

Step 1; fold up and over

4 Turn the dough round like this

Seal the edges with a rolling pin. Roll out gently again, repeat with the remaining two portions of fat

5 SHAPING

Cut into shapes as above

6 After glazing, roll up loosely from the wide base towards the point

7 The roll now looks like this

8 Now bend the ends of the crescent towards each other to form a shape like this

Rye Bread

This coarse-textured bread is a favourite of many and can be made at home provided you remember that it requires a starter (or sour) dough which must be prepared 12–24 hours before beginning the actual bread. Rye was grown for centuries as one of the staple grains in England; it has now largely disappeared and hence the rye loaf is not always easy to find, apart from in Jewish and Polish bakeries where it is still very popular. Rye gives a rather powerful but delicious flavour to baked bread, so it is often best to use a fairly high proportion of white flour to help counteract both the strong flavour and close texture caused by too much rye flour.

Starter Dough

150g (5oz) coarse rye flour

150g (5oz) fine rye flour

150ml (¼pt) sour milk or fresh milk soured with lemon juice

1 level teaspoon caster sugar

Second Dough

125ml (scant ¼pt) warm water (43°C/110°F)

1 tablespoon black treacle

25g (1oz) fresh yeast, or
    1 level tablespoon dried yeast and 1 level teaspoon sugar

300g (10 oz) strong white flour

15g (½oz) salt

Starch Glaze

2 level teaspoons cornflour

about 100ml (4fl oz) water

For the starter dough, mix all the ingredients together in a bowl, cover and leave in a cool place overnight or for up to 24 hours. The next day, blend the water and treacle together and either crumble in the fresh yeast or sprinkle in the dried yeast and sugar, together with 2 tablespoons white flour. Leave in a warm place for 10–20 minutes until frothy. Sift the remaining white flour and salt and add them to the yeast batter with the starter dough. Mix thoroughly to form a firm but slightly sticky dough. Turn on to a floured surface and knead until smooth and firm – about 10 minutes by hand or 3–4 minutes if using a large electric mixer fitted with a dough hook. Shape into a ball, place in an oiled polythene bag and put to rise in a warm place

for 1–1½ hours or until doubled in size. Turn out on to a floured surface, knock back and knead until smooth. Divide into 2 pieces, shape into cobs or batons (small bloomers – see page 25) and place on greased baking sheets. Cover with a sheet of oiled polythene and put to prove in a warm place until doubled in size.

Meanwhile, make the starch glaze by blending the cornflour in a little of the cold water, then boil the remainder and add quickly, stirring continuously until the glaze clears; leave to cool. Remove polythene from the loaves and brush them with cooled starch glaze. Preheat the oven to very hot (230°C/450°F, Gas Mark 8), reduce to fairly hot (200°C/400°F, Gas Mark 6) and put the loaves in for 30 minutes. Reduce the temperature to cool (150°C/300°F, Gas Mark 2), brush the loaves again with starch glaze and return to the oven for a further 30 minutes. Glaze loaves again and return to the oven for 2–3 minutes. Cool on a wire rack.

Note For a coarser-textured loaf use half fine rye flour and half strong white flour in the second dough instead of all white flour; 1–2 teaspoons caraway seeds can be added to this dough.

Suitable to freeze for 2–3 months.

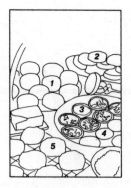

1 *Muffins;* 2 *Crumpets;* 3 *Potato scones;* 4 *Treacle drop scones;* 5 *Welsh cakes*

Rye Crispbread

450g (1lb) risen Rye Bread dough (see page 48)

50g (2oz) lard or 2 tablespoons oil

2 level teaspoons salt

1 level tablespoon coarse rye or crushed cornflakes

Place the dough in a bowl and add either the lard (cut into small pieces) or the oil, the salt and the rye or cornflakes. Knead and squeeze all the ingredients together until evenly blended. Roll the dough out thinly on a floured surface, place on greased baking sheets and cut into squares or rectangles with either a pastry wheel or a sharp knife. Cover with a sheet of oiled polythene and put to prove in a warm place until puffy. Remove polythene and bake in a fairly hot oven (200°C/400°F, Gas Mark 6) for about 15 minutes, then turn off the heat and crisp off in the cooling oven. Remove to a wire rack and leave to cool. Store in an airtight container.

Quick Rye Bread

Not a traditional rye loaf but a rye-flavoured bread, using only a small proportion of rye flour and no starter dough. This bread stays

1 *White cottage loaf;* 2 *Plaited poppy seed loaf;*
3 *Clover leaf rolls;* 4 *Mince pies;* 5 *Fruit pie;*
6 *Plaited Fish Puff;* 7 *Brown rolls (round and finger);* 8 *Kent huffkins*

fresh for longer than a wholemeal loaf and is delicious served with smoked fish and cheese. A few caraway seeds can be added to the dry ingredients or sprinkled on top of the loaf before baking, to give extra flavour.

550g (1¼lb) strong white flour

15g (½oz) salt

100g (4oz) rye flour or meal

25g (1oz) fresh yeast, or
1 level tablespoon dried yeast and 1 level teaspoon sugar

450ml (¾pt) warm water (43°C/110°F)

1 tablespoon oil

Grease two 900g (2lb) loaf tins. Sift the white flour and salt into a bowl and mix in the rye flour. Blend the fresh yeast with the warm water; for dried yeast, dissolve the sugar in the water, sprinkle the yeast on top and leave in a warm place until frothy – about 10 minutes. Add to the dry ingredients with the oil and mix to form a firm dough. Knead on a lightly floured surface until smooth and even for about 10 minutes by hand or 3–4 minutes in a large electric mixer fitted with a dough hook. Shape into a ball, place in an oiled polythene bag and put to rise in a warm place until doubled in size.

Remove the dough, knock back and knead until smooth, then shape to fit the 2 tins. Slash the tops, cover with oiled polythene and put to prove until the dough reaches the tops of the tins and springs back when lightly pressed with a floured finger. Remove polythene and bake in a very hot oven (230°C/450°F, Gas Mark 8) for 15 minutes, then reduce the temperature to moderately hot (190°C/375°F, Gas Mark 5) and continue for 15 minutes. Remove the loaves from the tins and return to the oven, lowered to moderate (170°C/325°F, Gas Mark 3), for a further 10 minutes. Cool on a wire rack.

Suitable to freeze for up to 6 months.

Scottish Morning Rowies

Also called Butteries, these rolls are quite different from the floury baps which are so popular in the south of Scotland. They are more like a flaky pastry made with yeast and need to be served very fresh and preferably warm.

25g (1oz) fresh yeast, or
    1 level tablespoon dried yeast and 1 level teaspoon sugar
about 300ml (½pt) warm water (43°C/110°F)
450g (1lb) strong white flour
½ level teaspoon salt
1 level tablespoon caster sugar
175g (6oz) softened butter

Blend the fresh yeast with the warm water; for dried yeast, dissolve the sugar in the water, sprinkle the yeast on top and leave in a warm place until frothy – about 10 minutes. Sift the flour, salt and sugar into a bowl, add the yeast liquid and mix to form a fairly soft dough. Turn on to a floured surface and knead until smooth and even – about 10 minutes by hand or 3–4 minutes in a large electric mixer fitted with a dough hook. Shape into a ball, place in an oiled polythene bag and put to rise in a warm place for about an hour or until doubled in size. Turn out, knead until smooth and roll out into a long strip 3 times as long as it is wide. Divide the butter into three and dot 1 portion over the top two-thirds of the dough. Fold the bottom third upwards and top third down like an envelope. Seal the edges, wrap in polythene and chill in the refrigerator for 15 minutes. Repeat with the other 2 portions of butter, giving the dough a quarter turn each time so that the fold is always at the right. Then roll out to about 1–2cm (½–¾in) thick and cut into 6–7.5cm (2½–3in) rounds or ovals. Place on greased or floured baking sheets, cover with oiled polythene and put to rise in a warm place for about 30 minutes or until doubled

in size. Remove polythene and bake in a fairly hot oven (200°C/400°F, Gas Mark 6) for about 20 minutes. Cool on a wire rack and eat warm.

Makes 12–15.

Cheese Bread

This is a modern invention, giving a delicious flavour and crisp cheesy crust to the baked bread. As bread has always been eaten with cheese this is a good combination, making super sandwiches with a variety of fillings, and the left-overs toast very well. Extra ingredients such as herbs, celery, chopped peanuts, onion, etc, can all be added to the basic dough.

450g (1lb) strong white flour
2 level teaspoons salt
1 level teaspoon dry mustard
pinch of pepper (optional)
100–175g (4–6oz) mature Cheddar cheese, finely grated or 2–3 tablespoons grated Parmesan cheese
15g (½oz) fresh yeast, or
    1½ level teaspoons dried yeast and 1 level teaspoon sugar
300ml (½pt) warm water (43°C/110°F)

Grease one 900g (2lb) or two 450g (1lb) loaf tins. Sift the flour, salt, mustard and pepper into a bowl and mix in most of the cheese. Blend the fresh yeast with the warm water; for dried yeast, dissolve the sugar in the liquid, sprinkle the yeast on top and leave in a warm place until frothy – about 10 minutes. Add the yeast liquid to the dry ingredients and mix to form a firm dough, adding extra flour if necessary, to leave the sides of the bowl clean. Turn on to a floured surface and knead until smooth and elastic and no longer sticky – about 10 minutes by hand or 3–4 minutes in a large electric mixer fitted with a dough hook. Shape into a ball, place in an oiled polythene bag and put to rise in a warm place for about an hour or until doubled in size.

Remove from the bag, knock back and knead until smooth, then either shape all the dough to fit the large tin or half the dough to fit each of the smaller tins, or divide into 50g (2oz) pieces and shape into rolls. Cover with oiled polythene and put to prove in a warm place until the dough reaches the tops of the tins or the rolls have doubled in size. Remove polythene, sprinkle with the remaining cheese and bake in a moderately hot oven (190°C/375°F, Gas Mark 5) allowing about 45 minutes for large loaves, 30 minutes for smaller loaves and 15–20 minutes for rolls. Cheese bread tends to overbrown and overbake rather suddenly – so take care and watch the bread. Cool on a wire rack.

Variations

Cheese and Celery Bread

2–3 raw sticks of celery can be minced and added to the dry ingredients, and the tops of the loaves or rolls sprinkled with a mixture of 1 teaspoon celery salt and 25g (1oz) grated cheese.

Cheese and Onion Bread

1 small raw minced onion can be added to the dry ingredients, and the tops of the loaves or rolls sprinkled with either grated cheese or a mixture of 1 teaspoon onion salt and 25g (1oz) finely grated cheese.

Cheese and Herb Bread

At the knocking back stage of making the bread, knead 3–4 tablespoons freshly chopped mixed herbs (or one type only) or 1½–2 tablespoons dried herbs into the dough and continue as for Cheese Bread.

Cheese and Peanut Bread

At the knocking back stage of making the bread, knead 50–75g (2–3oz) finely chopped salted peanuts into the dough. Continue as for Cheese Bread.

Tomato Bread

The colour of this bread is very unusual and a very modern idea. It is coloured and flavoured with tomato purée, and can be used for loaves or rolls. Decker sandwiches acquire a further dimension with a slice of tomato bread used with white and brown bread; salads and cheese blend well for filling sandwiches or rolls; and dinner party guests will be pleasantly surprised to find tomato rolls served in place of the more traditional brown or white rolls.

550g (1¼lb) strong white flour
1 level teaspoon salt
1 level teaspoon paprika
15g (½oz) fresh yeast, or
   1½ level teaspoons dried yeast and 1 teaspoon sugar
300ml (½pt) warm water (43°C/110°F)
142g (5oz) tube tomato purée
1 tablespoon oil
oatmeal, cracked wheat or sea salt crystals (optional)

Sift the flour, salt and paprika into a bowl. Blend the fresh yeast with half the water; for dried yeast, dissolve the sugar in half the water, sprinkle the yeast on top and leave in a warm place until frothy. Blend the tomato purée and oil in the remaining water, then add to the dry ingredients together with the yeast liquid. Mix to form a firm dough, adding a little extra flour if necessary, to leave the sides of the bowl clean. Turn on to a floured surface and knead until smooth and even – about 10 minutes by hand or 3–4 minutes if using a large electric mixer fitted with a dough hook. Shape into a ball, place in an oiled polythene bag and put to rise in a warm place until the dough has doubled in size and springs back when lightly pressed with a floured finger. Turn out on to a lightly floured surface, knock back, then knead until smooth and either shape to fit two greased 450g (1lb) loaf tins or make into rolls.

For rolls, divide the dough into 50g (2oz) pieces and shape into any of the shapes described on pages 34–6; alternatively make into flattish rolls by shaping each into a ball, flattening with the palm of your hand to about 2cm (¾in) thick and cutting a cross on each one. Loaves or rolls can be sprinkled with oatmeal, cracked wheat or sea salt, or left plain. Cover with oiled polythene and put to prove in a warm place until the dough reaches the tops of the tins or the rolls have doubled in size. Remove polythene and bake in a very hot oven (230°C/450°F, Gas Mark 8), allowing 30–40 minutes for loaves and 15–20 minutes for rolls, or until the bases sound hollow when tapped. Cool on a wire rack.

Suitable to freeze for 2–3 months.

Onion Bread

Onion lovers will like the flavour and crisp-textured top of this loaf. It can be served with butter and a chunk of cheese to make an excellent Ploughman's lunch platter when baked in a loaf, or as an accompaniment to soup, pâté, salads, etc, when baked into rolls. It is also good for picnics and packed lunches. Only freeze for up to 2 months as onions can become musty flavoured if stored for too long in the freezer.

350g (12oz) onions, peeled and thinly sliced
50g (2oz) butter or margarine
1 recipe quantity risen brown country bread dough (see page 32)
1 tablespoon double cream (optional)

Fry the onions very gently in the melted fat until soft but not coloured, stirring from time to time. Divide the dough in half and use 1 portion for a loaf and the other for rolls; do the same with the onions. For a loaf, shape half of 1 piece of dough to fit a greased 900g (2lb) loaf tin, pressing well down. Spread half of the fried onions over the dough and cover with the remaining piece of dough shaped to fit the tin. Mix the remainder of the onions with the cream (if used) and spread over the top of the loaf. Cover with oiled polythene and put to prove until doubled in size.

For the rolls, knead two-thirds of the onions into the dough; divide into 50–75g (2–3oz) pieces and shape each by rolling the dough to a long sausage and tying into a knot. Place on greased baking sheets, cover with oiled polythene and put to prove until doubled in size. Remove polythene and put a few pieces of onion on to each roll before baking. Bake in a hot oven (220°C/425°F, Gas Mark 7) allowing 30–40 minutes for the loaf (covering with foil or greaseproof paper when sufficiently browned) and 15–20 minutes for rolls. Cool on a wire rack. Serve warm or cold.

Suitable to freeze for up to 2 months.

Savoury Breads

Plain risen white bread dough (or brown country bread dough) can be used for savoury breads. Roll out, spread with a savoury mixture and then roll up like a Swiss roll before putting into the tin to prove and bake. This gives the sliced loaf an interesting marbled effect with the flavouring spread throughout the slice. Serve warm or cold, spread with butter. The basic recipe quantity will make two loaves. The dough can also be cut into 2·5cm (1in) slices after rolling up, to bake as rolls, keeping one cut side downwards.

Yeast Extract Loaf

Using half the basic risen dough – 450–550g (1–1¼lb) – knock back and knead until smooth and then roll out to a rectangle as wide as a 450g (1lb) loaf tin and about 1cm (½in) thick. Spread with 1–2 tablespoons yeast extract or meat extract leaving a 2·5cm (1in) margin clear all round. Beginning at the narrow end, roll up loosely like a Swiss roll. Put into the well greased tin, tucking the ends in and keeping the join underneath. Smooth the top, cover lightly with oiled polythene and put to prove in a warm place until the dough reaches the top of the tin. Bake in a very hot oven (230°C/450°F, Gas Mark 8) for 25–30 minutes until well browned and the base sounds hollow when tapped. Cool on a wire rack.

Herby Loaf

As above, but spread the dough with 50g (2oz) butter or margarine creamed with a good pinch of salt, pepper, crushed garlic (optional) and 3–4 tablespoons chopped fresh herbs or 2 tablespoons dried herbs.

Piquant Cheese Loaf

As Yeast Extract Loaf, but spread the dough with 25g (1oz) butter or margarine creamed with 75g (3oz) grated mature Cheddar cheese or 2 tablespoons grated Parmesan cheese and 1½–2 teaspoons made English or French mustard.

Olive Loaf

As Yeast Extract Loaf, but cover the rolled-out dough with sliced stuffed green olives or arrange whole stuffed green olives in rows across the dough. Roll up carefully to keep the olives in place.

Orange Bread

This bread has an unusual but pleasant flavour and is made from the usually discarded shells of the fruit from which the juice or flesh has been removed. It is good with cream, cottage or curd cheese, chocolate spread, marmalade, honey, etc, and makes an interestingly flavoured toast. Extra ingredients kneaded in at the knocking back stage make rather special teabreads.

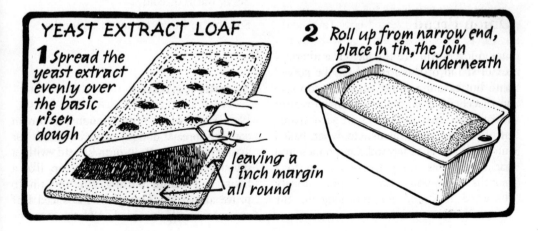

YEAST EXTRACT LOAF

1 Spread the yeast extract evenly over the basic risen dough

leaving a 1 inch margin all round

2 Roll up from narrow end, place in tin, the join underneath

3 medium or 2 large half orange shells

450g (1lb) strong white flour

2 level teaspoons salt

25g (1oz) caster sugar

25g (1oz) fresh yeast, or
   1 level tablespoon dried yeast and 1 level
   teaspoon sugar

150ml (¼pt) warm water (43°C/110°F)

1 egg, beaten

Grease two 450g (1lb) loaf tins. For the orange pulp, either mince or very finely chop the orange shells; alternatively, use the whole of a medium orange – flesh, juice and shell, but discarding any pips. Sift the flour, salt and sugar into a bowl. Blend the fresh yeast with the liquid; for dried yeast, dissolve the sugar in the liquid, sprinkle the yeast on top and leave in a warm place until frothy – about 10 minutes. Add the yeast liquid to the dry ingredients together with the beaten egg and orange pulp, and mix to form a softish dough, adding a little extra flour if necessary, to leave the sides of the bowl clean. Turn on to a floured surface and knead until smooth and even – about 10 minutes by hand or 3–4 minutes in a large electric mixer fitted with a dough hook. Shape into a ball, place in an oiled polythene bag and put to rise in a warm place until doubled in size. Remove from the bag, knock back and knead until even – about 2 minutes.

Shape the dough to fit the loaf tins or, if preferred, to fit one greased 900g (2lb) loaf tin. Cover with oiled polythene and put to prove in a warm place until the dough reaches the tops of the tins. Remove polythene and bake in a fairly hot oven (200°C/400°F, Gas Mark 6) for 30–35 minutes for small loaves; and 40–50 minutes for a large loaf, or until well browned and the base sounds hollow when tapped. Cool on a wire rack.

Variations

Orange Sultana Bread

Add 175g (6oz) sultanas (or raisins or mixed dried fruit) to the dry ingredients and proceed as for Orange Bread. The dough will take longer to rise because of the addition of the fruit.

Orange Treacle Bread

At the knocking back stage, knead 6–8 tablespoons black treacle into the dough, squeezing with your hands until it is evenly mixed and no longer sticky. Pour into two greased 450g (1lb) loaf tins and proceed as for Orange Bread.

Orange Nut Bread

At the knocking back stage, knead 175g (6oz) chopped walnuts (or mixed nuts) and 3–4 tablespoons thick honey into the dough until evenly mixed and no longer streaky. Divide between two greased 450g (1lb) loaf tins and proceed as above.

Orange Tutti-Frutti Bread

At the knocking back stage, knead and squeeze 100g (4oz) mixed dried fruit, 50g (2oz) walnuts and 2 tablespoons thick honey into the dough and proceed as above.

Rice Bread

This bread was baked in the eighteenth and nineteenth centuries because the addition of rice helped to keep the bread moist which was an essential factor before the introduction of freezers, especially if several loaves were to be baked at a time. The texture is quite light and fairly holey, but the bread is easy to make and has a good flavour. A smaller proportion of rice can be used now that it is becoming so expensive, to keep the cost of the bread down.

75g (3oz) raw long-grain rice
550g (1¼lb) strong white flour
15g (½oz) salt
15g (½oz) fresh yeast, or
    1½ level teaspoons dried yeast and 1 level teaspoon sugar
about 175ml (7fl oz) warm water (43°C/110°F)

Grease three 450g (1lb) loaf tins or one 900g (2lb) tin and one smaller tin. Cook the rice in plenty of boiling water until it is very tender and beginning to turn mushy; drain but keep warm. Sift the flour and salt into a bowl and mix in the warm rice. Blend the fresh yeast with half the warm water; for dried yeast, dissolve the sugar in half the water, sprinkle the yeast on top and leave in a warm place until frothy – about 10 minutes. Add to the dry ingredients with sufficient of the remaining water to form a fairly soft dough. Beat well with your hand or a wooden spoon and cover the bowl with a wet cloth or oiled polythene. Put to rise in a warm place until doubled in size and bubbly – about 1½ hours. Turn out on to a floured surface and knead very lightly adding a little extra flour if necessary, as this is a soft dough. Divide up and shape roughly to fit the tins. Cover with oiled polythene and put to prove until the dough reaches the tops of the tins. Remove polythene, bake in a very hot oven (230°C/450°F, Gas Mark 8) for 15 minutes, then reduce to fairly hot (200°C/400°F, Gas Mark 6) and continue for a further 15–20 minutes. Remove the loaves from the tins and return to the oven for a further 10–20 minutes or until the base sounds hollow when tapped and the loaf is firm. Cool on a wire rack.

Potato Bread

Potato bread used to be baked for various reasons; sometimes when there was a grain shortage, sometimes for its extra keeping qualities, and often just because people preferred the flavour and texture. The proportion of potato used varies greatly but about 100g (4oz) mashed potato to each 450g (1lb) flour is a good balance. The potato is best freshly boiled and finely mashed or sieved just before being mixed thoroughly with the flour; however, it can be used cold but it will then be more difficult to amalgamate with the flour and will not give such a light-textured loaf. The baked loaf has a particularly crisp crust.

about 175g (6oz) potatoes
salt
25g (1oz) butter or margarine
450g (1lb) strong white flour
15g (½oz) fresh yeast, or
    1½ level teaspoons dried yeast and 1 level teaspoon sugar
150ml (¼pt) warm milk (43°C/110°F)
150ml (¼pt) warm water (43°C/110°F)

Grease one 900g (2lb) loaf tin or two 450g (1lb) tins very thoroughly. Peel the potatoes and cook in well salted water until tender. Drain and either mash very thoroughly or sieve. (The potatoes should not be mushy or the extra water will spoil the texture of the loaf.) Weigh 100g (4oz) potato and beat in the fat. Add the sifted flour and 15g (½oz) salt, and mix thoroughly. Blend the fresh yeast with the milk; for dried yeast, dissolve the sugar in the milk, sprinkle the yeast on top and leave in a warm place until frothy – about 10 minutes. Add the yeast liquid and water to the dry ingredients and mix to form a fairly firm dough. Turn on to a floured surface and knead until smooth and even – about 10 minutes by hand or 3–4 minutes in an

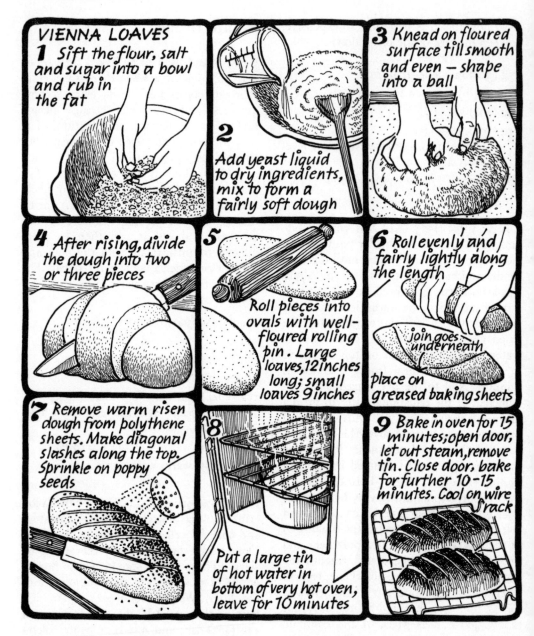

VIENNA LOAVES
1 Sift the flour, salt and sugar into a bowl and rub in the fat

2 Add yeast liquid to dry ingredients, mix to form a fairly soft dough

3 Knead on floured surface till smooth and even – shape into a ball

4 After rising, divide the dough into two or three pieces

5 Roll pieces into ovals with well-floured rolling pin. Large loaves, 12 inches long; small loaves 9 inches

6 Roll evenly and fairly lightly along the length

join goes underneath

place on greased baking sheets

7 Remove warm risen dough from polythene sheets. Make diagonal slashes along the top. Sprinkle on poppy seeds

8 Put a large tin of hot water in bottom of very hot oven, leave for 10 minutes

9 Bake in oven for 15 minutes; open door, let out steam, remove tin. Close door, bake for further 10–15 minutes. Cool on wire rack

electric mixer fitted with a dough hook. Shape into a ball, place in an oiled polythene bag and put to rise in a warm place until doubled in size. Turn out the dough, which will be rather soft, and knead until smooth. Either shape to fit the large loaf tin or the two smaller tins, or divide into 50g (2oz) pieces and shape into rolls, placing them on greased baking sheets. Cover with oiled polythene and put to prove in a warm place until the dough reaches the tops of the tins or the rolls have doubled in size. Remove polythene and bake in a hot oven (220°C/425°F, Gas Mark 7) for about 30 minutes for small loaves, 40–45 minutes for a larger loaf and about 15 minutes for rolls.

Cool on a wire rack. This bread makes excellent toast.

Variations

Cheese and Potato Bread

At the knocking back stage, knead in 100g (4oz) finely grated Cheddar cheese until smooth, then shape to fit the tins. A little cheese may also be sprinkled on the crust before baking.

Herb and Potato Bread

As above but knead in 2–3 tablespoons freshly chopped herbs or 1–2 tablespoons dried herbs.

Vienna Loaves

It is almost impossible to achieve the true flavour and texture of a French baguette loaf baked in France in a domestic cooker, but this recipe, together with the pan of water in the oven for part of the baking time, helps to create the steamy atmosphere necessary to give the crisp but soft-textured crust and soft crumb of the French loaf. Here strong flour is used, but sometimes ordinary household plain flour is preferred. It does keep fresh for longer than true French bread but is still best eaten as fresh as possible.

450g (1lb) strong white flour

1½ level teaspoons salt

1 level teaspoon caster sugar

25g (1oz) lard or margarine

25g (1oz) fresh yeast, or
  1 level tablespoon dried yeast and 1 level teaspoon sugar

300ml (½pt) warm milk and water, mixed (43°C/110°F)

poppy seeds (optional)

Sift the flour, salt and sugar into a bowl and rub in the fat. Blend the fresh yeast with the milk and water; for dried yeast, dissolve the sugar in the liquid, sprinkle the yeast on top and leave in a warm place until frothy. Add the yeast liquid to the dry ingredients and mix to form a fairly soft dough. Turn on to a lightly floured surface and knead until smooth and even – about 10 minutes by hand or 3–4 minutes in a large electric mixer fitted with a dough hook. Shape into a ball, place in an oiled polythene bag and put to rise in a warm place for 45–60 minutes or until doubled in size. Remove from the bag, knead until smooth and divide into 2 or 3 pieces. Roll each piece out thinly to an oval, keeping the rolling pin well floured to prevent tearing the dough – about 30cm (12in) for large loaves and 23cm (9in) for smaller ones. Beginning at a long side, roll up each piece evenly and fairly tightly. Place on greased baking sheets, either straight or curved, keeping the join underneath. Cover with oiled polythene and put to prove in a warm place for about 30 minutes or until doubled in size and puffy. Remove polythene, make several diagonal slashes along the top of each loaf and sprinkle with poppy seeds if liked. Put a large tin of hot water in the bottom of a very hot oven (230°C/450°F, Gas Mark 8) to produce a steamy atmosphere. Leave for 10 minutes then put the loaves in the oven and bake for 15 minutes. Open the door, let out the steam and take out the tin of water. Close the door and cook for a further 10–15 minutes or until the crust is crispy and a dark golden brown. Cool on a wire rack.

Makes 2 or 3 loaves

Suitable to freeze for up to 6 months.

Garlic or Herb Bread

Beat 100g (4oz) butter until soft then beat in 2–3 crushed cloves of garlic or ½–1 teaspoon garlic powder and a pinch of salt and pepper; for herb bread, add 2 tablespoons freshly chopped mixed herbs or 1 tablespoon dried herbs in place of the garlic. Cut the Vienna loaf into slanting slices about 2·5cm (1in) thick, leaving a hinge on the bottom crust. Spread the slices with savoury butter, putting each slice carefully back into position after spreading, then wrap the whole loaf loosely in foil. Put into a fairly hot oven (200°C/400°F, Gas Mark 6) for 15–20 minutes until really hot, opening the foil for the last 5 minutes to crisp up the crust.

Bran Bread

Centuries ago, bran bread was made to give to servants as it was the coarsest type available and would both satisfy huge appetites and provide the necessary roughage. It was made in vast quantities and baked into very large loaves. This is a very different recipe from the one used in those days, but it has an interesting texture and flavour. It is, however, a slow riser.

225g (8oz) strong white flour

100g (4oz) wholewheat flour

100g (4oz) broad bran

1 level teaspoon salt

2 level teaspoons sugar

about 300ml (½pt) warm milk and water mixed (43°C/110°F)

25g (1oz) fresh yeast, or
    3 level teaspoons dried yeast and 1 level teaspoon caster sugar

25g (1oz) butter or margarine, melted

Grease one 900g (2lb) loaf tin or two 450g (1lb) tins. Sift the white flour into a bowl, mix in the wholewheat flour, bran, salt and sugar, and warm slightly. Blend the fresh yeast with the warm liquid; for dried yeast, dissolve the sugar in the liquid, sprinkle the

yeast on top and leave in a warm place until frothy – about 10 minutes. Add to the dry ingredients with the melted butter and mix to a fairly soft dough. Knead on a lightly floured surface for about 5 minutes until smooth and elastic. Using a large electric mixer fitted with a dough hook, it will take only 2–3 minutes. Shape into a ball, place in an oiled polythene bag and put to rise in a warm place until doubled in size (1½–2 hours). Remove the dough, knock back, then knead until smooth and shape to fit the tins. Cover with oiled polythene and put to prove until the dough nearly fills the tins – about 1–1½ hours. Remove polythene, bake in a very hot oven (230°C/450°F, Gas Mark 8) for about 25 minutes or until the base sounds hollow. Cool on a wire rack.

Coconut Bread

This a relic from the eighteenth century when coconut, rather surprisingly, was a favourite flavouring. A fresh coconut can be grated and used for the recipe below but as they are not always easy to obtain, I have used desiccated coconut which is always readily available and much easier to prepare. The bread has a good flavour and an interesting texture.

75g (3oz) desiccated coconut

300ml (½pt) milk

15g (½oz) fresh yeast, or
    1½ level teaspoons dried yeast and 1 level teaspoon sugar

550g (1¼lb) strong white flour

1 level teaspoon salt

1 level tablespoon caster sugar

25g (1oz) butter, margarine or lard

Grease one 450g (1lb) loaf tin and one 900g (2lb) tin. Put the coconut and milk into a saucepan and heat very gently for 10 minutes, bringing only just up to the boil. Leave to stand until warm, then strain, pressing out all the liquid from the coconut with a potato masher. Make the liquid up to 300ml (½pt) with warm water, then blend the fresh yeast with it; for dried yeast, dissolve the sugar in the liquid, sprinkle the yeast on top and leave in a warm place for about 10 minutes or until frothy. Sift the flour, salt and sugar into a bowl and rub in the fat. Add the drained coconut and mix very thoroughly, then add the yeast liquid and mix to form a fairly soft dough. Beat until smooth and even by hand or with a wooden spoon for about 3 minutes, or in a large electric mixer fitted with a dough hook for 1–2 minutes. Cover the bowl with a damp cloth or oiled polythene and put to rise in a warm place until doubled in size.

Turn out the dough, knock back and knead until smooth. Either divide into 50g (2oz) pieces to make rolls, or shape one-third of the dough to fit the small tin and the remainder to fit the large tin, or shape into 2 cobs (see page 24) and put on greased baking sheets. Cover with a sheet of oiled polythene and put to prove in a warm place until the rolls or cobs have doubled in size, or the dough reaches the tops of the tins. Remove cover and bake in a hot oven (220°C/425°F, Gas Mark 7), allowing about 15 minutes for rolls, 30–35 minutes for a small loaf and 40–45 minutes for a large loaf.

Suitable to freeze for 2–3 months.

Caraway Bread

Caraway seeds were a great favourite for flavouring in the eighteenth century and although they almost disappeared early this century, they are now beginning to become more popular again. The plant originated in the East and was widely used as a spice by the Greeks. It can be grown in this country and indeed used to be on quite a large scale, but is now more often imported. As well as a flavouring for the famous seed cake, caraway seeds are widely used in continental breads and baking, and are found in the teatime yeast cakes called Wigs.

350g (12oz) strong white flour
1 level teaspoon salt
1–2 level teaspoons caraway seeds
100g (4oz) wholemeal flour
15g (½oz) fresh yeast, or
    1½ level teaspoons dried yeast and 1 tea-spoon sugar
300ml (½pt) warm water (43°C/110°F)
25g (1oz) lard or margarine
salted water

Sift the white flour and salt into a bowl and mix in the caraway seeds and brown flour. Blend the fresh yeast with half the warm water; for dried yeast, dissolve the sugar in half the water, sprinkle the yeast on top and leave in a warm place until frothy – about 10 minutes. Melt the lard or margarine in the remaining liquid and cool to lukewarm. Add the yeast liquid and other liquid to the dry ingredients and mix to form a fairly soft dough. Turn on to a floured surface and knead until smooth – about 10 minutes by hand or 3–4 minutes in a large electric mixer fitted with a dough hook. Shape into a ball, place in an oiled polythene bag and put to rise in a warm place until doubled in size. Remove to a floured surface, knock back and knead until smooth; divide into equal pieces and shape into two cobs or two batons (see pages 24–5). Place on greased baking sheets, cover with oiled polythene and put to prove until doubled in size. One larger cob or baton can be made, if preferred. Remove polythene, brush with salted water and bake in a fairly hot oven (200°C/400°F, Gas Mark 6) for 25–30 minutes for small loaves and about 10 minutes longer for a large loaf, or until the base of the loaf

HARVEST LOAF

sheaf

complete wheatsheaf

stalk

1 Roll out a sausage shape about 7 inches long and place on baking sheet. Next, shape about 6 ounces of dough into a semicircle; place at the top of the stalk, join and flatten to give the basic wheatsheaf shape

2 Roll long thin sausages, thinner than a pencil, about 7 inches long. Plait three of these together, lay the rest on the stalk then place the plaiting over the stalks, tuck in the ends

3 To make the ears of corn, roll a lot of small sausages, arrange on the crescent to completely cover the area

4 Brush carefully all over with beaten egg; then with oiled scissors snip each sausage to make it look like an ear of corn. Shape the remaining dough into a small mouse with a long tail and position it to look as though it is climbing up the sheaf of corn

The finished loaf

sounds hollow when tapped. Remove to a wire rack and brush again with salted water. Leave to cool. This dough can also be made into rolls.

Suitable to freeze for up to 2 months.

Harvest Bread

This is the traditional loaf made after the harvest as a thanksgiving for all the harvest having been safely gathered in. It can take the shape of a wheatsheaf or sometimes of a platter with the five loaves and two fishes in the centre. The whole loaf should be shaped on the baking sheet for it is almost impossible to move when made. This recipe makes a small loaf but for a large one double the quantities and use two baking sheets stuck together and positioned on the removed shelf of the oven so the loaf can be shaped and easily slipped into the oven.

1 recipe quantity risen basic white bread dough (see page 22)

beaten egg to glaze

Thoroughly grease a large baking sheet – preferably the base of the sheet if it has raised sides all round, to make it easier to slide the baked loaf off.

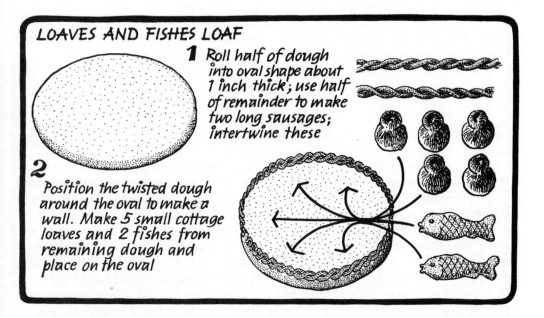

LOAVES AND FISHES LOAF

1 Roll half of dough into oval shape about 1 inch thick; use half of remainder to make two long sausages; intertwine these

2 Position the twisted dough around the oval to make a wall. Make 5 small cottage loaves and 2 fishes from remaining dough and place on the oval

Wheatsheaf Loaf

Using about 100g (4oz) dough, roll out to a sausage shape about 18cm (7in) long, place on the baking sheet as a base for the stalks of the corn and flatten a little. Next take about 175g (6oz) dough, shape into a semi-circle and place at the top of the basic stalk, curving it round and flattening it to give the basic wheatsheaf shape. Then divide the rest of the dough in half and put 25g (1oz) aside from 1 piece for the mouse. Divide the remainder of the smaller piece into portions and roll into long thin sausages, thinner than a pencil and about 18cm (7in) long. Plait three of these together; lay the others on the basic stalk to cover it completely. Wind the plaited dough around the centre of the stalks, tucking the ends underneath. For the ears of corn, divide the remaining dough into small pieces each about 15g (½oz) and roll into small sausages. Arrange these over the crescent in radiating circles to cover it completely. Brush all over the loaf carefully with beaten egg. Then with a pair of scissors brushed with oil, snip into each of the sausage shapes in several places to make the ears of corn. Use the remaining 25g (1oz) dough to shape into a minute mouse with a long tail and position it as if climbing up the sheaf of corn. Glaze again. Cover with oiled polythene and put to prove for only 10 minutes. Remove the polythene and bake in a hot oven (220°C/425°F, Gas Mark 7) for 15–20 minutes, then lower the temperature to moderate (170°C/325°F, Gas Mark 3) and continue baking for about 15 minutes until firm to the touch. Carefully slide on to a wire rack to cool.

Loaves and Fishes Loaf

Roll half of the dough into an oval shape about 2·5cm (1in) thick and place carefully on the greased baking sheet. Then use half the remaining dough to make into 2 long thin sausages. Twist these together to represent a rope and then position it all round the edge of the dough oval to make a wall. The rest of the dough is used to make 5 tiny cottage loaves and 2 flat fishes, with scissor snipping to represent the scales and minute pieces of dough for eyes. Position on the platter and brush the whole thing carefully with beaten egg. Cover with oiled polythene and put to prove and bake as above, but for about 5 minutes less time.

eighteenth and early nineteenth centuries, these pieces of 'toast-like' bread were eaten with cheese; nowadays they are very good served with pâté or soup and quite different from the usual rolls, French bread or toast.

Pulled Bread

On baking day when the loaves were freshly out of the oven, any extra loaf was often turned into pulled bread. This consisted of crisp pieces of bread which were made by pulling the crumb of a fresh loaf into pieces each about 4–5cm (1½–2in), by tearing it apart with two forks. These pieces were put on to a baking sheet and returned to a hot oven for about 10–15 minutes or until crisp and golden brown, but with the centres still a little soft. Originally, in the

Pizza

Pizzas have become anglicised over the last few years, particularly with the arrival of the pizza restaurants and snack bars. Many of those commercially available hardly resemble an Italian pizza at all, but the idea of a flat round open pie with a bread dough base instead of pastry, and a tomato and cheese topping, has caught on and everyone wants to try their hand at their own versions. Basic risen white bread dough can be used provided it is well brushed with oil, but

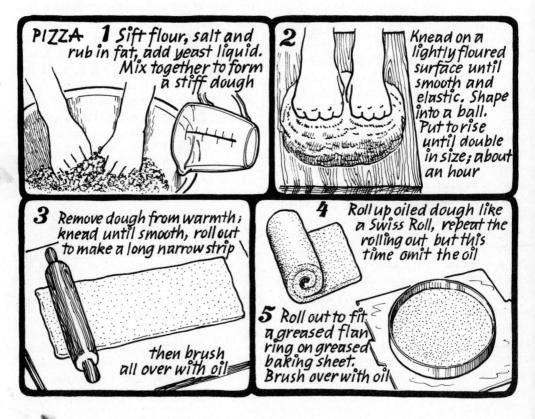

PIZZA **1** Sift flour, salt and rub in fat, add yeast liquid. Mix together to form a stiff dough

2 Knead on a lightly floured surface until smooth and elastic. Shape into a ball. Put to rise until double in size; about an hour

3 Remove dough from warmth; knead until smooth, roll out to make a long narrow strip then brush all over with oil

4 Roll up oiled dough like a Swiss Roll, repeat the rolling out but this time omit the oil

5 Roll out to fit a greased flan ring on greased baking sheet. Brush over with oil

whatever the dough, it must be rolled out thinly. In Italy a pizza means any sort of pie or tart, usually open but sometimes covered, with either a pastry or yeast dough base. They can also be made in shallow square or oblong tins.

15g (½oz) fresh yeast, or
   1½ level teaspoons dried yeast and 1 level teaspoon sugar
about 150ml (¼pt) warm water (43°C/110°F)
225g (8oz) strong white flour
1 level teaspoon salt
15g (½oz) lard or margarine
oil

Toppings
see below

Blend the fresh yeast with the water; for dried yeast, dissolve the sugar in the water, sprinkle the yeast on top and leave in a warm place until frothy – about 10 minutes. Sift the flour and salt into a bowl and rub in the fat. Add the yeast liquid and mix to form a fairly stiff dough. Knead on a lightly floured surface until smooth and elastic – about 10 minutes by hand or 3–4 minutes in an electric mixer fitted with a dough hook. Shape into a ball, place in an oiled polythene bag, and put to rise in a warm place until doubled in size – about 1 hour, or longer in cooler conditions.

Remove dough, knead until smooth and roll out to a long narrow strip. Brush all over with oil and roll the dough up like a Swiss roll; repeat the rolling process again but without oil. For 1 large pizza, roll out all the dough to fit a greased 30cm (12in) plain flan ring on a greased baking sheet; for 2 smaller ones, divide the dough in half and roll each piece to fit a 20cm (8in) flan ring. Brush all over with oil, add the topping to the pizza and then put to prove in a warm place for about 15 minutes. Remove polythene, bake in a hot oven (220°C/425°F,

Gas Mark 7) for about 20–25 minutes, then reduce the temperature to moderate (180°C/350°F, Gas Mark 4) and continue for 15–20 minutes for a large pizza and 10–15 minutes for smaller ones. Remove flan rings and serve hot or cold.

Serves 4–6

Toppings

Onion and Tomato
350g (12oz) onions, peeled and sliced
1–2 cloves garlic, crushed (optional)
2 tablespoons oil
450g (1lb) tomatoes, peeled and sliced or an 822g (1lb 13oz) can tomatoes
salt and pepper
1–2 level teaspoons oregano or basil
175g (6oz) cheese, thinly sliced (Mozzarella, Bel Paese or Gouda)
1 can anchovy fillets, drained
a few black or stuffed green olives

Fry the onions and garlic gently in oil until soft but only lightly coloured. Add the fresh tomatoes or partly drained canned tomatoes and cook for about 10 minutes until thick. Season well. Spread over the pizza base, sprinkle with herbs and cover with sliced cheese. Arrange anchovies on top in a lattice pattern, filling in some of the gaps with olives.

Pepper and Salami
2 large onions, peeled and sliced
1 green pepper, seeded and chopped
1–2 cloves garlic, crushed (optional)
2 tablespoons oil
salt and pepper
175g (6oz) salami, thinly sliced
350g (12oz) tomatoes, peeled and sliced
100g (4oz) grated cheese (Emmenthal, Gouda or Cheddar)

Fry the onions, pepper and garlic in oil until soft but only lightly coloured. Season well and spread over the pizza base. Arrange slices of salami on top and cover with the tomatoes. Sprinkle with grated cheese.

Bacon and Mushroom

1 onion, peeled and sliced

1 clove garlic, crushed (optional)

2 tablespoons oil

175g (6oz) mushrooms, sliced

350g (12oz) fresh tomatoes, peeled and sliced

1 level teaspoon mixed herbs

salt and pepper

100g (4oz) mature Cheddar cheese, grated

175g (6oz) streaky bacon rashers, rinded

pickled walnuts or olives to garnish

Fry the onion and garlic in oil until soft then add the mushrooms and continue for 2–3 minutes. Spoon over the pizza dough, cover with tomatoes and sprinkle first with herbs and seasoning and then the grated cheese. Arrange rashers of bacon in a lattice or cartwheel design on the pizza. Garnish with walnuts or olives when baked.

Note Half the bacon can be chopped and fried with the onions, if preferred.

Prawn Creole

1 large onion, peeled and sliced

1 clove garlic, crushed (optional)

2 tablespoons oil

1 red pepper, seeded and thinly sliced

822g (1lb 13oz) can peeled tomatoes, partly drained

1 level tablespoon tomato paste

2 teaspoons Worcestershire sauce

salt and pepper

100–175g (4–6oz) peeled prawns

100g (4oz) Mozzarella cheese, sliced

a few whole prawns to garnish

Fry the onion and garlic in the oil until soft. Drain and lay over the pizza base. Fry the pepper in same oil then add the tomatoes, tomato paste, Worcestershire sauce and seasoning to the pan and simmer gently for 5–10 minutes or until thick; stir in the prawns and spoon over the onion. Lay the cheese on top before baking. Garnish with whole prawns after baking.

Teatime Favourites

The British recipes for yeasted fare and baking are thought by many to be the best the country has to offer. The richer and sweet loaves and buns, in other words the teatime favourites, are plentiful and there are many recipes which are often similar in appearance and ingredients but found in different areas, each having its own regional characteristics and name. An example of this is Bara Brith, the famous speckled currant bread of Wales which is similar to the Selkirk Bannock of Scotland, the Barm Brack of Ireland and the simply named Currant Bread of England. The ingredients in each version include dried fruit, peel, spices, butter and sometimes eggs, but the proportions vary and the loaves are often baked in different shapes.

Perhaps the most traditional of all are the Crumpets, Pikelets and Muffins which used to be sold in the streets by the muffin-man or crumpet-seller. He carried his wares wrapped in a cloth in a wicker tray or basket which was often balanced on his head; he rang a bell to announce his presence, and even now children will chant the famous song about him, 'Oh, have you seen the muffin-man?' Crumpets are available commercially but the home-made version is that much better still, often with more holes for the butter to sink into. Muffins largely disappeared after the muffin-man ceased to trade early this century but now some supermarkets have begun to stock them again and consequently this has aroused an interest in baking them at home.

There are many other favourites which have survived, some from as long ago as the fifteenth and sixteenth centuries, whilst others are much younger. Wigs date well back, being popular when caraway seeds were greatly favoured; London and Chelsea Buns became famous at the Old Chelsea Bun House in Pimlico where everyone from royalty downwards would go to eat their buns and watch the world go by; whilst the Lardy and Dough Cakes were invented to use up the left-over plain bread dough from baking day.

This selection of recipes has been drawn from around the country and includes the famous and not so well known yeasted teatime specialities. Although they are all suitable to serve for tea or high tea they don't have to be served only at teatime; try a Yeasted Pastry or Fruit Finger Bun at coffee time, or a slice of Iced Twist for a late evening snack – but not if you are trying to count the calories and lose weight!

Malt Bread

This sticky loaf, full of sultanas, is a great favourite of many, especially children, when it is served spread with butter at teatime. Although called a bread and made with yeast, I think it really is one of our English tea-table specialities and much more of a cake than a bread. It is made with household flour and not the strong bread flour.

100g (4oz) malt extract

1 level tablespoon black treacle

25g (1oz) butter or margarine

450g (1lb) plain flour (not strong flour)

1 level teaspoon salt

175g (6oz) sultanas

25g (1oz) fresh yeast, or
    1 level tablespoon dried yeast and 1 level
    teaspoon caster sugar

150ml (¼pt) warm water (43°C/110°F)

honey to glaze (optional)

Grease two 450g (1lb) loaf tins. Put the malt, treacle and fat into a saucepan and heat gently until melted and thoroughly blended. Cool until lukewarm. Sift the flour and salt into a bowl and mix in the sultanas. Blend the fresh yeast with the water; for dried yeast, dissolve the sugar in the water, sprinkle the yeast on top and leave in a warm place until frothy – about 10 minutes. Add the malt mixture and yeast liquid to the dry ingredients and mix to form a soft sticky dough. It may be necessary to add a little more flour to leave the sides of the bowl just clean, but add very sparingly for this has to be a very soft dough to get the required result. Knead on a floured surface for about 5 minutes or if using a large electric mixer fitted with a dough hook, for only 1–2 minutes. Divide the dough in half and shape each piece to fit a tin. Place in oiled polythene bags and put to rise until the dough reaches the tops of the tins and springs back when lightly pressed with a floured finger. Malt bread is a slow riser – it will take about 1½ hours in a warm place. Remove from the bags and bake in a fairly hot oven (200°C/400°F, Gas Mark 6) for 35–40 minutes until well risen and browned, and the base sounds hollow when tapped. Turn on to a wire rack to cool. For a sticky top brush with honey.

Note For a darker malt loaf, replace 1 tablespoon malt extract with black treacle and add a little gravy browning to the dough.

Suitable to freeze for up to 4 months.

Muffins

It is thought that the muffin-man and the crumpet-seller were the oldest of all the street traders. They were a familiar sight in the streets of London, ringing their bells and carrying their goods to sell to all, right up to the early 1930s. Muffins must be eaten very fresh, preferably on the day made or possibly the next, and they should be toasted then pulled apart after gently splitting round the sides, never cut. Always serve them hot or warm. No one is really sure when both muffins and crumpets first appeared for although recipes only date from the eighteenth century, they are spoken of before then. There are many variations in the proportions of the main ingredients necessary for making muffins; this recipe, using half ordinary plain flour and half strong bread flour, gives a good texture and rise. A good tip is to warm the flour in the oven before beginning to make muffins.

225g (8oz) plain flour

225g (8oz) strong white flour

1 level teaspoon salt

2 level teaspoons caster sugar

300ml (½pt) warm milk (43°C/110°F)

Muffins

15g (½oz) fresh yeast, or
  2 level teaspoons dried yeast
1 egg, beaten
2 tablespoons oil
ground rice or rice flour

Sift the flours and salt into a bowl and if time allows, warm in the oven for a few minutes. Dissolve the sugar in the warm milk and either blend in the fresh yeast or sprinkle the dried yeast on top and leave in a warm place until frothy. Add the yeast liquid to the flour, together with the beaten egg and oil, and mix to form a soft dough. As this is a very soft dough it is easier to knead in an electric mixer fitted with a dough hook for 3–4 minutes; by hand, use as little extra flour as possible and knead for about 10 minutes. Put into a floured bowl (or leave in the mixing bowl), cover with polythene or a damp cloth and put to rise in a warm place until the dough has doubled in size and springs back when

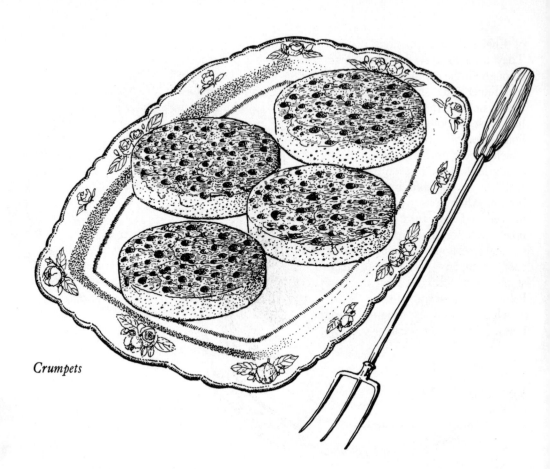

Crumpets

lightly pressed with a floured finger. Remove from the bowl to a surface dredged with a mixture of flour and ground rice. Knock back and roll out to a thickness of 1cm (½in). Cut into 7·5cm (3in) rounds with a plain cutter and place on a baking sheet well dredged with ground rice. Sprinkle muffins lightly with more ground rice and put to prove in a warm place until almost doubled in size. Heat a griddle or heavy-based frying pan over a gentle heat, rub with lard or oil and place a few muffins carefully on it. Cook gently for 8–10 minutes or until the undersides are firm and an even dark golden brown. Turn over and cook for a further 8–10 minutes or until similarly browned and firm.

To eat at once, break into the sides of the muffin all round, toast each side and then pull open. Spread generously with butter or cover with thin slices of butter, reassemble and cut in half. To eat later, first cool them on a wire rack then toast on each side. Split them in half and spread thickly with butter; reassemble, cut in half and eat warm. If the muffins are becoming stale cut into two or three horizontal slices and toast each separately.

Makes about 12

Crumpets

Another of the delicacies sold by the muffin-man or crumpet-seller, crumpets are favoured by all – young and old – and are one of England's most famous teatime treats. They used to vary from region to region throughout the country, some being as large as a dinner plate, some with a proportion of brown flour in the batter, and others small like those we know today and very full of holes. Today's crumpet has small holes – which appear in the top as the batter cooks on a griddle, is of an even thickness all over and has a very thin brown crust on the bottom, whereas its predecessors were often uneven and very thin, some even without holes. Use ordinary plain flour not the strong bread flour for the best results. When cool, crumpets should be toasted on the smooth side first and then the holey side, before being spread thickly with butter which soaks into the crumpet through the holes. Serve hot or warm.

450g (1lb) plain flour (not strong)

1 level teaspoon salt

2 level teaspoons sugar

550ml (1pt) warm milk and water mixed (43°C/110°F)

15g (½oz) fresh yeast, or
  2 level teaspoons dried yeast

¼ level teaspoon bicarbonate of soda

2 teaspoons warm water

Sift the flour and salt into a bowl. Dissolve the sugar in the warm liquid and either blend in the fresh yeast or sprinkle the dried yeast over the top and leave in a warm place until frothy – about 10 minutes. Add the yeast liquid to the flour and mix to form a smooth batter, then beat hard for about 5 minutes, using a flat whisk, a wooden spoon or an electric mixer. Cover the bowl with polythene or a damp cloth and put in a warm place until the batter has doubled in size – about an hour. Dissolve the soda in the warm water and beat into the risen batter until smooth again. Repeat the rising. Grease 7·5cm (3in) plain metal rings and place them on a lightly greased and heated griddle or heavy-based frying pan. Add 3–4 tablespoons of batter to each ring and cook gently until the crumpets rise up, set and become full of holes – about 10 minutes. Continue until the base is a light brown then remove rings, turn over carefully and continue for 2–3 minutes until dried out. Cool on a wire rack. To serve, toast the crumpets on both sides, spread liberally with butter and serve hot.

Makes 12–14 crumpets

Note Some people prefer to use all water instead of a mixture of milk and water, saying it can give a lighter-textured crumpet.

Pikelets

Crumpets and pikelets were often thought to be the same thing, with the name pikelet meaning more or less the same in the North of England as a crumpet in the South. However, a pikelet was usually cooked without the rings necessary to make crumpets and was much thinner – more like a thick pancake – but it was still cooked on a griddle and had the holes in the surface caused by the air bubbles bursting during cooking. Whatever they are called, both are very good to eat and quite simple to make. The thinner crumpets or pikelets should be cooked, toasted lightly, spread with butter and then stacked up into piles of five or six to take to the table, so that the butter runs through the whole lot.

To make pikelets, use the crumpet batter (see this page) but add a little more liquid to it. Spoon a thin layer on to a greased hot griddle or heavy frying pan, turning over when lightly browned to complete the cooking. Either toast and serve at once, or leave to cool and toast and butter when required.

Plain Teacakes

Teacakes are flat round buns made with a yeast dough and are either plain or have various additions of fruit, nuts, peel, etc. Some are really quite large whilst others are much smaller. The amount of fruit (or not as may be) and the size of the teacake vary in different parts of the country.

450g (1lb) strong white flour

pinch of salt

40g (1½oz) butter or margarine

40g (1½oz) caster sugar

15g (½oz) fresh yeast, or
  1½ level teaspoons dried yeast and 1 level teaspoon sugar

about 200ml (8fl oz) warm milk (43°C/ 110°F)

1 egg, beaten

Glaze

2 level tablespoons caster sugar

4 tablespoons milk

Sift the flour and salt into a bowl, rub in the fat and stir in the sugar. Blend the fresh yeast with half the warm milk; for dried yeast, dissolve the sugar in half the liquid, sprinkle the yeast on top and leave in a warm place until frothy. Add the yeast liquid, egg and sufficient of the remaining milk to the dry ingredients to form a fairly soft dough. Knead on a lightly floured surface until smooth and even and no longer sticky – about 10 minutes by hand or 3–4 minutes in a large electric mixer fitted with a dough hook. Shape into a ball, place in an oiled polythene bag and put to rise until doubled in size. Remove from bag, knock back and knead until smooth, then divide into 6 pieces. Shape each piece into a flat round cake and place on greased baking sheets. Cover with oiled polythene and put to prove in a warm place for about 15 minutes or until puffy. Remove polythene and bake in a very hot oven (230°C/ 450°F, Gas Mark 8) for 10–15 minutes or until well browned. Meanwhile melt the sugar in the milk for the glaze and as the teacakes emerge from the oven, brush the tops once or twice with the glaze. Cool on wire racks. Serve split and buttered with jam or honey, or, if preferred, toasted and buttered.

Makes 6

Note For smaller teacakes divide the dough into 8 or 10 pieces.

Suitable to freeze for up to 6 months.

Yorkshire Teacakes

Originally, these teacakes from Yorkshire were said to be plain and they always appeared on the high-tea table. Nowadays, they often have fruit added which makes them more interesting. To serve teacakes correctly, they are split and buttered when fresh. They can also be toasted on both sides, then split in half and toasted inside; the bottom half is spread with butter and the teacake is inverted for a few minutes to prevent all the butter sinking into the bottom half! Whether this is correct or not, it makes the teacakes quite delicious.

15g (½oz) fresh yeast, or
  1½ level teaspoons dried yeast and 1 level teaspoon caster sugar

300ml (½pt) warm milk (43°C/110°F)

450g (1lb) strong white flour

1 level teaspoon salt

40g (1½oz) butter, margarine or lard

25g (1oz) caster sugar

75g (3oz) currants

25g (1oz) mixed peel (optional)

Blend the fresh yeast with the milk; for dried yeast, dissolve the sugar in the milk, sprinkle the yeast on top and leave in a warm place for about 10 minutes or until frothy. Sift the flour and salt into a bowl, rub in the fat and then mix in the sugar, currants and peel (if used). Add the yeast liquid and mix to form a fairly soft dough. Turn on to a floured surface and knead until smooth and even – about 10 minutes by hand or 3–4 minutes in a large electric mixer fitted with a dough hook. Shape into a ball and place in a lightly oiled polythene bag. Put to rise in a warm place until doubled in size. Turn out and knead lightly, then divide into 5 or 6 equal-sized pieces. Roll each piece out to a circle 15–18cm (6–7in) in diameter and place on greased baking sheets. Cover with a sheet of oiled polythene and put to prove in a warm place until doubled in size. Remove polythene and bake in a fairly hot oven (200°C/400°F, Gas Mark 6) for about 20 minutes until browned. Cool on a wire rack. The tops can be brushed with clear honey or syrup if a sticky top is required. To serve, split the teacakes in half and spread with butter, or toast as above.

Note This recipe can be used to make 10–12 small teacakes, baking as above but for only 15 minutes.

Suitable to freeze for up to 6 months.

Variations

Nutty Teacakes

Replace the currants with chopped walnuts or other nuts.

Ginger Teacakes

Replace the currants with finely chopped stem, preserved or crystallised ginger.

Orange or Lemon Teacakes

Add the grated rind of 1 orange or 1 lemon to the dry ingredients.

Sally Lunn

There are many versions of this famous teacake, which is supposed to come from Bath, and the name seems to be a derivative of the French *soleil lune* or 'sun and moon' which can be used to describe it in a way, for it has a rich golden top and white crumb. The proportions of fat and eggs to flour give the main variations of texture and flavour. The Sally Lunn can also be served in several ways: today it is most often topped with a glacé icing which runs down the sides, and is then cut in slices and spread with butter and perhaps honey or jam; traditionally, it is sliced up thickly whilst still hot, has melted butter poured or clotted cream spread over the slices, and is then reassembled prior to eating, preferably while still warm. It stales fairly quickly but toasts extremely well.

50g (2oz) butter
200ml (8fl oz) milk
1 level teaspoon caster sugar
15g (½oz) fresh yeast, or
   1½ level teaspoons dried yeast
450g (1lb) strong white flour
1 level teaspoon salt
2 eggs, beaten

Glaze
2 level tablespoons sugar
2 tablespoons water

Glacé Icing (optional)
see page 77

Grease two 13–15cm (5–6in) round cake

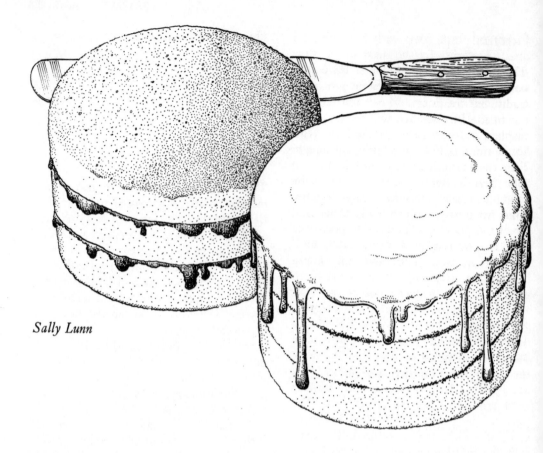

Sally Lunn

tins and coat lightly with flour. Melt the butter slowly in a pan, then stir in the milk, heating it if necessary, to about blood heat. Stir in the sugar and blend in the fresh yeast or sprinkle the dried yeast on top and leave to stand for about 10 minutes or until frothy. Sift the flour and salt into a bowl, make a well in the centre, then add the yeast mixture and beaten eggs. Mix to form a soft dough then turn on to a lightly floured surface and knead until smooth and even – about 5 minutes by hand or 3–4 minutes in a large electric mixer fitted with a dough hook. Divide the dough in half and shape into rounds to fit the tins. Put in the tins, cover with oiled polythene and put to rise in a warm place for 1–1½ hours or until the dough reaches the tops of the tins. Remove the polythene and bake in a hot oven (220°C/425°F, Gas Mark 7) for about

15–20 minutes or until a light golden brown. Boil the sugar and water together for 2 minutes then brush over the cake whilst still in the tin. Cool slightly then turn out and glaze the top again. Either leave until cold and serve as it is or cover the top with a thin glacé icing, or, to be traditional, cut the cake into 3 horizontal slices, spread each with a little softened butter or clotted cream, reassemble and eat whilst still warm.

Suitable to freeze (without adding butter, cream or glacé icing) for up to 3 months.

Variation
A little finely grated lemon rind or mixed spice can be added to the dry ingredients.

74

Cornish Splits

These yeasted scone-like buns are famous both in Cornwall and Devon as part of the traditional cream tea. They are split open and filled with clotted or whipped cream and raspberry (or other) home-made jam. Devonshire Splits are supposedly smaller than the Cornish variety, maybe Cornish folk had larger appetites. The name 'Thunder and Lightning' describes these splits when filled with cream and treacle.

15g (½oz) fresh yeast, or
  1½ level teaspoons dried yeast and 1 level teaspoon sugar
300ml (½pt) warm milk (43°C/110°F)
450g (1lb) strong white flour
1 level teaspoon salt
25g (1oz) caster sugar
40–50g (1½–2oz) butter or margarine

To serve
clotted or whipped cream
raspberry jam
icing sugar (optional)

Blend the fresh yeast with half the warm milk; for dried yeast, dissolve the sugar in half the milk, sprinkle the yeast on top and leave in a warm place until frothy – about 10 minutes. Sift the flour and salt into a bowl. Dissolve the sugar and fat in the remaining milk then cool to lukewarm before adding to the dry ingredients with the yeast liquid. Mix to form a soft dough and beat until smooth. Turn on to a floured surface and knead until smooth – about 10 minutes by hand or 3–4 minutes if using a large electric mixer fitted with a dough hook. Shape into a ball, place in an oiled polythene bag and put to rise in a warm place until doubled in size. Turn out on to a floured surface, knead lightly and divide into 15–16 pieces. Shape each into a small round cake and place on greased baking sheets. Cover with oiled polythene and put to prove until doubled in size. Remove polythene and bake in a hot oven (220°C/425°F, Gas Mark 7) for 15–20 minutes. Cool on a wire rack. Before serving, split the buns in half, spread with cream and jam, reassemble and dredge the tops with icing sugar, if liked. They may also be served hot when they are simply split and spread with butter.

Makes 15–16

Suitable to freeze (unfilled) for up to 6 months.

London Buns

These are plain long finger buns coated with pink or white glacé icing. At one time they had mixed fruit added which made a more interesting bun, but it is the plain mixture which is so popular today; a little dried fruit can be added at the knocking back stage, if liked. These buns originated somewhere in London, where exactly is not known, but they were also sold at the Chelsea Bun House of Pimlico Road along with their more famous counterpart the Chelsea Bun.

1 recipe quantity risen Cornish Split dough (see above)
75g (3oz) mixed dried fruit (optional)

Glacé Icing
225g (8oz) icing sugar
warm water
red food colouring

If using fruit, knead and squeeze it into the risen dough until evenly distributed. For plain or fruited buns, divide the dough into 50–75g (2–3oz) pieces and make each into a sausage shape using the palms of your hands. Place on well greased baking sheets

75

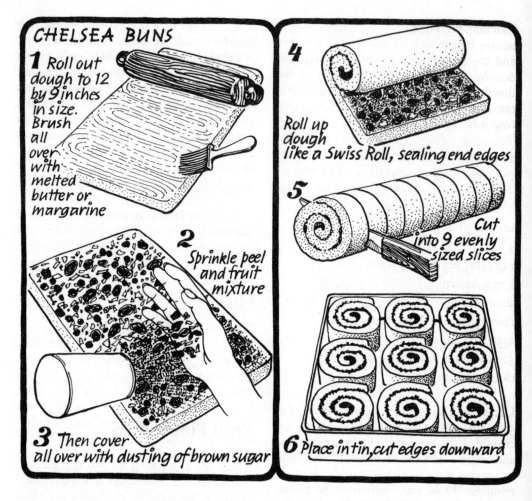

CHELSEA BUNS

1 Roll out dough to 12 by 9 inches in size. Brush all over with melted butter or margarine

2 Sprinkle peel and fruit mixture

3 Then cover all over with dusting of brown sugar

4 Roll up dough like a Swiss Roll, sealing end edges

5 Cut into 9 evenly sized slices

6 Place in tin, cut edges downward

either well apart for crisp-sided buns or about 2·5cm (1in) apart for soft-sided buns which will join up during baking. Cover with a sheet of oiled polythene and put to prove in a warm place until doubled in size. Remove polythene and bake in a hot oven (220°C/425°F, Gas Mark 7) for about 15 minutes or until well risen and a pale golden brown. Cool on a wire rack. Make up the glacé icing by sifting the icing sugar into a bowl and adding sufficient warm water to mix to a thick coating consistency. Spread white icing over the top of half the buns, then add a few drops of red colouring to the remaining icing to give a pale pink and use to spread over the remaining buns. Leave to set.

Suitable to freeze (without the icing) for up to 6 months.

Chelsea Buns

These originated at the old Chelsea Bun House where thousands of the buns, which came to be known as Chelsea Buns, were baked every day. The Bun House was in fact in Pimlico but the name Chelsea stuck to the buns. It was frequented by all types of people including George III and his Queen who enjoyed eating their buns and watching the world go by. These traditional square buns which are baked close together and are pulled apart to eat, revealing soft doughy sides, are made by rolling up the dough with a layer of dried fruit and sometimes spices, similar to a Swiss roll, and cutting it into slices before baking.

225g (8oz) strong white flour

15g (½oz) fresh yeast, or
   1½ level teaspoons dried yeast and 1 level teaspoon caster sugar

100ml (4fl oz) warm milk (43°C/110°F)

½ level teaspoon salt

15g (½oz) butter or margarine

1 egg, beaten

about 50g (2oz) melted butter or margarine

100g (4oz) mixed dried fruit

25g (1oz) mixed chopped peel

50g (2oz) soft brown sugar

clear honey to glaze

Grease an 18cm (7in) square cake tin. Put 50g (2oz) of the flour into a bowl with the crumbled fresh yeast – or the dried yeast and sugar – and the warm milk, and leave in a warm place until frothy – about 10–20 minutes. Whilst the yeast batter ferments, sift the remaining flour and the salt into a bowl and rub in the 15g (½oz) fat. Add the dry ingredients and the egg to the yeast batter and mix thoroughly to form a soft dough. Turn on to a lightly floured surface and knead until smooth and elastic – this should take about 5 minutes by hand or 2–3 minutes if kneaded in a large electric mixer fitted with a dough hook. Shape into a ball and place in a lightly oiled polythene bag tied at the neck. Put to rise in a warm place until doubled in size – 1–1½ hours. This is a richer dough so it takes a little longer to rise. Remove the dough from the polythene and knead on a floured surface until smooth. Roll out to a rectangle about 30×23cm (12×9in). Brush the whole surface with melted butter or margarine

and then sprinkle evenly with mixed fruit and peel and then with brown sugar.

Beginning at a long edge, roll up the dough like a Swiss roll, keeping it even, and seal the end with water. Cut into 9 even-sized slices and place, cut side downwards, in the prepared tin. They should not quite touch. Cover with oiled polythene and put to prove in a warm place until they have doubled in size and feel springy. Remove polythene and bake in a moderately hot oven (190°C/375°F, Gas Mark 5) for 30–35 minutes or until golden brown and firm to the touch. Turn the buns out still in one piece on to a wire rack and whilst still warm, brush the tops with clear honey. Pull apart when cold.

Makes 9

Suitable to freeze for 2–3 months.

Fruit Finger Buns

These are a variation on the currant bun but are shaped into fingers and when baked are coated with glacé icing. Spices and other flavourings can be added to the mixture if liked.

The London Bun sometimes contained fruit and was similar to but less fruited than this recipe, but is now more often unfruited. This type of bun is popular in the North of England.

1 recipe quantity risen currant bread dough
   (see page 44)

40g (1½oz) butter or margarine (optional)

2 level teaspoons ground cinnamon or mixed spice (optional)

Glacé Icing
225g (8oz) icing sugar, sifted

2–3 tablespoons warm water or fruit juice

77

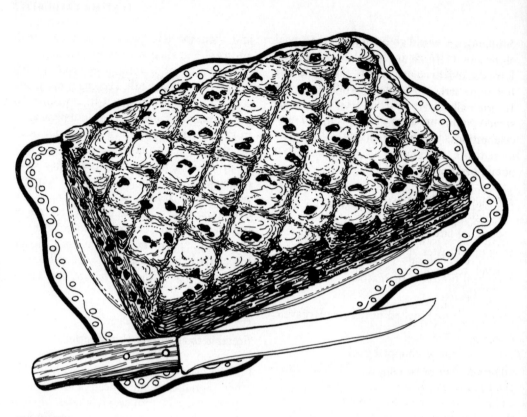

Lardy Cake

Knock back the risen currant bread dough and divide into 50g (2oz) pieces. For extra spiciness, cream the fat and spice together until fluffy. Roll each piece of dough to a circle about 10cm (4in) in diameter, spread a little spiced butter in the centre if liked, and roll the dough up fairly loosely. Place on greased baking sheets with the join underneath. Cover with oiled polythene and put to prove in a warm place until almost doubled in size – about 30–45 minutes (this dough takes longer to rise because of the fruit). Remove polythene and bake in a hot oven (220°C/425°F, Gas Mark 7) for 15–20 minutes until well browned and firm. Cool on a wire rack. Make the glacé icing by beating sufficient water or fruit juice into the icing sugar to give a coating consistency, then pour or spoon a little icing over each bun. Leave to set.

78

Makes 12–14

Suitable to freeze (without the icing) for up to 2 months.

Lardy Cake

This cake, based on risen white bread dough, is made in a similar way to a flaked pastry, adding flakes of pure lard, sugar, dried fruit and spice to the rolled-out dough which is then rolled up. The process is repeated several times before baking in a shallow rectangular tin. It has to be scored deeply into diamonds before baking, for tradition says that a lardy cake is always broken along the cracks – never cut! It was particularly popular in the North and

Midlands as well as the Wiltshire, Hampshire and Oxfordshire areas in the south. Lardy cake is extremely rich and indigestible but quite irresistible when properly made. It originally used to be a speciality cake served only at harvest-time and other celebrations, for the rich and expensive ingredients it requires were difficult to obtain or afford.

½ recipe quantity risen basic white bread dough (see page 22)

100g (4oz) lard (or more if liked)

100g (4oz) caster sugar

1 level teaspoon mixed spice or ground cinnamon

pinch of ground nutmeg

100g (4oz) mixed dried fruit

little oil

Grease a shallow rectangular tin about 28 × 18cm (11 × 7in). Knock back the risen dough and roll out to a rectangle about 0·5cm (¼in) thick. Cover the dough with half the lard cut into small flakes. Mix the sugar and spices together and sprinkle half over the dough followed by half the dried fruit. Roll up loosely like a Swiss roll, then roll out again thinly to a rectangle. Dot with flakes of the remaining lard, sprinkle with most of the remaining sugar and all the fruit. Roll up again loosely. Repeat the rolling out and rolling up process once or twice more without adding anything, then place in the prepared tin. Press out to fill the tin completely, especially at the corners. Cover with oiled polythene and put to prove in a warm place until almost doubled in size. Remove polythene, brush with oil and sprinkle with the remaining sugar. Score the top fairly deeply into diamonds with a sharp knife. Bake in a hot oven (220°C/425°F, Gas Mark 7) for about 30 minutes. Turn out carefully on to a wire rack. Serve fresh, broken into pieces, or warm gently and serve as a pudding with custard or cream.

Do not freeze.

Sussex Plum Heavies

These are a Sussex version of the famous Lardy Cake, but made into buns with the extra ingredients kneaded rather than rolled and folded into the dough. They have similar ingredients to and are prepared in the same way as Galettes which are like small flat Lardy Cakes which have been snipped round the edges before baking. The mixture can also be baked in a round cake tin or loaf tin to make a Dough Cake.

½ recipe quantity risen basic white bread dough (see page 22)

50g (2oz) lard, softened

100g (4oz) currants

50g (2oz) soft brown sugar

1 level teaspoon mixed spice

Put the risen dough into a bowl with all the other ingredients and knead and squeeze with your hands until evenly mixed. Divide into 50g (2oz) pieces and shape into round buns. Place fairly well apart on greased baking sheets, cover with oiled polythene and put to prove in a warm place until doubled in size. Remove polythene and bake in a hot oven (220°C/425°F, Gas Mark 7) for about 15 minutes until well risen and browned. Cool on a wire rack. Eat whilst fresh.

Makes 10-12

Dough Cake

Shape the fruited dough to fit a greased 450g (1lb) loaf tin or a 18cm (7in) round cake tin. Put to prove, then sprinkle with caster sugar and bake in a hot oven (220°C/425°F, Gas Mark 7) for about 30 minutes until the base sounds hollow when tapped. 50g (2oz) chopped nuts can also be kneaded into the dough, or 40-50g (1½-2oz) chopped preserved or crystallised ginger.

Do not freeze.

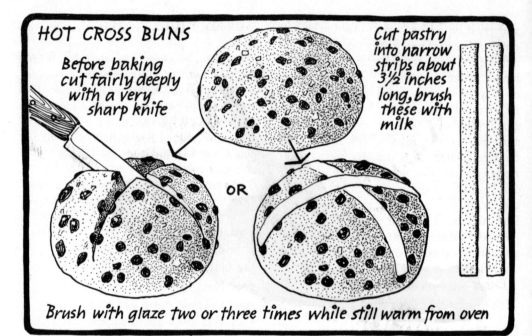

HOT CROSS BUNS

Before baking cut fairly deeply with a very sharp knife

Cut pastry into narrow strips about 3½ inches long, brush these with milk

OR

Brush with glaze two or three times while still warm from oven

Hot Cross Buns

Known as the Good Friday or Easter buns, hot cross buns are famous for their spiciness, abundance of fruit and the symbolic cross on top. They are slow risers because of the weight of fruit and richness of the dough, but are worth the effort to make. The crosses can be marked simply with a knife or be made out of narrow strips of short-crust pastry. Equally good warmed or cold, they also toast beautifully for eating up any left over during Easter week.

450g (1lb) strong white flour
25g (1oz) fresh yeast, or
  1 level tablespoon dried yeast
1 level teaspoon caster sugar
150ml (¼pt) milk
4 tablespoons water
½ level teaspoon salt
½ level teaspoon each ground nutmeg, mixed
  spice and ground cinnamon

50g (2oz) caster sugar
50g (2oz) chopped mixed peel
100g (4oz) currants
50g (2oz) butter or margarine, melted and
  cooled
1 egg, beaten

Pastry Crosses (optional)
¼ recipe quantity shortcrust pastry (see
  page 122)

Glaze
3 level tablespoons caster sugar
4 tablespoons milk and water, mixed

Put 100g (4oz) flour in a bowl with the yeast (fresh or dried) and 1 teaspoon sugar. Warm the milk and water to 43°C/110°F, stir into the flour mixture and leave in a warm place for about 10–15 minutes or until frothy. Sift the remaining flour and salt into a bowl and mix in the spices, sugar, peel and currants. Add the melted fat, egg and yeast liquid, and mix to form a softish dough. Turn on to a lightly floured surface and knead until smooth and even and no longer sticky – about 10 minutes by hand or 3–4 minutes if using a large electric mixer fitted with a dough hook. Shape into a ball, place in a lightly oiled polythene bag and put to rise in a warm place until doubled in size – this will take 1½–2 hours. Remove from the polythene, knock back and knead for about 2 minutes, then divide the dough into 12 or 14 even-sized pieces. Roll each into a ball and place well apart on greased baking sheets. Cover with oiled polythene and put to prove in a warm place until doubled in size – about 30 minutes.

Either cut a deep cross on top of each bun with a very sharp knife, before baking in a moderately hot oven (190°C/375°F, Gas Mark 5) for 20–25 minutes until golden brown; or whilst the buns are proving, make up the pastry, cut into very narrow strips about 9cm (3½in) long, brush the strips with milk and position two across each risen bun to make the cross. Bake in the same way. Whilst the buns are cooking, boil the sugar and milk and water together for 2 minutes. Remove buns to a wire rack and brush with the glaze 2 or 3 times whilst still warm. Leave to cool.

Makes 14–16

Suitable to freeze for 6–8 weeks.

Wigs

There are many spellings of this ancient spiced teacake that dates as far back as the fifteenth century. Wigs were once a Lent speciality, but the recipe gradually became much richer and they were often served with ale or wine at other times of the year. The caraway seeds and spices are traditional but for those who are not too keen on the flavour of caraway, the quantity of seeds can be reduced even more than in this recipe. Caraway was very popular up to about the eighteenth or nineteenth centuries but is now largely forgotten in cake baking except in the old-fashioned seed cake which still survives, and the many foreign breads and cakes. Wigs should be triangular in shape and this is best achieved by baking in a round which is cut into wedges.

450g (1lb) strong white flour
pinch of salt
50g (2oz) caster sugar
1½ level teaspoons caraway seeds
½ level teaspoon ground ginger or cinnamon
½ level teaspoon mixed spice
15g (½oz) fresh yeast, or
   1½ level teaspoons dried yeast and 1 level
   teaspoon sugar
300ml (½pt) warm milk (43°C/110°F)
50g (2oz) softened butter

Sift the flour and salt into a bowl and mix in the sugar, caraway seeds and spices. Blend the fresh yeast with the warm liquid; for dried yeast, dissolve the sugar in the liquid, sprinkle the yeast on top and leave in a warm place for about 10 minutes or until frothy. Add to the dry ingredients with the softened butter and mix to form a fairly soft dough. Knead or beat well with your hand or in an electric mixer until smooth. Cover the bowl with polythene or a damp cloth and put to rise in a warm place until doubled in size – about 1½ hours. Remove the cover, knead the dough (which is rather soft) on a floured surface until smooth, then divide it into 2 pieces and shape into 2 rounds about 20–23cm (8–9in) in diameter. Place on well greased baking sheets and cut each round into 8 or 10 wedges. Cover with oiled polythene and put to prove for 20–30 minutes until puffy. Remove polythene and bake in a moderately hot oven (190°C/375°F, Gas Mark 5) for about 15 minutes. Cool on a wire rack then break into wedges to serve. Serve warm or cold, as they are, or split and buttered.

Makes 16–20

Do not freeze.

Saffron Cake or Buns

Saffron – the dried flower stigmas of a specially grown crocus flower – has a pleasant honey aroma with a slightly bitter taste, and is bright yellow. In medieval times saffron was used in stews and made-up dishes mainly for its colour, since the flavour was usually greatly overpowered by the other ingredients. Even now the stigmas are soaked in warm liquid to extract the colour and flavour and this liquid is used (as it has been for centuries) for making bread or cakes. Apart from baking, saffron is also used today in making fish stews and soups and the famous Spanish paella – but sparingly, for it is a very expensive spice and not always easy to obtain except from the continental delicatessens. Saffron buns or cakes are still a speciality of Cornwall where they can easily be found.

about 250ml (scant ½pt) milk

good pinch of saffron

450g (1lb) strong white flour

pinch of salt

good pinch of mixed spice

100g (4oz) butter or margarine

100g (4oz) lard

15g (½oz) fresh yeast, or
   1½ level teaspoons dried yeast and 1 level
   teaspoon caster sugar

75g (3oz) caster sugar

50g (2oz) raisins

50g (2oz) currants

50g (2oz) chopped mixed peel

Warm half the milk and infuse the saffron in it for about 30 minutes. Sift the flour, salt and spice into a bowl and rub in the butter or margarine and lard until the mixture resembles fine breadcrumbs. Blend the fresh yeast with the remaining milk warmed to 43°C/110°F; for dried yeast, dissolve the sugar in the milk, sprinkle the yeast on top and leave in a warm place for about 10 minutes or until frothy. Add the saffron liquid and yeast liquid to the dry ingredients and mix to form a soft dough. Beat well with your hand or a wooden spoon for 2–3 minutes, or for 1–2 minutes if using an electric mixer fitted with a dough hook. Cover the bowl with a damp cloth or piece of oiled polythene and put to rise in a warm place until doubled in size. Remove cover and knead in the sugar, dried fruit and peel until evenly distributed. Either put into a well greased 21–23cm (8½–9in) round cake tin or a 900g (2lb) loaf tin, or for saffron buns, put tablespoons of the mixture on to greased baking sheets, keeping them fairly well apart. Cover with oiled polythene and put to prove until doubled in size. Remove polythene and bake the cake in a fairly hot oven (200°C/400°F, Gas Mark 6) for 15 minutes, then reduce the temperature to moderately hot (190°C/375°F, Gas Mark 5) and continue for about 40 minutes or until well risen and browned, and the base sounds hollow when tapped. Saffron buns take about 15–20 minutes in a fairly hot oven (200°C/400°F, Gas Mark 6). Cool cake or buns on a wire rack.

Makes 1 cake or 16–18 buns

Suitable to freeze for up to 3 months.

Doughnuts

These large, sticky, sugar-covered buns with a hidden centre of thick red jam are still devoured by schoolchildren as they have been for years. They are taboo to the weight-watching members of the family for the dough combined with frying in deep fat and the sugar coating simply pile on the calories. The only way to eat a doughnut is when it's really fresh – essentially on the day made. It appears that they were at one time a speciality of the Isle of Wight, sometimes filled with candied peel and dried fruit instead of the more usual jam.

225g (8oz) strong white flour

½ level teaspoon salt

15g (½oz) fresh yeast, or
   1½ level teaspoons dried yeast and 1 level teaspoon caster sugar

about 4 tablespoons warm milk (43°C/110F°)

15g (½oz) softened butter

1 egg, beaten

about 8 teaspoons thick red jam

deep fat or oil for frying

caster sugar and ground cinnamon (optional) for coating

Sift the flour and salt into a bowl. Blend the fresh yeast with the milk; for dried yeast, dissolve the sugar in the milk, sprinkle the yeast on top and leave in a warm place until frothy – about 10 minutes. Add the yeast liquid to the dry ingredients together with the softened butter and egg, and mix to form a dough which is fairly soft but leaves the sides of the bowl clean; add a little more milk if necessary. Knead on a lightly floured surface for about 10 minutes until smooth, or use a large electric mixer fitted with a

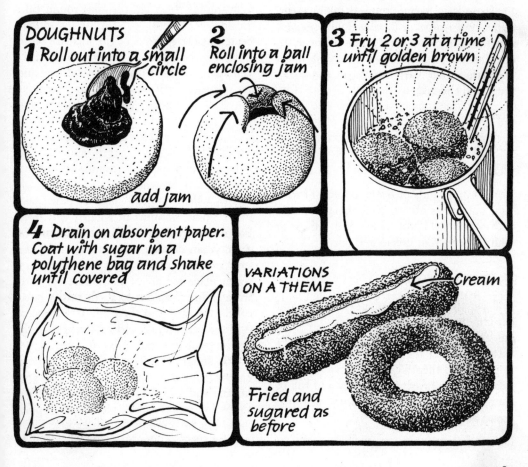

DOUGHNUTS
1 Roll out into a small circle
add jam

2 Roll into a ball enclosing jam

3 Fry 2 or 3 at a time until golden brown

4 Drain on absorbent paper. Coat with sugar in a polythene bag and shake until covered

VARIATIONS ON A THEME
Cream
Fried and sugared as before

dough hook for 3–4 minutes. Put into a lightly floured bowl, cover with oiled polythene and put to rise in a warm place for about an hour or until doubled in size. Remove from the bag and knock back to remove all air bubbles, then knead until smooth. Divide the dough into 8–10 pieces and roll each into a small circle. Put a teaspoon of jam in the centre of each and pull in the edges to enclose the jam. Roll carefully into a ball and place on a greased and floured baking sheet. Cover with oiled polythene and put to prove in a warm place until nicely puffy – about 10–15 minutes. Meanwhile heat a pan of deep fat to 182°C/360°F or until a cube of bread will brown in about 45 seconds. Fry the doughnuts, two or three at a time, for 5–10 minutes until a deep golden brown all over, turning with a metal spoon as necessary. Drain on absorbent paper and roll in caster sugar, either plain or flavoured with ground cinnamon. Leave to cool. The best way to coat them in sugar is to put the doughnut in a polythene bag with the sugar and shake until well covered.

Makes 8–10

Variations

Cream Doughnuts

Shape into rounds or ovals, do not fill with jam, but fry as above. Roll them in sugar and when cold slit open and fill with whipped cream or cream and jam.

Ring Doughnuts

Roll out the dough to 1cm ($\frac{1}{2}$in) thick and cut into 7·5cm (3in) plain rounds. Then cut out the centres with a 2·5–4cm (1–1$\frac{1}{2}$in) cutter. Transfer the rings to a baking sheet to prove and then fry for about 5 minutes. Coat in sugar, brush with honey and roll in chopped nuts or decorate with whipped cream and fruit.

Do not freeze.

Yeasted Pastries

Similar to the delicious Danish Pastries, these are made with a soft-textured yeasted flaky pastry achieved by folding and rolling in the butter and by using ordinary plain flour rather than the strong type usually required in yeast cookery. The fillings and toppings can be varied to suit any taste.

25g (1oz) fresh yeast, or
   1 level tablespoon dried yeast and 1 level teaspoon caster sugar
150ml ($\frac{1}{4}$pt) warm water (43°C/110°F)
450g (1lb) plain flour (not strong flour)
1 level teaspoon salt
50g (2oz) lard
25g (1oz) caster sugar
2 eggs, beaten
275g (10oz) butter
beaten egg to glaze

Fillings
see opposite

Glacé Icing
see pages 75–6

Toppings
see page 86

Blend the fresh yeast with the water; for dried yeast, dissolve the sugar in the water, sprinkle the yeast on top and leave in a warm place for about 10 minutes or until frothy. Sift the flour and salt into a bowl, rub in the lard and then mix in the sugar. Add the yeast liquid and beaten eggs to the dry ingredients and mix to form a soft elastic dough, adding a little more water if necessary. Turn on to a lightly floured surface and knead by hand until smooth – about 2–3 minutes. Put into an oiled polythene bag and chill in the refrigerator for 10 minutes. Soften the butter until it can be

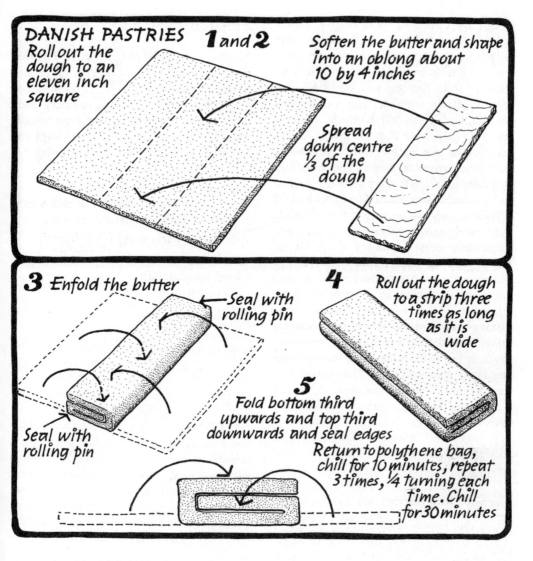

DANISH PASTRIES **1** and **2**

Roll out the dough to an eleven inch square

Soften the butter and shape into an oblong about 10 by 4 inches

Spread down centre ⅓ of the dough

3 Enfold the butter

Seal with rolling pin

Seal with rolling pin

4 Roll out the dough to a strip three times as long as it is wide

5 Fold bottom third upwards and top third downwards and seal edges

Return to polythene bag, chill for 10 minutes, repeat 3 times, ¼ turning each time. Chill for 30 minutes

shaped into an oblong about 23 × 10cm (10 × 4in). Remove the dough from the bag and roll out to a 28cm (11in) square and spread the butter down the centre of it. Enclose the butter by folding the flaps of dough to overlap in the middle. Seal the top and bottom with the rolling pin, then roll out to a strip 3 times as long as it is wide. Fold the bottom third upwards and the top third downwards and seal the edges. Return to the polythene bag and chill for 10 minutes. Repeat the rolling, folding and

resting 3 more times, giving the pastry a quarter turn each time so that the fold is at the side. Chill for 30 minutes and the dough is then ready for use, or it can be frozen at this stage. Prepare the fillings.

Fillings

Spiced Nuts Toast 50g (2oz) hazelnuts or almonds and chop roughly. Mix with 25g (1oz) each of butter and soft brown sugar and ½ level teaspoon ground mixed spice.

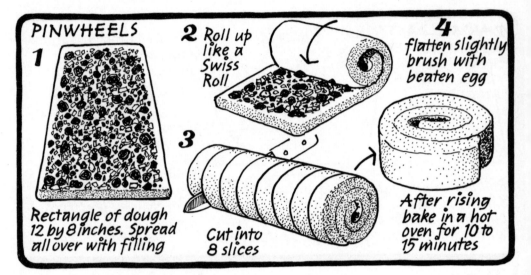

Mixed Fruit Cream 25g (1oz) soft brown sugar with 25g (1oz) butter and beat in a pinch of ground allspice or cinnamon and 25g (1oz) each of currants, sultanas and chopped mixed peel.

Ginger Cream 25g (1oz) caster sugar with 25g (1oz) butter, ½ teaspoon ground ginger and 40–50g (1½–2oz) crystallised or preserved ginger, finely chopped.

Marzipan Mix together 50g (2oz) each of ground almonds and caster sugar and bind to a pliable paste with a few drops of almond essence and sufficient beaten egg.

Stewed Apple Peel and slice 2 cooking apples and cook to a pulp with the minimum of water and a knob of butter. Beat until smooth or sieve, sweeten to taste and flavour with a pinch of any spice or add a few currants, sultanas or raisins.

Toppings
Use toasted or plain almonds, flaked or chopped; chopped or sliced glacé cherries; chopped angelica; toasted hazelnuts, roughly chopped; pieces of chopped ginger; clear honey.

Pinwheels

Roll out a quarter of the dough thinly and trim to a rectangle about 30×20cm (12×8in). Spread all over with either spiced nuts, mixed fruit, ginger or stewed apple filling and roll up like a Swiss roll, beginning at the narrow end. Seal end with water. Cut into 8 slices and place, cut side down, on a greased baking sheet. Flatten slightly, brush with beaten egg, cover with oiled polythene and put to prove in a warm place for about 15 minutes or until puffy. Remove polythene and bake in a hot oven (220°C/425°F, Gas Mark 7) for 10–15 minutes until golden brown.

Remove to a wire rack and while still warm either brush with clear honey or drizzle with white glacé icing. Sprinkle with nuts, ginger or glacé cherries.

Windmills

Roll out a quarter of the dough thinly and cut into 7·5cm (3in) squares. Make diagonal cuts from each corner to within 2·5cm (1in) of the centre of each square. Place a round ball of marzipan in the centre and fold each alternate corner of the square to

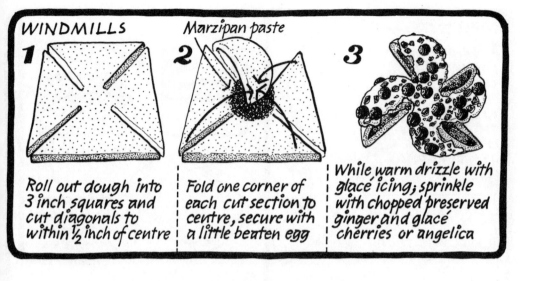

WINDMILLS

1 Roll out dough into 3 inch squares and cut diagonals to within ½ inch of centre

2 Marzipan paste — Fold one corner of each cut section to centre, secure with a little beaten egg

3 While warm drizzle with glacé icing; sprinkle with chopped preserved ginger and glacé cherries or angelica

the centre, securing the tips with beaten egg. Place on a greased baking sheet and glaze, prove and bake as for Pinwheels, but for about 20 minutes. Remove to a wire rack; while warm, drizzle with glacé icing and sprinkle with chopped preserved ginger and glacé cherries or angelica.

Diamonds

Roll out a quarter of the dough and cut into strips 13×6cm ($5 \times 2\frac{1}{2}$in). Spread any of the fillings in a narrow strip down the centre of each strip, then fold up the opposite corners to enclose the filling, damping edges with beaten egg. Place on greased

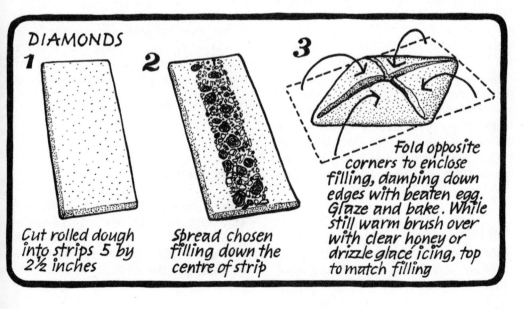

DIAMONDS

1 Cut rolled dough into strips 5 by 2½ inches

2 Spread chosen filling down the centre of strip

3 Fold opposite corners to enclose filling, damping down edges with beaten egg. Glaze and bake. While still warm brush over with clear honey or drizzle glacé icing, top to match filling

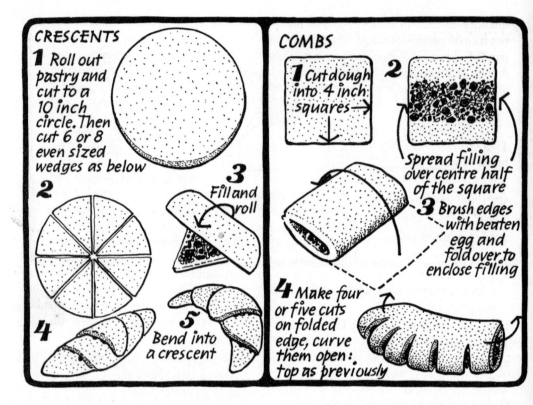

baking sheet and glaze, prove and bake as for Pinwheels, but for about 20 minutes. Remove to a wire rack and brush with clear honey or drizzle with glacé icing while still warm. Sprinkle with a topping to match the filling.

Crescents

Roll out a quarter of the dough and cut to a circle 23cm (10in) in diameter, then cut into 6 or 8 even-sized wedges. Put about a teaspoon of any of the fillings at the wide base of each wedge and roll up towards the point. Bend into a crescent, place on a greased baking sheet and glaze, prove and bake as for Pinwheels.

Combs

Roll out a quarter of the dough thinly and cut into 10cm (4in) squares. Spread marzipan – or any of the other fillings – over the centre part of half of each square. Brush the edges with beaten egg and fold over the other half to enclose the filling. Make 4 or 5 cuts into the folded edge of the pastry and place on a greased baking sheet, curving the cut edge to open out the comb a little. Glaze, prove and bake as for Pinwheels, but for about 20 minutes. Remove to a wire rack, drizzle with glacé icing while still warm and sprinkle with toasted nuts.

Each design makes 6–8 pastries

Bara Brith

This is a Welsh currant bread usually made with yeast, but there is a teabread version made using baking powder. 'Bara' is the Welsh word for bread and 'Brith' means speckled and the resulting bread is very good, but a slow riser for it has a large quantity of fruit in it. Each Welsh family has its own particular recipe which has been handed down and some are richer than others. It is similar to the Selkirk Bannock of Scotland and the Irish Barm Brack, and is served sliced and buttered.

450g (1lb) strong white flour
pinch of salt
75g (3oz) butter, margarine or lard
50g (2oz) soft brown sugar
½ level teaspoon mixed spice
25g (1oz) mixed peel
225g (8oz) currants or mixed dried fruit
25g (1oz) fresh yeast, or
   1 level tablespoon dried yeast and 1 level
   teaspoon sugar
200ml (8fl oz) warm milk (43°C/110°F)
1 egg, beaten
clear honey to glaze

Grease one 900g (2lb) loaf tin or two 450g (1lb) tins. Sift the flour and salt into a bowl and rub in the fat. Mix in the sugar, spice, peel and dried fruit. Blend the fresh yeast with the warm milk; for dried yeast, dissolve the sugar in the milk, sprinkle the yeast on top and leave in a warm place until frothy – about 10 minutes. Add the yeast liquid to the dry ingredients with the egg and mix to form a softish dough. Knead well on a floured surface until smooth. Shape into a ball and place in an oiled polythene bag; put to rise in a warm place until doubled in size – this will take up to 2 hours. Turn out and knead for 1–2 minutes then shape to fit the tins. Cover with oiled polythene and put to prove in a warm place until the dough springs back when lightly pressed with a floured finger. Remove polythene and bake in a fairly hot oven (200°C/400°F, Gas Mark 6) for 20 minutes, then reduce the temperature to moderately hot (190°C/375°F, Gas Mark 5) and continue for about 45–50 minutes or until the base sounds

hollow when tapped. Smaller loaves will take about 30 minutes at the lower temperature. Turn on to a wire rack, brush the top of each loaf with a wet brush dipped in clear honey and leave to cool.

Suitable to freeze for up to 3 months.

Barm Brack

The Irish version of a spicy currant loaf, Barm Brack is much richer than the other currant breads for it has a much higher proportion of beaten egg added to the dough. This bread is usually baked in a round cake tin but can also be made in a loaf tin.

½ recipe quantity risen basic white bread
   dough (see page 22)
75g (3oz) caster sugar
50g (2oz) softened butter or lard
2–3 eggs, beaten
175g (6oz) currants, raisins or sultanas
50g (2oz) chopped mixed peel
1 level teaspoon caraway seeds (optional)
½–1 level teaspoon mixed spice (optional)

Grease two 18–20cm (7–8in) round cake tins or two 900g (2lb) loaf tins. Place the dough in a bowl with all the other ingredients and knead and squeeze with your hands until they are evenly distributed. Shape to fit the tins, cover with oiled polythene and put to prove in a warm place until well risen or doubled in size. Remove cover and bake in a hot oven (220°C/425°F, Gas Mark 7) for 20–25 minutes, then reduce to moderate (180°C/350°F, Gas Mark 4) and continue for about 30–45 minutes or until the base sounds hollow when tapped. Cool on a wire rack.

Suitable to freeze for up to 3 months.

Bath Buns

Bath Buns

These are one of the old traditional favourite buns of England. They can be somewhat stodgy if not baked with care, but have a delicious sticky, sugary top and plenty of sultanas. Originally they were not a fruited bun, but were flavoured with caraway. They were very popular at the Great Exhibition of 1851 but due to the huge quantities that were baked, the quality of the buns deteriorated and the bun became the poor relation of the original Bath bun, created in Bath.

450g (1lb) strong white flour
25g (1oz) fresh yeast, or
  1 level tablespoon dried yeast
50g (2oz) caster sugar
150ml (¼pt) milk
4 tablespoons water
½ level teaspoon salt
50g (2oz) mixed chopped peel
175g (6oz) sultanas
50g (2oz) butter, melted
2 eggs, beaten

Topping
Sugar lumps, lightly crushed

Put 100g (4oz) flour into a bowl with the yeast (fresh or dried) and 1 teaspoon of the sugar. Warm the milk and water to about 43°C/110°F, add to the yeast and mix to a smooth batter. Leave in a warm place for about 15 minutes or until frothy. Sift the remaining flour and salt into a bowl and mix in the remaining sugar, peel and sultanas. Stir in the melted butter, most of the beaten eggs (reserve a little for glazing) and the yeast batter and mix to form a soft dough. Turn on to a floured surface and knead until smooth – about 5 minutes by hand or 3–4 minutes in a large electric mixer fitted with a dough hook. Place in a lightly floured bowl, cover with oiled polythene and put to rise in a warm place for 45–60 minutes or until doubled in size. Remove polythene and beat the dough with a wooden spoon or your hand until smooth and free of air bubbles. Put tablespoons of the mixture well apart on to well greased baking sheets, cover with oiled polythene and put to prove in a warm place until doubled in size. Remove polythene, glaze buns with the reserved beaten egg and sprinkle with crushed sugar. Bake in a moderately hot oven (190°C/375°F, Gas Mark 5) for about 15 minutes or until well risen and golden brown. Cool on a wire rack.

Makes about 16

Suitable to freeze for up to 3 months.

Selkirk Bannock

A bannock is a type of Scottish scone, often including oatmeal, which is sometimes baked and sometimes cooked on a griddle. It can also be made from a yeast dough when dried fruit, sugar, spices and butter are added, and it makes a change from the usual type of scone. In Scotland, bannocks are always served at high tea.

225g (8oz) strong white flour
25g (1oz) softened butter
150ml (¼pt) warm milk (43°C/110°F)
15g (½oz) fresh yeast, or
  1½ level teaspoons dried yeast and 1 level
  teaspoon caster sugar
pinch of salt
25g (1oz) caster sugar
100g (4oz) mixed dried fruit
½ level teaspoon mixed spice (optional)
milk to glaze

Put 50g (2oz) flour into a large bowl with the softened butter, the warm milk and either the fresh yeast or the dried yeast and the 1 teaspoon sugar. Mix to form a batter and leave in a warm place until frothy – about 25 minutes. Sift the remaining flour and salt into a bowl and mix in the sugar, dried fruit and spice, if used. Add these ingredients to the yeast batter and mix to form a firm dough. Turn on to a lightly floured surface and knead until smooth and

even – about 10 minutes by hand or 3–4 minutes using a large electric mixer fitted with a dough hook. Shape into a ball, place in an oiled polythene bag and put to rise in a warm place for about an hour or until doubled in size. Turn out of the bag, knead lightly and shape to a circle about 1cm (½in) thick. Place on a greased baking sheet and cut into 8 wedges. Cover with a sheet of oiled polythene and put to prove in a warm place until doubled in size. Remove polythene, brush with milk and bake in a fairly hot oven (200°C/400°F, Gas Mark 6) for about 20 minutes or until well risen and golden brown. Remove to a wire rack and leave to cool. To serve, cut or break into wedges, split and spread with butter, and add jam or honey, if liked.

This bannock freezes well for up to 3 months; it is worth making several at a time if you have a freezer.

Variations
Ginger Bannock

Replace 50g (2oz) dried fruit with finely chopped stem, preserved or crystallised ginger and the spice with ground ginger.

Walnut Bannock

Replace the dried fruit with chopped walnuts and add the finely grated rind of an orange or lemon in place of the spice; sprinkle the bannock with 1 tablespoon demerara sugar before baking.

Wholemeal Bannock

Replace half the white flour with wholemeal or other brown flour and continue as above.

Oatmeal Bannock

Replace 50g (2oz) flour with medium or fine oatmeal and continue as above.

Fruited Bap Loaves

By using a basic risen white bread dough and kneading in varying ingredients after the initial rising, you can achieve very pleasant and unusual teabreads to serve sliced as a cake for the tea-table. Some can have a honey-glazed top, others glacé icing or some be left plain to serve spread with butter.

Fig and Lemon Bap

½ recipe quantity risen basic white bread dough (see page 22)

25g (1oz) soft brown sugar

finely grated rind of 1 lemon

75–100g (3–4oz) figs, finely chopped

1 level tablespoon demerara or granulated sugar

Place all the ingredients except the demerara sugar in a bowl and knead and squeeze with your hands until everything is evenly distributed throughout the dough. Shape into a bap loaf – a circle about 5cm (2in) thick and 15–18cm (6–7in) in diameter. Place on a greased baking sheet, cover with a sheet of oiled polythene and put to prove until the dough has doubled in size and springs back when lightly pressed with a floured finger. Remove polythene, sprinkle with demerara sugar and bake in a hot oven (220°C/425°F, Gas Mark 7) for 25–30 minutes. Cool on a wire rack.

Gingered Bap

½ recipe quantity risen basic white bread dough (see page 22)

1 level teaspoon ground ginger

50g (2oz) crystallised, stem or preserved ginger, finely chopped

25g (1oz) caster sugar

50g (2oz) sultanas or mixed dried fruit

clear honey to glaze

Mix all the ingredients into the dough as above. Prove and bake in the same way but brush the hot loaf with a wet brush dipped in honey to give a sticky glazed top.

Rum and Raisin Bap

½ recipe quantity risen basic white bread dough (see page 22)

1 tablespoon rum

25g (1oz) caster sugar

75–100g (3–4oz) raisins

a little glacé icing (see pages 76–7)

Make, prove and bake as above. As the bap cools spread a thin layer of glacé icing over the top and leave to set.

Fruited Orange Bap

½ recipe quantity risen basic white bread dough (see page 22)

25g (1oz) caster or soft brown sugar

finely grated rind of 1 orange

75–100g (3–4oz) mixed dried fruit

clear honey to glaze

Make, prove and bake as for Gingered Bap, brushing the top with honey whilst still warm.

These baps are suitable to freeze for up to 3 months.

Spicy Tea Ring

This type of yeasted tea ring is very popular in England but it probably originated in Scandinavia. It is most attractive and looks more difficult to make than it is. The spices can be varied to suit your taste and it can be left plain with a honey glaze or be topped with glacé icing, toasted almonds, glacé cherries and angelica.

SPICY TEA RING

1 Roll out to a rectangle 12 by 9 inches

2 Brush melted butter over the dough's surface

3 Sprinkle combined sugar and spice all over

4 Beginning at long edge roll up like a Swiss Roll

5 Bend into a ring, cut 12 slanting slashes

6 Twist slices to show cut surfaces

7 While still warm brush with clear honey, or pour over lemon glacé icing; sprinkle with nuts, cherries and angelica

225g (8oz) strong white flour

½ level teaspoon caster sugar

15g (½oz) fresh yeast, or
   1½ level teaspoons dried yeast

100ml (4fl oz) warm milk (43°C/110°F)

½ level teaspoon salt

50g (2oz) butter or margarine

½ egg, beaten

75g (3oz) soft brown sugar

2–3 level teaspoons ground cinnamon

good pinch each of ground nutmeg and ground allspice

clear honey or lemon glacé icing (see page 96)

glacé cherries, angelica and/or toasted almonds

Put 65g (2½oz) flour into a bowl with the sugar, yeast (fresh or dried) and warm milk, and leave in a warm place until frothy – about 15 minutes. Sift the remaining flour and salt into a bowl and rub in half of the fat. Add the beaten egg and yeast batter and mix to form a fairly soft dough. Turn on to a lightly floured surface and knead until smooth and even – about 10 minutes by hand or 3–4 minutes in a large electric mixer fitted with a dough hook. Shape into a ball, place in a lightly oiled polythene bag and put to rise in a warm place for about an hour or until the dough has doubled in size and springs back when lightly pressed with a floured finger. Remove from the polythene, and knock back and knead for 2 minutes or until smooth. Roll out to a rectangle about 30×23cm (12×9in). Melt

93

the remaining butter and brush all over the dough. Combine the sugar and spices, and sprinkle over the whole of the dough. Beginning at a long edge, roll up the dough like a Swiss roll, bending it into a ring and sealing the ends together. Place on a well greased baking sheet. Brush a pair of scissors with oil and cut slanting slashes about two-thirds of the way through the ring at 2·5cm (1in) intervals. Carefully twist each slice so the cut surface faces upwards, but keep the ring an even shape. Cover with oiled polythene and put to prove in a warm place for about 30 minutes or until well risen and puffy. Remove the polythene and bake in a moderately hot oven (190°C/375°F, Gas Mark 5) for 30–35 minutes until well risen and golden brown. Transfer to a wire rack. Whilst still warm, either brush with clear honey or pour lemon glacé icing over the top of the ring and sprinkle with a mixture of nuts, cherries and angelica.

Freeze (without the icing) for up to 1 month only, because of the spice.

Variations
Finely grated orange or lemon rind, finely chopped dates, mixed fruit or nuts can be sprinkled over the sugar, before rolling up.

Christmas Bread

Many countries bake a specially fruited yeast loaf or cake for the Christmas celebrations. The shape varies from loaves or simple round and square cakes – some deep, some shallow – to plaits, twists or rolled-up loaves which resemble a Swiss roll. Some are simply glazed with honey, some coated with glacé, royal or fondant icing and others just heavily dredged with icing sugar. This recipe is similar to the German Stollen but is less rich; it is flavoured with almonds, angelica, glacé cherries, peel and raisins.

50g (2oz) raisins
40g (1½oz) glacé cherries, quartered
25g (1oz) angelica, chopped
50g (2oz) mixed peel
25g (1oz) flaked almonds or chopped blanched almonds
25g (1oz) fresh yeast, or
  1 level tablespoon dried yeast and 1 level teaspoon sugar
150ml (¼pt) warm milk (43°C/110°F)
2 tablespoons warm water
450g (1lb) strong white flour
75g (3oz) caster sugar
100g (4oz) butter, softened
1 egg, beaten
few drops almond essence
finely grated rind of half an orange or lemon (optional)
icing sugar for dredging

Combine the raisins, cherries, angelica, peel and almonds. Blend the fresh yeast with the milk and water; for dried yeast, dissolve the sugar in the liquid, sprinkle the yeast on top and leave in a warm place until frothy – about 10 minutes. Sift the flour into a bowl and mix in 50g (2oz) sugar. Add the yeast liquid, 75g (3oz) softened butter, beaten egg, almond essence and fruit rind (if used) to the dry ingredients and mix to form a softish dough. Knead on a lightly floured surface until smooth – about 10 minutes by hand or 3–4 minutes using a large electric mixer fitted with a dough hook. Shape into a ball, place in an oiled polythene bag and put to rise in a warm place until doubled in size – about an hour. Remove the dough, knock back and knead in the fruit mixture until evenly distributed. Roll out to a rectangle about 30×20cm (12×8in). Melt the remaining butter and brush over the dough, then sprinkle with the remaining sugar. Roll up the dough loosely, beginning with a long side. Place on a greased baking sheet with the join on top. Press down gently, cover with oiled polythene and put to prove until doubled in size; it may take a little longer than usual because of all the additional ingredients. Remove polythene and bake in a moderately hot oven (190°C/375°F, Gas Mark 5) for about 45 minutes or until golden brown and the base sounds hollow when tapped. Cool on a wire rack, then dredge heavily with icing sugar. Serve cut into slices.

Suitable to freeze for up to 4 months but dredge with icing sugar after thawing out.

Iced Twist

This is a rich yeasted dough full of dried fruit and flavoured with orange rind, which is made into a plait and then joined up to make a ring. It takes longer to rise than plain bread. The top can be simply brushed with clear honey or have a coating of glacé icing sprinkled with chopped nuts and glacé cherries.

225g (8oz) strong white flour
pinch of salt

25g (1oz) butter or margarine
50g (2oz) light soft brown or caster sugar
75g (3oz) mixed dried fruit
grated rind of 1 small orange
15g ($\frac{1}{2}$oz) fresh yeast, or
   1$\frac{1}{2}$ level teaspoons dried yeast and 1 level teaspoon caster sugar
5 tablespoons warm milk (43°C/110°F)
1 egg, beaten
beaten egg or milk to glaze
clear honey or glacé icing
chopped nuts and glacé cherries (optional)

Sift the flour and salt into a bowl, rub in the fat until the mixture resembles fine breadcrumbs, and then mix in the sugar, dried fruit and orange rind. Dissolve the fresh yeast in the warm milk; for dried yeast, dissolve the sugar in the milk, sprinkle the yeast on top and leave in a warm place until frothy – about 10 minutes. Add the yeast liquid and the egg to the dry ingredients and mix to a fairly soft dough. Turn on to a lightly floured surface and knead until smooth and elastic and no longer sticky – about 10 minutes by hand or 3–4 minutes if using a large electric mixer fitted with a

Iced Twist

dough hook. Shape into a ball and place in a lightly oiled polythene bag. Put to rise in a warm place until the dough has doubled in size and springs back when lightly pressed with a floured finger. (This may take 1½–2 hours.) Remove from the polythene and knead on a lightly floured surface for about 2 minutes until smooth. Divide into 3 equal pieces and roll each into a thin sausage about 30cm (12in) long. Place the strands side by side in front of you and beginning in the middle, plait the strands towards you; pinch the ends together. Turn the plait right over and away from you so the unplaited strands now face you, and complete the plait. Twist the plait into a ring, damp the ends and press well together. Place on a greased baking sheet, cover with oiled polythene and put to prove in a warm place for about 30 minutes or until doubled in size and puffy. Remove polythene, brush with beaten egg or milk and bake in a hot oven (220°C/425°F, Gas Mark 7) for 15–20 minutes until golden brown. Remove to a wire rack and either brush with clear honey whilst still warm, or leave to cool then pour a little glacé icing over the top and sprinkle with chopped nuts and cherries.

Note The dough can be baked as a plait, if preferred, and the orange rind can be omitted or replaced by lemon rind.

The baked twist can be frozen (without the icing and topping) for 2–3 months.

Glacé Icing

100–175g (4–6 oz) icing sugar, sifted

2–3 teaspoons orange or lemon juice or water

colouring (optional)

Add sufficient liquid to the icing sugar to blend to a smooth coating consistency, adding colouring, if liked. If too runny, add a little extra icing sugar.

CHAPTER 5

Scones and Teabreads

The traditional afternoon tea-table appears somewhat bare unless there is a plate of some type of scone included, and equally well needs a few slices of a buttered teabread somewhere amongst the other goodies.

Scones have always been popular in some form or another, for these light plain cakes – which are usually split open and spread first with butter and then often with jam or honey – are quick and simple to make. They can in fact be served straight from the oven, still hot, or be heated through in the oven after being taken hastily from the deep-freeze to serve to unexpected guests. Scones stay fresh for a day or so after baking but then they are best refreshed in the oven before serving; they also freeze very well, so batch baking is ideal. They probably originated in Scotland or one of the other Celtic countries and are still served there as part of the high-tea table. In and around the nineteenth century, they were served with butter and honey for breakfast as part of the huge, almost banquet-like meal which included more or less any type of food you can imagine, and was favoured by the gentry of that time, particularly on Sundays.

Scones are baked all over the country and in some parts, particularly the North of England, Scotland, Ireland and Wales, are open-baked on a griddle, girdle or bakestone, the name meaning much the same thing in the different areas – oatcakes, potato scones, drop scones, etc, are also baked this way. Whatever it is called, the griddle is a thick solid piece of flat cast-iron, usually round and either with a half hoop handle so it could be hung over the fire or with three or four legs on which it stood over the fire. Originally it was always used over an open fire which often burnt peat; nowadays, when open fires are not so common it is sometimes used on a kitchen range or the hob of a gas or electric cooker. (On gas burners it is advisable to use an asbestos mat under it.)

In Wales this is called a bakestone and apart from metal, may also be a flat stone or piece of slate. In Scotland and the North of England it is more often called a girdle, whilst in Ireland it is called a girdle or griddle. Some of our modern cookers now include a built in 'griddle' which is ideal for this type of baking. However, a large heavy-based frying pan can be used with equal success in its stead, provided it is greased well and heated gently until evenly hot.

A teabread is not quite a cake, but is not a true bread either; however, the combination of the two describes this moist teatime favourite adequately, both in name and flavour. It makes a change from the many yeasted teacakes and fancy breads which are so often served for tea, and to my mind is a very important addition to the varieties of teatime fare. It is served cut into slices and spread with butter, sometimes being quite highly flavoured and full of fruit or other ingredients, whilst at other times it is much plainer with one pre-dominant flavour. Teabreads are an ideal stand-by, for not only do they keep moist for a fair time if wrapped first in greaseproof paper or cling film and then foil, but they are also good 'freezers'. However, remember that frozen teabreads need time to thaw before serving to your guests!

Note When sour milk for scones is not available, fresh milk can be soured by adding 2–3 teaspoons lemon juice to each 150ml (¼pt) milk.

Plain Oven Scones

Scones probably originated in Scotland, forming part of the traditional high tea. Nowadays they are popular all over the country both for high teas and the most elegant of tea parties. Recipes vary greatly, with most families having their own special recipe which may have been in the family for generations.

This recipe is for a plain scone, but others follow for rich scones and those with dried fruit and other flavourings.

225g (8oz) plain flour
good pinch of salt
1 level tablespoon baking powder
2 level teaspoons caster sugar (optional)
50g (2oz) butter or margarine
about 150ml ($\frac{1}{4}$pt) milk (preferably sour)

Sift the flour, salt and baking powder into a bowl and mix in the sugar, if used. Add the fat and rub in until the mixture resembles fine breadcrumbs. Make a well in the centre and stir in sufficient milk to mix to a fairly soft dough. Turn on to a floured surface and knead only very lightly if necessary, to remove any cracks. Roll or pat out to about 2cm ($\frac{3}{4}$in) thick and cut into 5cm (2in) rounds with a floured plain or fluted cutter. Place on greased or floured baking sheets, brush the tops with milk, if liked, and bake in a very hot oven (230°C/450°F, Gas Mark 8) for about 10 minutes or until well risen and browned. Cool on a wire rack.

Makes about 10

Note In place of the baking powder, 2 teaspoons cream of tartar and 1 teaspoon bicarbonate of soda may be used; alternatively, forget all raising agents and use self-raising flour.

Suitable to freeze for up to 4 months.

Rich Floury Scones

These light-textured scones are so simple and quick to make, using self-raising flour, butter, milk and an egg. Fresh milk is fine but sour milk or buttermilk will give even better results; dried fruit can be added or not as you wish. The secret of the texture is to take the scones from the oven, turn out on to a wire rack covered with a clean cloth and wrap in the cloth, leaving until ready to eat or until cold. This forces the steam back into the scones. They are also baked close to each other so that they join up and when pulled apart reveal soft sides.

225g (8oz) self-raising flour
pinch of salt
50g (2oz) butter or margarine
25g (1oz) caster sugar
1 egg, beaten
about 5 tablespoons milk (preferably sour)
flour for dredging

Sift the flour and salt into a bowl. Rub in the fat until the mixture resembles fine breadcrumbs, then stir in the sugar. Add the beaten egg and sufficient milk to mix to a soft dough. Turn out on to a floured surface and gently flatten the dough to about 2cm ($\frac{3}{4}$in) thick. Cut into 5cm (2in) plain or fluted rounds with a well floured cutter, or cut into triangles. Place on a greased or floured baking sheet so that each scone almost touches its neighbour. Dredge with flour and bake in a very hot oven (230°C/450°F, Gas Mark 8) for 12–15 minutes or until well risen and golden brown.

Slide all in one piece on to a wire rack covered with a clean cloth, and wrap up. Leave to cool then pull apart as required. Serve warm or cold, split and buttered, and with jam or honey.

Makes 8–10

RICH FLOURY SCONES

1 Sift flour and salt into bowl. Rub in fat till mixture resembles fine breadcrumbs, then stir in sugar

2 Add beaten egg and enough milk to make a soft dough

3 Flatten dough to about ¾ inch

4 Cut into 2 inch plain or fluted rounds using well floured cutter

5 Place on greased or floured baking sheet so that each scone almost touches its neighbours. Dredge with flour. Bake in very hot oven. 12-15 minutes

6 Slide in one piece onto wire rack covered with clean cloth and wrap up. Leave to cool

Variations

Savoury Scones

Omit the sugar and add either 2–3 teaspoons finely chopped fresh herbs; 1–1½ teaspoons dried herbs; 50g (2oz) finely grated mature Cheddar cheese; or 1 tablespoon grated Parmesan cheese.

Sultana or Raisin Scones

Add 50g (2oz) sultanas or raisins to the dry ingredients.

Citrus Scones

Add the finely grated rind of 1 orange or lemon to the dry ingredients.

Walnut Scones

Add 40g (1½oz) finely chopped walnuts to the dry ingredients.

All scones freeze well for up to 4 months except herb scones which should only be frozen for up to 3 months.

Wholemeal Scone Round

Brown scones, like brown bread, are becoming more and more favoured both for flavour and health. They are just as simple as white scones but need a little extra raising agent to keep them light.

100g (4oz) self-raising flour
1 level teaspoon baking powder
good pinch salt
100g (4oz) wholemeal flour
1 level tablespoon caster sugar
50g (2oz) butter or margarine
about 150ml (¼pt) milk (preferably sour)

Sift the white flour, baking powder and salt into a bowl. Add the brown flour and sugar, then the fat and rub in until the mixture resembles breadcrumbs. Add sufficient milk to mix to a softish dough. Turn on to a floured surface and flatten with your hands to a round about 2·5cm (1in) thick. Transfer to a greased or floured baking sheet and cut into 8 wedges. Dredge with flour and bake in a very hot oven (230°C/450°F, Gas Mark 8) for about 15 minutes. Cool on a wire rack and break into pieces as required.

Note 50g (2oz) sultanas or raisins can be added to the dry ingredients. For savoury scones, omit the sugar and add either a few herbs or little grated cheese to the dry ingredients, then sprinkle the top with flour, coarse sea salt or grated cheese.

Suitable to freeze for up to 4 months.

Orange Scone Bar

As a change from individual scones or scone rounds, this recipe is shaped into a long thin bar and served cut in slices to spread with butter. When becoming stale, it refreshes well if lightly covered with foil and put in a moderate oven for 5–7 minutes.

350g (12oz) self-raising flour
pinch of salt
75g (3oz) butter or margarine
40g (1½oz) caster sugar
50g (2oz) currants
25g (1oz) shelled walnuts, chopped
grated rind of 1 orange
1 egg, beaten

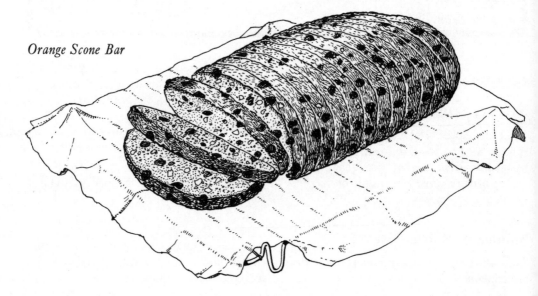

Orange Scone Bar

about 150ml (¼pt) milk (preferably sour)

1–2 tablespoons demerara sugar (optional)

Sift the flour and salt into a bowl and rub in the fat until the mixture resembles fine breadcrumbs. Stir in the sugar, currants, walnuts and orange rind. Add the egg and sufficient milk to mix to a fairly soft dough. Turn on to a floured surface and form into a brick shape about 4cm (1½in) deep. Transfer to a greased baking sheet and sprinkle the top with demerara sugar, if liked. Bake in a hot oven (220°C/425°F, Gas Mark 7) for about 25 minutes or until well risen, golden brown and firm. Turn on to a wire rack covered with a clean cloth, wrap up and leave to cool. Serve cut in slices, plain or buttered.

Suitable to freeze for up to 4 months.

Spicy Sultana Scones

Soft-textured scones, cut into squares, which saves time, and batch baked to give soft sides. Sultanas are used here but other dried fruits such as raisins, currants, chopped dates or figs can be used equally well.

350g (12oz) self-raising flour

pinch of salt

1½ level teaspoons ground cinnamon or mixed spice

75g (3oz) butter or margarine

40g (1½oz) caster or soft brown sugar

50–75g (2–3oz) sultanas, chopped dates or figs, etc

1 large egg, beaten

about 150ml (¼pt) milk (preferably sour)

milk to glaze

Sift the flour, salt and spice into a bowl, rub in the fat until the mixture resembles fine breadcrumbs, then mix in the sugar and sultanas (or other fruit). Add the egg and sufficient milk to mix to a fairly soft dough. Knead lightly until evenly mixed, turn on to a floured surface and roll out or press lightly with your hand to a square about 2cm (¾in) thick. Slide carefully on to a greased baking sheet, then cut into about 4cm (1½in) squares with a sharp knife, easing the scones a little away from each other but so they still almost touch. Brush with milk and bake in a very hot oven (230°C/450°F, Gas Mark 8) for 12–15 minutes until golden brown and firm to the touch. Wrap in a clean cloth and cool on a wire rack. Serve split and buttered.

Makes about 16

Suitable to freeze for up to 2 months only because of the spice.

Variations

Plain Scones

Omit the spice and fruit.

Coffee Scones

Replace 1 tablespoon milk with coffee essence or strong black coffee.

Lemon Scones

If preferred, omit the spice and fruit and add the finely grated rind of 1–2 lemons.

Walnut Scones

If preferred, replace the fruit with 75g (3oz) chopped walnuts and omit spice.

Oatmeal Scones

As a change from the usual recipes, oatmeal gives a nutty flavour and coarser texture to these quickly made scones.

225g (8oz) self-raising flour
1 level teaspoon baking powder
1 level teaspoon salt
175g (6oz) oatmeal, fine or medium
40g (1½oz) butter or margarine
1 tablespoon lemon juice
about 175ml (6fl oz) milk

Sift the flour, baking powder and salt into a bowl, add the oatmeal and rub in the fat. Add the lemon juice to the milk (to turn it sour), then add sufficient liquid to the dry ingredients to mix to a softish dough. Divide in half and shape each piece to a flat round about 2·5cm (1in) thick. Place on well floured baking sheets, cut each round into 6 wedges and dredge lightly with flour. Bake in a hot oven (220°C/425°F, Gas Mark 7) for about 15 minutes or until firm to the touch and lightly browned. Transfer to a wire rack and serve warm if possible, with butter and jam, cheese or savoury spreads.

Makes.12

Cheese Scones

Savoury scones are a boon for picnics and buffet lunches in place of bread or rolls. Provided they are served fresh and with plenty of butter, they will tempt everyone, and the variations are endless. Toppings can range from grated cheese, poppy or sesame seeds or coarse sea salt, to a simple egg or milk glaze.

225g (8oz) self-raising flour
½ level teaspoon salt
1 level teaspoon dry mustard
pinch of cayenne pepper
50g (2oz) butter or margarine
50g (2oz) finely grated mature Cheddar cheese or 2 tablespoons grated Parmesan cheese
about 125ml (¼pt) milk (preferably sour)
poppy or sesame seeds

Sift the flour, salt, mustard and cayenne into a bowl and rub in the butter or margarine until the mixture resembles fine breadcrumbs. Stir in the cheese until evenly mixed, then add sufficient milk to mix to a soft but not sticky dough, using a round-bladed knife. Turn on to a floured surface, knead lightly and roll out to about 1cm (½in) thick. Cut into 5–6cm (2–2½in) plain or fluted rounds with a floured cutter. Place on a greased baking sheet, brush the tops with milk and sprinkle with poppy or sesame seeds. Bake in a very hot oven (230°C/450°F, Gas Mark 8) for about 10 minutes or until well risen and golden brown. Cool on a wire rack.

Makes 8–10 scones

Suitable to freeze for up to 3 months.

Variations

Cheese and Onion

Add 2 level tablespoons minced raw onion or 1–2 level tablespoons chopped chives to the dry ingredients.

Cheese and Ham

Add 25g (1oz) minced ham and 2 level teaspoons chopped parsley to the dry ingredients.

Plain Scones

Omit the cheese, mustard and cayenne.

Peanut Scones

Replace the cheese with 50g (2oz) finely chopped salted peanuts, omit the mustard and cayenne, and sprinkle the tops with rock salt or chopped peanuts.

Soda Bread

Speed always being important nowadays and bread-making becoming more and more popular, it is possible to combine the two and make soda bread. Using bicarbonate of soda and cream of tartar or tartaric acid, instead of yeast, to aerate breads, cakes and scones, became popular more than a hundred years ago in Ireland, Scotland and England. The famous Irish soda bread is probably the best known, and although the special flavour it obtains from being baked over a peat fire is impossible to achieve in a modern cooker, it is still well worth making and is extremely quick. The liquid used should for preference be buttermilk, but as this is not always easy to obtain, sour milk or fresh milk soured with lemon juice can be used. Soda bread is baked daily in Ireland for it dries out quickly so needs really to be eaten the day it is made, but it toasts well when stale. The flour can vary from all wholewheat through proportions of brown and white flour to all white flour, depending on taste.

225g (8oz) plain white flour

1–2 level teaspoons salt

2 level teaspoons bicarbonate of soda

2 level teaspoons cream of tartar

225g (8oz) wholewheat or wholemeal flour

50g (2oz) lard or margarine

300ml (½pt) milk, sour milk or buttermilk

1 tablespoon lemon juice (if using fresh milk)

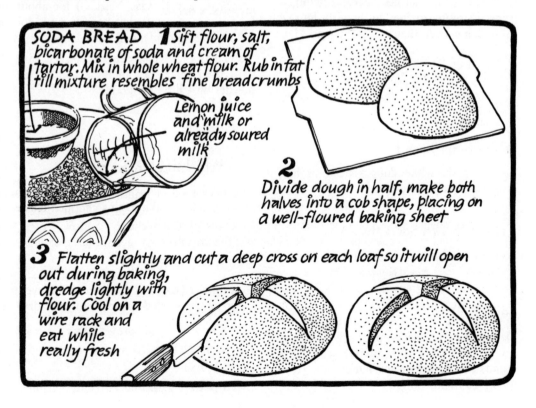

SODA BREAD **1** Sift flour, salt, bicarbonate of soda and cream of tartar. Mix in whole wheat flour. Rub in fat till mixture resembles fine breadcrumbs

Lemon juice and milk or already soured milk

2 Divide dough in half, make both halves into a cob shape, placing on a well-floured baking sheet

3 Flatten slightly and cut a deep cross on each loaf so it will open out during baking, dredge lightly with flour. Cool on a wire rack and eat while really fresh

Sift the white flour, salt, bicarbonate of soda and cream of tartar into a bowl then mix in the wholewheat flour. Rub in the fat until the mixture resembles fine bread-crumbs and make a well in the centre. Add the lemon juice to the fresh milk (which will make it curdle) then add this or the already sour milk or buttermilk to the dry ingredients and mix to a soft but manage-able dough. Turn on to a floured surface and divide the dough in half. Shape each piece into a round cob and place on a well floured baking sheet. Flatten slightly and cut a deep cross on each loaf so it will open out during baking, and dredge lightly with flour. Bake in a hot oven (220°C/425°F, Gas Mark 7) for about 30 minutes or until well risen and golden brown. Some people prefer the method of inverting a large deep cake tin over each loaf before putting it into the oven, then baking for 30 minutes, remove the tins and continue for a further 5–10 minutes – this is supposed to increase the volume of the loaf, especially when using white flour. Cool on a wire rack and eat whilst very fresh.

Note If buttermilk is available, the cream of tartar can be omitted.

Variations

White Soda Bread

Use all plain white flour instead of half brown and half white flour.

Coarse Brown Soda Bread

Use all wholewheat flour instead of half brown and half white flour.

Soda Rolls

Flatten out the made-up dough to about 2·5cm (1in) thick and cut into 5cm (2in) rounds or equivalent-sized triangles. Bake for 15–20 minutes.

Baking Powder Rolls

A quick stand-by when rolls are needed but there is not sufficient time to allow yeast to rise. They are best served very fresh and slightly warm.

225g (8oz) plain flour
2 level teaspoons baking powder
good pinch of salt
2 level teaspoons caster sugar
about 200ml (7fl oz) milk (preferably sour)
milk to glaze

Sift the flour, baking powder, salt and sugar into a bowl. Add the milk gradually, mixing to form a firm dough. Knead lightly, then divide into 6–8 pieces. Shape each into a roll and place on a greased baking sheet. Brush the tops with milk and prick each roll twice with a fork. Bake in a hot oven (220°C/425°F, Gas Mark 7) for about 10 minutes. Cool on a wire rack.

Makes 6–8

Note 75g (3oz) flour can be replaced with wholemeal flour, but increase the baking powder by ½ level teaspoon.

Treacle Drop Scones

The bakestone or griddle makes delicious drop scones. These differ from Scotch Pancakes by the addition of black treacle, and the use of brown sugar in place of white sugar to give a rich flavour.

100g (4oz) self-raising flour
pinch of salt
2 level teaspoons soft brown sugar
2 tablespoons black treacle
1 egg, beaten
125ml (scant ¼pt) milk

Sift the flour and salt into a bowl and mix in the sugar. Heat the treacle gently until it just flows, then add to the dry ingredients with the egg and half the milk. Beat until smooth, gradually adding the remaining milk. Heat a bakestone, griddle or heavy-based frying pan and rub lightly with oil or lard. Drop dessertspoons of the batter on to the griddle and cook for 3–4 minutes until bubbles rise to the surface and the undersides are lightly browned. Turn over and continue for 2–3 minutes until lightly browned. Remove to a clean tea towel and wrap them up to keep warm whilst cooking the remainder. Serve warm or cold, spread with butter.

Makes about 18

Note To measure treacle easily, first rub the spoon with oil.

Suitable to freeze for up to 2 months.

Variations

Scotch Pancakes or Drop Scones

Omit the black treacle and use 1 level tablespoon caster sugar in place of the soft brown sugar.

Griddle or Girdle Scones

These are very quick and easy to make and cook. The Welsh and Scots are very fond of

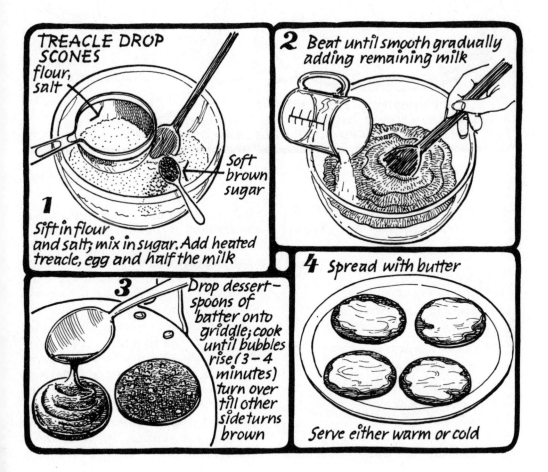

1. **TREACLE DROP SCONES** flour, salt / Soft brown sugar / Sift in flour and salt; mix in sugar. Add heated treacle, egg and half the milk

2. Beat until smooth gradually adding remaining milk

3. Drop dessert-spoons of batter onto griddle; cook until bubbles rise (3–4 minutes) turn over till other side turns brown

4. Spread with butter / Serve either warm or cold

POTATO SCONES

1 Boil peeled potatoes; cool a little, mash, add salt. Beat in butter, finally work in flour to make a smooth dough

2 Roll out thinly (about ¼ inch) on a floured surface

3 Cut into plain rounds using a 2½ to 3 inch cutter

4 Place on a preheated greased griddle or heavy-based frying pan, cook till golden brown then turn over. Wrap in clean cloth while cooking remainder

cooking scones this way and if you don't have a griddle, a heavy-based frying pan will do just as well.

225g (8oz) plain flour
2 level teaspoons cream of tartar
1 level teaspoon bicarbonate of soda
good pinch of salt
2 level teaspoons caster sugar
40g (1½oz) butter, margarine or lard
50g (2oz) sultanas (optional)
about 150ml (¼pt) milk
1 teaspoon lemon juice

Sift the flour, cream of tartar, soda and salt into a bowl and mix in the sugar. Rub in the fat until the mixture resembles fine breadcrumbs, then stir in the sultanas, if used. Combine the milk and lemon juice (to turn it sour) and add sufficient to the dry ingredients to form a fairly soft but manageable dough. Knead very lightly, divide the dough in half and roll each piece to a flat round about 1cm (½in) thick. Heat a bakestone, griddle or heavy-based frying pan and dredge with flour. Cut each scone round into 6 wedges, place on the griddle and cook gently for about 5 minutes or until well risen and evenly browned. Turn over carefully and continue for a further 5 minutes until brown. Cook the remaining scones in the same way. Cool on a wire rack and serve, preferably still warm, with plenty of butter.

Makes 12

Potato Scones

These scones used to be very popular and are very good if properly made. Some people prefer to use freshly boiled hot potatoes whilst others insist on leaving them to get cold first – I think they should still be lukewarm for it gives a lighter scone. The proportion of flour can also vary greatly. Any left-over or stale scones can be fried to serve with bacon and eggs or grills.

450g (1lb) floury potatoes
salt
25–50g (1–2oz) butter or margarine
75g (3oz) plain flour

Peel the potatoes, cook in boiling salted water until tender and then drain thoroughly. Leave to cool a little then mash very thoroughly or rub through a sieve. Season well with salt, beat in the butter or margarine and finally work in the flour to give a smooth dough. Roll out thinly to about 0·5cm ($\frac{1}{4}$in) on a floured surface and cut into plain rounds using a 6–7·5cm (2$\frac{1}{2}$–3in) cutter. Place on a pre-heated greased bakestone, griddle or heavy-based frying pan and cook for 4–5 minutes until golden brown. Turn over and continue until browned. Wrap first batch in a clean cloth whilst cooking the remainder, and serve warm or cold spread with butter.

Makes 8–10

Note For a coarser-textured scone, roll out on a mixture of fine oatmeal and flour.

Welsh Cakes

These are another type of fruited griddle cake which, although found all over Wales, are more popular in the south of the country. They are rolled thicker than some of the griddle scones or cakes and are cut into fairly large rounds. Although not traditional, they may also be baked in a fairly hot oven (200°C/400°F, Gas Mark 6) for about 10 minutes.

225g (8oz) plain flour
pinch of salt
1 level teaspoon baking powder
good pinch of mixed spice, ground nutmeg or mace
125g (5oz) butter or margarine
75g (3oz) caster sugar
40g (1$\frac{1}{2}$oz) currants
40g (1$\frac{1}{2}$oz) sultanas
1 egg, beaten
about 2 tablespoons milk

Sift the flour, salt, baking powder and spice into a bowl and rub in the butter or margarine. Mix in the sugar, currants and sultanas and add the egg and sufficient milk to mix to a pliable dough, similar to shortcrust pastry. Turn on to a floured surface and roll out to about 1cm ($\frac{1}{2}$in) thick. Cut into plain or fluted 7·5cm (3in) rounds. Cook on a griddle, heavy-based frying pan or bakestone (greased and pre-heated to moderate) for about 3–4 minutes each side or until golden brown. Do not cook too quickly or the insides will still be soggy when the outsides are ready. They may then be dredged with caster sugar before being cooled on a wire rack. Eat whilst fresh, either warm or cold, with butter.

Makes about 12

Note They may also be sprinkled with ground cinnamon mixed with caster sugar.

Singing Hinny

A speciality of Northumberland, this is a large round cake or scone made from a type of scone dough which is cooked on a griddle where it sings and fizzles as it cooks – hence the name. A 'hinny' is an endearment for a friend, meaning probably that these scones are much appreciated. They are also called 'small coal fizzers' in some parts of the county, probably because they were baked over the small coals on the fire. The Yorkshire people call their version of fruit griddle scones 'Fat Rascals' which is a very suitable name.

150g (6oz) plain flour
½ level teaspoon salt
1 level teaspoon baking powder
25g (1oz) caster sugar
25g (1oz) ground rice
25g (1oz) lard or butter
40–50g (1½–2oz) currants
150ml (¼pt) single cream and milk mixed

Sift the flour, salt and baking powder into a bowl and mix in the sugar and ground rice. Rub in the fat finely, then mix in the currants. Add sufficient of the liquid to mix to a pliable dough. Turn on to a floured surface and roll out to about 1cm (½in) thick. Cut into about 10cm (4in) rounds and place on a pre-heated greased griddle or heavy-based frying pan. Prick with a fork in several places and cook slowly for 5–6 minutes each side until golden brown; the hissing and fizzling start when they are turned over. Serve warm, split in half and spread with butter.

Makes about 6

French Toast

In place of scones or bread, stale bread can be prepared and cooked in this way to produce a new type of crisp toast to serve with jam, honey, marmalade, cheese, etc.

6–8 slices stale bread, brown or white
2 eggs
200ml (8fl oz) milk
1–2 tablespoons caster sugar
lard for frying

Either leave the bread as it is or remove the crusts. Beat the eggs, milk and sugar together and soak the slices of bread in it until soft. Grease a griddle or heavy-based frying pan liberally with lard, then add the drained pieces of bread and cook gently until browned on both sides. Serve warm.

Oatcakes

Oatcakes, although probably most famous in Scotland, also come from Wales (Bara Ceirch), Yorkshire and other northern regions of England. They are usually cooked on a bakestone or griddle but are sometimes cooked in the oven; they can also be dried out in a cool oven with the door ajar, instead of on the metal rack or toaster which used to be hung in front of the kitchen fire.

225g (8oz) oatmeal, medium or fine
½ level teaspoon salt
pinch of bicarbonate of soda
1 tablespoon bacon fat or lard, melted
hot water

Put the oatmeal in a bowl with the salt and soda. Add the melted fat and sufficient hot water to mix to a stiff paste. Knead into a smooth ball, then roll out half the dough thinly, on a surface dredged with fine oatmeal. Cut into a round about 18–20cm (7–8in) in diameter then divide this into 4, 6 or 8 wedges. Put on a pre-heated, lightly

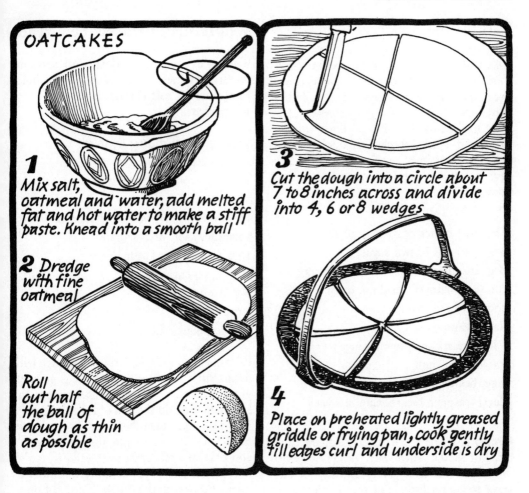

OATCAKES

1 Mix salt, oatmeal and water, add melted fat and hot water to make a stiff paste. Knead into a smooth ball

2 Dredge with fine oatmeal

Roll out half the ball of dough as thin as possible

3 Cut the dough into a circle about 7 to 8 inches across and divide into 4, 6 or 8 wedges

4 Place on preheated lightly greased griddle or frying pan, cook gently till edges curl and underside is dry

greased bakestone, griddle or heavy-based frying pan, lower the heat and cook gently until the edges begin to curl up and the undersides are dry. To dry the tops of the oatcakes, either put in a warm oven or toast lightly under the grill, or if you have an open fire, stand the oatcakes in front of it. Repeat with the second piece of dough. They will store in an airtight container for several weeks.

Makes 8–16

Bara Ceirch

The traditional Welsh oatcakes are made in the same way as the Scottish variety but are rolled thinner. The ingredients are the same, with the addition of 2 teaspoons melted butter or margarine and 1½ teaspoons caster sugar. The oatcakes are brushed with a glaze of an egg beaten with 1 tablespoon water and 1 teaspoon sugar, and are usually shaped into thin rounds about 7.5cm (3in) in diameter.

Note Oatcake dough is difficult to handle and for those who opt for an easier, if not traditional recipe, replace 50g (2oz) oatmeal with plain flour.

Parkin

This teabread or cake originated in York-shire and Lancashire where the oatmeal necessary to make it authentic is a well used ingredient. It is a moist gingerbread made with half oatmeal and half flour, brown sugar and black treacle (although golden syrup is sometimes used). It needs a few days to mature and is served cut into squares.

100g (4oz) butter or margarine
100g (4oz) soft brown sugar
100g (4oz) black treacle or golden syrup
100g (4oz) oatmeal, medium or fine
100g (4oz) plain flour
½ level teaspoon salt
1½ level teaspoons ground ginger
4 tablespoons milk
1 egg, beaten
½ level teaspoon bicarbonate of soda

Grease and line a 20cm (8in) square cake tin. Put the fat, sugar and treacle or syrup into a pan and heat gently until dissolved; leave to cool a little. Put the oatmeal in a bowl, sift in the flour, salt and ginger, and mix well. Add the treacle mixture, 3 table-spoons milk and the egg, then beat well until smooth. Dissolve the bicarbonate of soda in the remaining milk, add to the batter and beat thoroughly until it is well incorporated. Pour into the tin and bake in a moderate oven (170°C/325°F, Gas Mark 3) for 1–1¼ hours until firm to the touch. Turn on to a wire rack and leave to cool. Wrap in foil or store in an airtight container for 3–4 days before cutting. Parkin may also be spread with butter.

Note 1 level teaspoon each of ground cinnamon and mixed spice may be used in place of the ground ginger, and half the white flour replaced with wholemeal flour.

Wholemeal Fruited Teabread

This is a one-stage tealoaf with a coarse texture obtained by the addition of whole-meal flour. A soft margarine must be used for success.

100g (4oz) self-raising flour
1½ level teaspoons baking powder
¾ level teaspoon ground ginger
pinch of salt
100g (4oz) wholewheat or wholemeal flour
100g (4oz) soft margarine
100g (4oz) caster sugar
100g (4oz) currants
25g (1oz) mixed peel
2 eggs, beaten
3 tablespoons milk

Grease a 900g (2lb) loaf tin and dredge with flour. Sift the white flour, baking powder, ginger and salt into a bowl, then mix in the brown flour. Add the rest of the ingredients, mix well and then beat for 2–3 minutes until smooth. Turn into the prepared tin and bake in a moderate oven (180°C/350°F, Gas Mark 4) for 50–60 minutes until well risen and firm to the touch. Turn out on to

1 *Steak and kidney pie;* 2 *Raised game pie;*
3 *Raw short crust pastry;* 4 *Spider pie;*
5 *Cornish pasties*

a wire rack to cool. Serve sliced and buttered.

Suitable to freeze for up to 3 months.

moderate oven (170°C/325°F, Gas Mark 3) for 1–1¼ hours until well risen and firm to the touch. Turn out on to a wire rack and leave to cool. Wrap in foil for 2–3 days if time allows, for the loaf to mature. To serve, cut in slices and spread with butter.

Note For a mellower flavour, replace 50g (2oz) malt extract with golden syrup.

Suitable to freeze for up to 3 months.

[partial obscured recipe text]

...our of a yeasted
...er to make. It is
...es more sticky
...s before use.

...self-raising flour
...h of salt
100g (4oz) sultanas
50g (2oz) mixed peel or sultanas (optional)
1 egg, beaten

Grease and line a 900g (2lb) loaf tin. Put the malt extract, syrup, fat and milk into a saucepan, then heat gently until dissolved and runny but not too hot. Sift the flour and salt into a bowl and mix in the sultanas and mixed peel (if used). Add the malt liquid and beaten egg, and beat until smooth. Pour into the prepared tin and bake in a

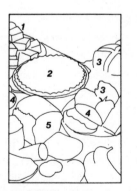

1 *Parkin*; 2 *Bacon and Egg Pie*; 3 *Soda bread*;
4 *Baps*; 5 *White tin loaf*

Marmalade and Walnut Teabread

Marmalade is so traditionally British and here it is combined with other ingredients to make a tasty teabread. Although orange marmalade and rind are used here, lemon marmalade and rind can be used for a variation.

225g (8oz) plain flour
pinch of salt
1 level tablespoon baking powder
100g (4oz) butter or margarine
50g (2oz) caster sugar
50g (2oz) chopped walnuts or hazelnuts
grated rind of ½ orange
2 eggs, beaten
3 level tablespoons orange marmalade (not jelly variety)
2–3 tablespoons milk

Grease and line a 450g (1lb) loaf tin. Sift the flour, salt and baking powder into a bowl and rub in the fat until the mixture resembles fine breadcrumbs. Stir in the sugar, nuts and orange rind. Add the eggs, marmalade and sufficient milk to mix to a fairly soft batter. Turn into the prepared tin and bake in a moderate oven (180°C/ 350°F, Gas Mark 4) for 1¼–1½ hours until well risen, firm to the touch and golden.

brown. Turn out and cool on a wire rack. Suitable to freeze for up to 3 months.

Cranberry Teabread

Cranberries are very popular in America and have begun to appear regularly in this country in one form or another. The small red berry is full of flavour and gives a good colour to anything to which it is added. When blended with nuts and orange, the resulting teabread will disappear from the plate almost as soon as it is put there.

200g (8oz) plain flour
1½ level teaspoons baking powder
½ level teaspoon bicarbonate of soda
good pinch of salt
50g (2oz) butter or margarine
150g (6oz) soft brown or caster sugar
grated rind of 1 orange
50g (2oz) chopped walnuts
4 tablespoons cranberries, chopped (fresh, frozen or canned)
50g (2oz) raisins
6 tablespoons orange juice
1 large egg

Grease and line a 900g (2lb) loaf tin. Sift the flour, baking powder, bicarbonate of soda and salt into a bowl and rub in the fat until the mixture resembles fine breadcrumbs. Mix in the sugar, orange rind, walnuts, cranberries and raisins. Beat the orange juice and egg together and mix into the dry ingredients. Turn into the prepared tin and bake in a moderate oven (180°C/350°F, Gas Mark 4) for 1–1¼ hours until well risen, firm to the touch and golden brown. Turn on to a wire rack to cool. Serve in slices, either plain or spread with butter.

Note In place of chopped cranberries, 3–4 tablespoons drained cranberry sauce may be used.

Suitable to freeze for up to 3 months.

Cidered Teabread

The fruit in this teabread is given a good flavour by the sweet cider in which it is both soaked and boiled before the loaf is mixed. The bread keeps moist for a good while and can be served plain or buttered.

250g (9oz) mixed dried fruit
75g (3oz) dates, chopped
300ml (½pt) sweet cider
275g (10oz) self-raising flour
50g (2oz) shelled walnuts, chopped (optional)
175g (6oz) soft brown sugar
grated rind of 1 lemon
2 eggs, beaten

Grease and line a 900g (2lb) loaf tin. Put the mixed fruit and dates into a bowl with the cider and mix well; cover and leave to stand overnight. Transfer to a saucepan and heat until it just comes to the boil, then cool until lukewarm. Sift the flour into a bowl and mix in the nuts (if used), sugar and lemon rind. Add the cidered fruit and the eggs, and beat until smooth. Turn into the tin, level the top and bake in a moderate oven (170°C/325°F, Gas Mark 3) for 1½–1¾ hours until well risen, golden brown and firm to the touch. Turn out on to a wire rack and leave to cool. Serve in slices, either plain or buttered.

Suitable to freeze for up to 3 months.

Orange and Apple Tealoaf

Made by the one-stage method with a soft margarine, this is very simple to make and has an unusual orange and honey flavour, and contains small pieces of apple.

225g (8oz) self-raising flour
pinch of salt
100g (4oz) soft margarine
50g (2oz) caster sugar
3 tablespoons clear honey
grated rind of 1 large orange
1 eating apple, peeled, cored and coarsely grated
2 eggs, beaten
clear honey to glaze

Grease a 900g (2lb) loaf tin and dredge lightly with flour. Sift the flour and salt into a bowl. Add the other ingredients, mix well and then beat for 2–3 minutes until smooth. Turn into the prepared tin and bake in a moderate oven (180°C/350°F, Gas Mark 4) for 1–1¼ hours until well risen and firm to the touch. Turn on to a wire rack, brush the top of the loaf with honey and leave to cool. Serve in slices, plain or buttered.

Suitable to freeze for up to 3 months.

Apricot Tealoaf

This recipe is a one-stage tealoaf with all the ingredients mixed together; for success it requires a soft or luxury margarine. Dried apricots are expensive but this loaf uses only a small quantity and the flavour comes through very strongly.

75g (3oz) dried apricots, chopped
150ml (¼pt) water
200g (8oz) self-raising flour
100g (4oz) soft margarine
100g (4oz) caster sugar
2 eggs
grated rind of ½ lemon

Grease and line a 900g (2lb) loaf tin. Put the apricots and water in a saucepan, bring up to the boil and simmer gently for 5 minutes, then leave to cool, when most of the liquid will be absorbed. Place the apricots in a bowl with the sifted flour and all the other ingredients, and beat for 2–3 minutes until smooth. Turn into the prepared tin, level the top and bake in a moderate oven (180°C/350°F, Gas Mark 4) for about 50 minutes or until well risen, golden brown and firm to the touch. Cool on a wire rack. Serve in slices, plain or buttered.

Note 50g (2oz) chopped hazelnuts or walnuts, or currants, raisins or sultanas may be added to this tealoaf.

Suitable to freeze for up to 3 months.

Bara Brith Teabread

As already shown in the Teatime Favourites section, Bara Brith is usually made with a yeast dough. However, this Welsh speciality currant bread can be made without yeast and the result is a delicious teabread with a completely different texture.

200g (8oz) self-raising flour
pinch of salt

1 level teaspoon mixed spice
50g (2oz) butter or margarine
75g (3oz) caster sugar
grated rind of 1 lemon
100g (4oz) currants
75g (3oz) black treacle
1 egg, beaten
½ level teaspoon bicarbonate of soda
100ml (4fl oz) milk

Grease and line a 900g (2lb) loaf tin. Sift the flour, salt and spice into a bowl and rub in the fat until the mixture resembles fine breadcrumbs, then stir in the sugar, lemon rind and currants and mix well. Add the treacle, egg and the bicarbonate of soda dissolved in the milk, and beat until evenly mixed and smooth. Turn into the prepared tin and bake in a moderate oven (180°C/350°F, Gas Mark 4) for about 1¼ hours or until firm to the touch. Turn on to a wire rack and leave to cool. Wrap in foil or store in an airtight container for at least 24 hours before use. Serve sliced and buttered.

Suitable to freeze for up to 3 months.

Barm Brack Teabread

This Irish tealoaf is usually made with a yeasted dough but another version can be made by soaking the currants (or dried fruit) in tea before mixing. The texture is especially moist and the loaf keeps well.

150g (6oz) soft brown or caster sugar
250g (10oz) currants or mixed dried fruit
50g (2oz) mixed peel
400ml (¾pt) freshly made tea, cooled
1 egg, beaten
300g (12oz) self-raising flour
1 level teaspoon mixed spice (optional)

Grease and line a 900g (2lb) loaf tin. Put the sugar, dried fruit and peel into a bowl and pour on the tea. Cover the bowl and leave to stand for at least 6 hours and preferably overnight. Stir in the beaten egg, then sift in the flour and spice, and beat until smooth. Turn into the prepared tin and cook in a moderate oven (180°C/350°F, Gas Mark 4) for about 1¼ hours or until well risen and firm to the touch. Turn out and cool on a wire rack.

Suitable to freeze for up to 3 months.

Pastry Making

Pastry making is an art, but one that is easily achieved; the secret is to keep everything cool. The fat should be cold and firm – but not too hard – so that it will cut into pieces and then rub easily into the flour or stay in small flakes or cubes if it is for one of the flaked pastries. The water used for mixing must be cold; a marble slab is ideal for rolling out since it is always cold, but as not everyone has marble in their kitchen, any cool surface will do; and utensils should be cold. In order for everything to blend properly, the ingredients must all be at the same temperature. If the pastry becomes too soft to roll, then rest it in a polythene bag in the refrigerator for a short while before proceeding. The exceptions to the 'cool' rule are, of course, hot water pastry and choux pastry, for in both cases the fat is melted in the liquid and brought up to the boil before being added to the flour.

Plain flour should be used for all pastry except suet crust pastry; this requires a raising agent in the form of baking powder, or self-raising flour which is more often used. The flaked pastries, such as puff, flaky and rough puff, can also be made with a strong plain flour as used in yeast cookery. The flour and salt (for flavouring) should be sifted into a bowl to incorporate as much air as possible. Pastry should be handled as little as possible and when rubbing in, only the fingertips should be used. The addition of too much liquid will give a sticky, unmanageable dough which becomes very brittle when baked, and if extra flour is added, it will upset the balance of ingredients and spoil the texture. It is very important to keep the exact proportions to obtain the correct results, so weigh ingredients with care. You will see that the metric and imperial equivalents in the pastry recipes are quite different from some of the others in this book; this is to achieve the correct balance and must be followed. Use only the minimum amount of flour on the rolling-out surface for if too much is incorporated, the dough will be spoiled; brush off any surplus flour after rolling out.

The type of fat used is important too. In general, for short and flaked pastries an equal mixture of butter or margarine and lard gives the best results. Using all lard gives a good short texture but the pastry will lack the flavour which a proportion of butter or margarine provides. Eggs are used in choux pastry to achieve the essential light airiness, and in flan pastry to help bind and enrich.

All pastry should be rolled in one direction only, ie straight in front of you, so turn the pastry round gradually whilst continuing to roll, to keep a good shape. Never turn it over or overstretch it during rolling or it will simply shrink back again during baking. The rolling should be light but firm; do not roll out more than necessary. When making flaky, puff or rough puff pastry, always keep it rolled to an even rectangle, keeping the corners square, to ensure an even rise during baking.

There are various methods of incorporating the fat into the flour for making the different types of pastry. Rubbing in is used for the shortcrusts and rich flan pastries; suet crust has the suet finely chopped or grated into the flour before binding with the liquid; the flaked pastries are made by rolling flakes or pieces of fat into the dough and folding and rolling the pastry several times to incorporate air as well as distribute the fat evenly to achieve the characteristic layers when baked; whilst choux and hot water crust pastries have the fat melted in hot liquid before it is added to the flour.

All pastries should be baked in a hot oven, ranging from 200–230°C/400–450°F, Gas Mark 6–8. with the rich flaked pastries requiring the highest temperature.

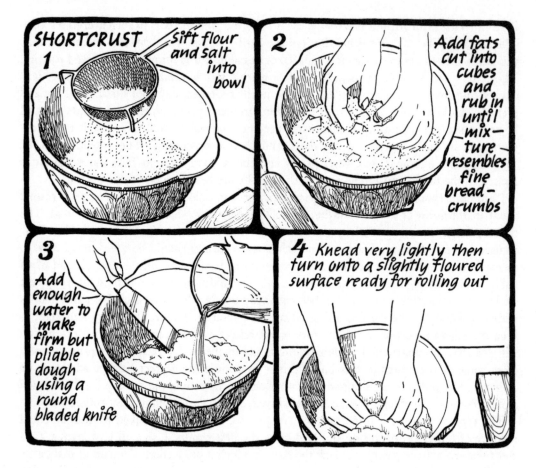

Shortcrust Pastry

This is a pastry suitable for nearly any purpose – sweet or savoury. It is made by the standard rubbing-in method with quantities of half fat to flour. It is usual for the fat to be half margarine and half lard or white fat but other proportions can be used to suit your taste. Butter can also be used, but if all butter or margarine is used the pastry will be very short and difficult to handle, although it will have an excellent flavour. The rubbed-in mixture will keep in an airtight container in the refrigerator for up to 2 weeks, whilst the made-up pastry will keep for 2–3 days wrapped in foil or polythene.

200g (8oz) plain flour
good pinch of salt
50g (2oz) butter or margarine
50g (2oz) lard or white fat
about 4 tablespoons cold water

Sift the flour and salt into a bowl. Add the fats cut into cubes, and rub in until the mixture resembles fine breadcrumbs. Add sufficient water to mix to a firm but pliable dough, using a round-bladed knife or a fork. Knead very lightly then turn on to a lightly floured surface ready for rolling out. The pastry can be wrapped in polythene or foil and chilled for 2–3 days but is best if used within 12 hours.

Note Pastries are usually measured by their weight of flour; for example, 200g (8oz) shortcrust pastry is made from 200g (8oz) plain flour, etc.

Suitable to freeze raw for up to 6 months.

Rich Flan Pastry

This is a slightly sweet pastry which is suitable for sweet dishes such as flans, tartlets and pies. It will keep in the refrigerator for 24 hours before use.

125g (5oz) plain flour
pinch of salt
75g (3oz) butter or margarine
1–1½ level teaspoons caster sugar
1 egg yolk
about 4 teaspoons cold water

Sift the flour and salt into a bowl. Rub the fat in carefully until the mixture resembles breadcrumbs, then stir in the sugar. Add the egg yolk and sufficient water to mix to a firm but pliable dough. Knead lightly and, if possible, wrap in polythene and chill for 10–20 minutes before use.

Suitable to freeze for up to 1 month.

Puff Pastry

Home-made puff pastry takes a little extra time to make but is well worth the effort. This pastry is the richest of all, using equal quantities of fat and flour, and has the greatest and most even rise of all because of the air rolled and folded into it. The best fat to use is butter, but margarine or a combination of butter or margarine and lard can also be used. The made-up pastry will keep wrapped in foil in the refrigerator for several days. Use the first rolling for the greatest rise – Vol-au-Vents, Cream Slices, etc – and the trimmings can be re-rolled for smaller pastries such as Cream Horns, Eccles Cakes, Sacristans etc.

450g (1lb) plain flour
1 level teaspoon salt
450g (1lb) butter, firm but not too hard
about 300ml (½pt) iced water

Sift the flour and salt into a bowl. Remove a quarter of the butter and rub in until the mixture resembles fine breadcrumbs. Bind to a fairly soft dough with iced water and knead lightly into a ball. Roll out on a lightly floured surface to about a 30cm (12in) square. Shape the remaining butter into a block and put it on one half of the pastry. Fold the pastry over the butter and seal the edges with the rolling pin, then 'rib' it by pressing the rolling pin across the pastry at regular intervals – this helps distribute the air evenly. Turn the pastry so that the fold is to the right and roll it out to a long strip, 3 times as long as it is wide. Fold the bottom third upwards and the top third downwards so it is evenly folded into three. Seal the edges, rib the pastry, then put it into a lightly oiled polythene bag. Chill for 30 minutes. Repeat the rolling and chilling process 5 times more, giving the pastry a quarter turn each time so that the fold is always on the right. Chill for at least 30 minutes after the final rolling. The pastry is even better if rolled out 3 times one day and the final 3 times the next day – if time permits. The pastry is now ready for use.

Suitable to freeze for up to 6 months.

See diagrams overleaf.

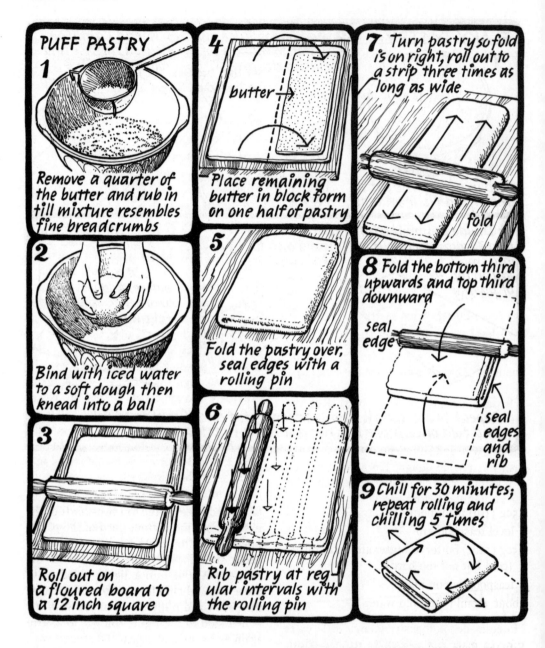

PUFF PASTRY

1 Remove a quarter of the butter and rub in till mixture resembles fine breadcrumbs

2 Bind with iced water to a soft dough then knead into a ball

3 Roll out on a floured board to a 12 inch square

4 Place remaining butter in block form on one half of pastry — *butter*→

5 Fold the pastry over, seal edges with a rolling pin

6 Rib pastry at regular intervals with the rolling pin

7 Turn pastry so fold is on right, roll out to a strip three times as long as wide — *fold*

8 Fold the bottom third upwards and top third downward — *seal edge* — *seal edges and rib*

9 Chill for 30 minutes; repeat rolling and chilling 5 times

Flaky Pastry

This is the most common of the 'flaked' pastries and has an excellent flavour and lightness. It is another rich pastry which rises well but is not so rich as puff pastry. It requires a proportion of three-quarters fat to flour and, as the name implies, is made by putting flakes of fat over the pastry dough during the rolling and folding process. Flaky pastry is used for sausage rolls, pies, pasties, etc, and anywhere that a medium-rising pastry is required. Again, all butter is best for flavour but a mixture of butter or margarine and lard can be used satisfactorily.

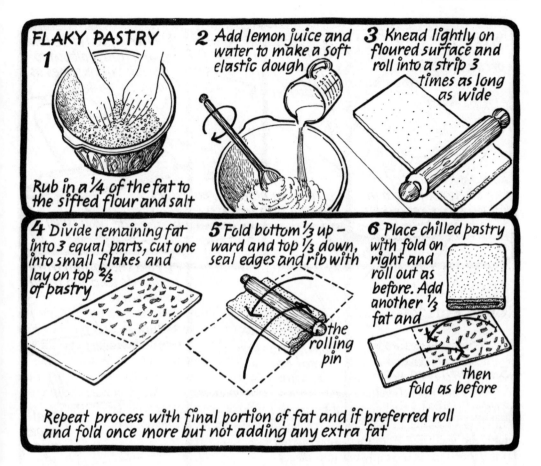

FLAKY PASTRY 1

Rub in a ¼ of the fat to the sifted flour and salt

2 Add lemon juice and water to make a soft elastic dough

3 Knead lightly on floured surface and roll into a strip 3 times as long as wide

4 Divide remaining fat into 3 equal parts, cut one into small flakes and lay on top ⅔ of pastry

5 Fold bottom ⅓ upward and top ⅓ down, seal edges and rib with the rolling pin

6 Place chilled pastry with fold on right and roll out as before. Add another ⅓ fat and then fold as before

Repeat process with final portion of fat and if preferred roll and fold once more but not adding any extra fat

450g (1lb) plain flour

1 level teaspoon salt

350g (12oz) butter or butter and lard, mixed (cold but not too hard)

1 teaspoon lemon juice

about 300ml (½pt) cold water

Sift the flour and salt into a bowl and rub in 75g (3oz) of the fat until the mixture resembles fine breadcrumbs. Add the lemon juice and sufficient water to the dry ingredients to mix to a fairly soft elastic dough. Knead lightly on a floured surface then roll out to a strip 3 times as long as it is wide. Divide the remaining fat into 3 equal amounts and use 1 portion to cut into small flakes and lay over the top two-thirds of the pastry. Fold the bottom third of the pastry upwards and top third downwards, seal the edges and rib (see puff pastry) with the rolling pin. Put into a lightly oiled polythene bag and chill for 15 minutes. Remove the pastry and put in front of you with the folded side to the right; roll out to a strip again as before and repeat the process with the second portion of fat. Fold up as before and chill. Repeat with the final portion of fat and, if liked, roll and fold once more without adding any fat. Replace in the polythene and chill for ¾–1 hour when the pastry will be ready for use. It will keep for 2–3 days in the refrigerator before use.

Suitable to freeze for up to 6 months.

ROUGH PUFF *1 Put cut fat into sifted flour and salt but do not break it up when mixing. Add lemon juice and water*

2 On floured surface roll out a strip three times as long as wide. Fold into three, seal edges and rib. Give ¼ turn so the fold is at the side. Roll, fold and turn another four times

Rough Puff Pastry

This is similar in texture to flaky pastry but is quicker and easier to make; it can be used in place of flaky pastry in most recipes. The proportions are again three-quarters fat to flour and either all butter or a mixture of butter or margarine and lard should be used, but note that none of the fat is rubbed in; it is simply cut into pieces and mixed into the flour before the rolling and folding process.

450g (1lb) plain flour

1 level teaspoon salt

350g (12oz) firm butter or butter and lard, mixed

1 teaspoon lemon juice

about 300ml (½pt) cold water

Sift the flour and salt into a bowl. Cut the fat into neat pieces about 1cm (½in) square, and mix into the flour without breaking up the fat at all. Add the lemon juice and sufficient water to mix to a fairly stiff dough. Turn on to a floured surface and roll out carefully to a strip 3 times as long as it is wide. Fold neatly into three as for the other flaked pastries, seal the edges and

rib with the rolling pin (see p 123). Give the pastry a quarter turn so that the fold is at the side and repeat the rolling and folding process 4 more times. If possible wrap in polythene and chill after 3 rollings, then when made, chill for 30 minutes before use. Rough puff pastry will keep in the refrigerator for 3 days before use.

Suitable to freeze for up to 6 months.

Wholemeal Pastry

For those who like the flavour of brown flour, it will make a very nice shortcrust pastry which is particularly good for pies and flans.

200g (8oz) wholemeal flour

1 level teaspoon salt

50g (2oz) butter or margarine

50g (2oz) lard or white fat

cold water to mix

Put the flour and salt into a bowl and rub in the fats until the mixture resembles breadcrumbs. Add sufficient water to mix to a firm but pliable dough. If possible wrap

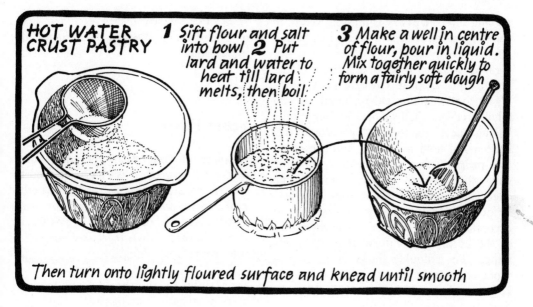

HOT WATER CRUST PASTRY **1** Sift flour and salt into bowl **2** Put lard and water to heat till lard melts, then boil. **3** Make a well in centre of flour, pour in liquid. Mix together quickly to form a fairly soft dough

Then turn onto lightly floured surface and knead until smooth

in foil or polythene and chill for 15–30 minutes before use.

Note Half plain white flour and half brown may also be used.

Hot Water Crust Pastry

This pastry is made with lard and boiling water to give a very pliable and strong dough which can be 'raised' to make a pie that will hold its shape during cooking and baking, and can accept the extra handling necessary during shaping without the texture being spoiled. It is used for savoury pies, in particular game, pork and veal and ham pies, and can either be raised by hand or used in a cake tin or special hinged metal pie mould.

450g (1lb) plain flour
1½ level teaspoons salt
100g (4oz) lard
200ml (7fl oz) water or milk and water, mixed

Sift the flour and salt into a bowl. Put the lard and water into a saucepan and heat gently until the lard melts, then bring up to the boil. Make a well in the centre of the flour and pour in the liquid, mixing quickly to form a fairly soft dough. Turn on to a lightly floured surface and knead until smooth. Use as required but quickly, whilst still warm. Keep the dough not being used in a bowl covered with a cloth to prevent hardening.

To Shape a Raised Pie

Cake Tin or Mould Grease a 15cm (6in) round cake tin (preferably with a loose bottom). Reserve a third of the dough for the lid and keep covered in a bowl. Roll the larger piece of dough to fit the cake tin and carefully lower in to cover the base and sides evenly. Add the filling (see individual recipes) then cover with a lid made from the reserved pastry. Trim and crimp the edges and make a hole in the centre of the lid. Decorate with pastry trimmings, then glaze and bake as stated in the recipe. Line a pie mould in the same way as a cake tin, making sure the pastry is pressed well in to show the patterns on the sides when baked.

To Raise by Hand Reserve a quarter of the dough and keep it covered in a bowl. Using the remaining pastry, mould it into a hollowed-out shell shape, standing it on a baking sheet. As the pastry cools it will harden and hold its shape. Add the filling (see recipes), then cover with a lid made from the reserved pastry, damping the edges and pressing them well together. Trim off surplus pastry and crimp or decorate the edge; make a hole in the centre of the lid and decorate with pastry trimmings. Tie a double thickness of greaseproof paper right round the pie to help it keep its shape during cooking. Bake as described in specific recipes.

Suet Crust Pastry

So simple to make by mixing shredded suet and flour together and binding with water, this pastry is the exception to the rule, for it must be made with self-raising flour. It can be used for sweet and savoury dishes and may be steamed, boiled or baked. It tends to be on the tough side when baked so use only on pre-cooked fillings to keep the cooking time to a minimum. Commercially shredded suet or your own finely grated suet from the butcher can be used at a proportion of half suet to flour.

200g (8oz) self-raising flour
½ level teaspoon salt
100g (4oz) shredded suet
about 150ml (¼pt) cold water

Sift the flour and salt into a bowl and mix in the suet evenly. Add sufficient cold water to mix to a light elastic dough. Knead lightly and roll out to 0·5cm (¼in) thick if used for baking.

Note For savoury dishes, chopped herbs or grated onion can be added to the dry ingredients.

Yeast Pastry

In place of flaky pastry, a yeast dough pastry can be used. It is especially good for sausage rolls and savoury puffs – whether a plaited or plain design – and for sweet pastries such as Banbury or Eccles Cakes. It can be made when there is a surplus of risen white bread dough.

450g (1lb) risen white bread dough (about ⅓ recipe quantity) see page 22
175g (6oz) lard and firm margarine or butter, mixed

Knock back the dough and roll out thinly on a floured surface to a strip 3 times as long as it is wide. Divide the fat into three and use 1 portion to dot over the top two-thirds of the pastry. Fold into three as for puff pastry by bringing the plain pastry third upwards and the top portion downwards. Seal the edges with the rolling pin and place in an oiled polythene bag. Chill for 15 minutes, then roll out to a strip

1   *Treacle tart;* 2   *Rhubarb and apple Cobbler;*
3   *Mincemeat and apple jalousie;* 4   *Lardy cake*

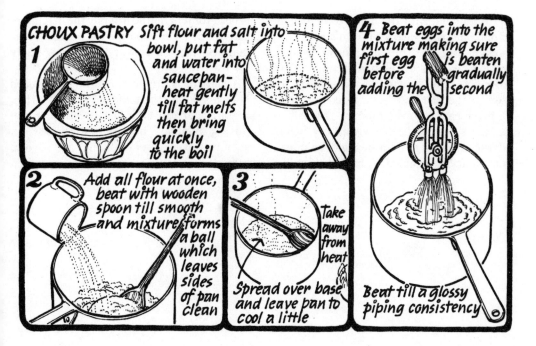

CHOUX PASTRY
1 Sift flour and salt into bowl, put fat and water into saucepan- heat gently till fat melts then bring quickly to the boil

2 Add all flour at once, beat with wooden spoon till smooth and mixture forms a ball which leaves sides of pan clean

3 Take away from heat. Spread over base and leave pan to cool a little

4 Beat eggs into the mixture making sure first egg is beaten before gradually adding the second. Beat till a glossy piping consistency

again making sure the folded edge is to the right-hand side. Repeat the dotting with fat, folding, resting and rolling out until all the fat is used, then repeat once more without adding any fat. Chill for at least 2 hours or preferably overnight before use. Roll out thinly and use as required, but put in a warm place for 15–20 minutes before baking in a very hot oven (230°C/450°F, Gas Mark 8).

1 *Chelsea buns;* 2 *Cream horns;* 3 *Cherry almond flan;* 4 *Cream slices;* 5 *Chocolate eclairs*

Choux Pastry

This is called a pastry but is more of a paste as it has to be piped or spooned into shape before baking. It is used for sweet and savoury dishes and as well as being baked in the oven, it can be deep fried for some recipes. Its success depends largely on the amount of air beaten into it with the eggs; also the flour must be added all at once and it must be cooked until the paste leaves the sides of the saucepan clean. Great care must be taken if opening the oven door during baking for a sudden draught can ruin choux pastry.

65g (2½oz) plain flour
pinch of salt
50g (2oz) butter or margarine
150ml (¼pt) water
2 standard eggs, beaten

Sift the flour and salt into a bowl. Put the fat and water into a saucepan and heat gently until the fat melts, then bring quickly up to the boil. Add the flour to the pan all at once and beat with a wooden spoon until smooth and the mixture forms a ball, leaving the sides of the pan clean. Remove from the heat, spread the paste over the base of the pan and leave to cool a little. Beat the eggs into the mixture gradually – making sure it is beaten vigorously before adding more egg – until a glossy piping consistency is obtained. A hand-held mixer is best, for it helps incorporate the maximum amount of air needed for the characteristic lightness of choux pastry. It is now ready for use.

Choux balls can be piped and then frozen before baking (thaw out completely when required) or can be baked and then frozen for 2–3 months. They are best refreshed in a warm oven after thawing and before filling.

CHAPTER 7

Savoury Pies and Pastries

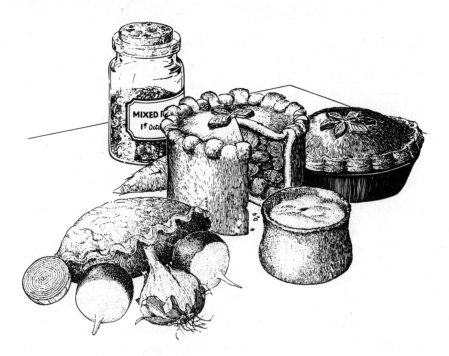

A 'pie' as defined in the Oxford Dictionary is a dish of meat or fruit, etc, enclosed in, or covered with, paste and baked. A 'pasty' is a pie of meat, fruit, jam, etc, enclosed in paste and baked without a dish. And 'pastry' is a baked flour paste; articles of food are made wholly or partly of this.

These definitions describe this section of recipes, for it includes all types of pies, pasties, flans, tarts, etc, having a savoury filling. Some of them simply have a top pastry crust, others are double crusted, a few are open flans or tarts and there are a selection of pasties and raised pies.

Most types of pastry are suitable for savoury pies of one type or another. Puff, flaky and rough puff give the light, crisp and airy pastry often preferred, but are best used as a covering crust only, with cooked or partly cooked fillings, for for a plaited or plain enclosed puff, pasty or pie baked without a tin. Shortcrust pastries are probably the ones most often used for single or double crusts and all types of flans and tarts; suet crust is best used for steamed or boiled puddings but can also be baked on a pie with a precooked filling; choux pastry can be baked into buns or éclairs and filled with savoury fillings; whilst yeast pastry is used in some of the ways that the puffed pastries are used. Hot water crust is probably the king or queen of the pastries when used to make the famous game or other raised meat pies; these date back in popularity to Elizabethan times when they were an important focal point of the huge banquets and cold spreads of that era.

As with most of the food of the British Isles, many of the savoury recipes began as regional fare, only spreading further afield as they became better known, and as people travelled about more and more, consequently tasting and liking the foods from other areas.

When the Normans invaded England, they introduced savoury pastry pies to the country. The fillings then would not have appealed to us today, for they contained mixtures such as eggs, ginger, bone marrow, raisins and saffron. In spite of this, the pie gradually became popular and the fillings improved, using all types of meat, but were highly seasoned with herbs and spices – probably to kill the smell of the slowly decomposing meats used in those times! Now the fillings are unlimited and range from the rather unusual Stargazey Pie of Cornwall, using whole pilchards or herrings whose heads peep out of the pastry; the Cornish Pasties which arouse plenty of tempers over the correct way of making them; and the Welsh leek pies and pasties which are often combined with chicken or lamb; to the West Country Artichoke Pie which is made as an accompaniment to roast meats but also with the original ingredients of dates and grapes included, and makes a fine meal in itself. Several pies combine pork or bacon with onion and apples, and others are filled with game or fish, but whatever the filling or the type of pastry used, there are sure to be many which will please and many more which can be adapted to your personal taste. The one fault found in all pastry dishes is that they are definitely not slimming!

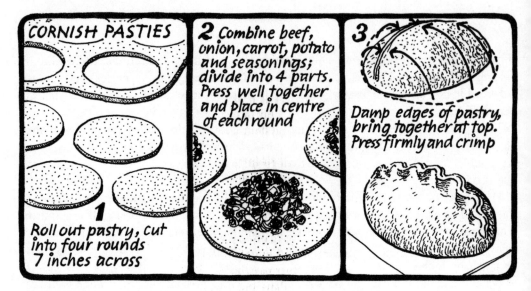

1 Roll out pastry, cut into four rounds 7 inches across

2 Combine beef, onion, carrot, potato and seasonings; divide into 4 parts. Press well together and place in centre of each round

3 Damp edges of pastry, bring together at top. Press firmly and crimp

Cornish Pasties

The Cornish pasty is thought to have originated as a packed lunch for the tin miners. Although it is now traditionally savoury, at one time a savoury filling was put in one end and a sweet or fruit mixture at the other to give a complete portable meal. It is said that only a true Cornish woman can bake a proper pasty and indeed recipes do vary considerably. However, by using a good lean beef, chopping the vegetables finely and making a perfect shortcrust pastry, there should be no problems in baking excellent pasties.

175g (6oz) best raw minced beef or finely chopped rump steak
1 onion, peeled and finely chopped
1 small carrot, peeled and grated (optional)
100g (4oz) peeled potato, finely chopped
salt and pepper
1 recipe quantity shortcrust pastry (see page 122)
beaten egg to glaze

Roll out the pastry and cut into four 18cm (7in) rounds. Combine the beef, onion, carrot, potato and seasoning, divide into four and place 1 portion in the centre of each piece of pastry, pressing it well together. Damp the edges of the pastry and bring together at the top. Press firmly together and crimp. Stand pasties on lightly greased baking sheets and brush with beaten egg. Bake in a hot oven (220°C/425°F, Gas Mark 7) for about 30 minutes or until golden brown. Serve hot, warm or cold.

Serves 4

Leek and Bacon Pasties

Thinly slice 2–3 leeks and blanch in boiling water for 2 minutes. Rinse under cold water and drain very well. Mix with 4 chopped bacon rashers, 1 tablespoon breadcrumbs, 1 tablespoon top of the milk and seasonings; continue as above.

Egg and Cheese Pasties

Make 150ml ($\frac{1}{4}$pt) thick white sauce, then stir in a large pinch of curry powder, seasonings, 50g (2oz) chopped mushrooms,

100g (4oz) grated mature Cheddar cheese, 2 chopped hard-boiled eggs and 2 tablespoons grated onion. Leave to cool then continue as for Cornish Pasties.

Forfar Bridies

These are a Scottish version of the Cornish Pasty, sold mainly in the Angus area of Scotland. They are made and baked in the same way, but the filling is meatier. For the filling, mix together 300g (10oz) raw minced beef or finely chopped rump steak, 25g (1oz) shredded suet, 1 finely chopped onion, 1 teaspoon Worcestershire sauce, salt and pepper, and a pinch of grated nutmeg.

Leek Turnovers

With the leek being one of the national emblems of Wales, it is easy to see why leeks often feature in Welsh recipes. This turnover or pasty is baked with open ends so the whole leek can be used. Sometimes a little bacon is added for flavour but is not necessary. They are ideal picnic fare.

6 leeks, trimmed and well washed

1 teaspoon lemon juice

2 tablespoons cream

100g (4oz) lean bacon rashers, rinded and chopped (optional)

salt and pepper

1 recipe quantity shortcrust pastry (see page 122)

beaten egg or milk to glaze

Trim the leeks to about 15cm (6in) in length and chop the remaining green part. Cook the whole leeks for 5 minutes in boiling salted water with the lemon juice added; add the chopped leek for the last 2 minutes. Drain very thoroughly and cool. Mix the chopped leek, cream, bacon (if

used) and seasoning. Roll out the pastry and cut into 6 rectangles about 15 × 10cm (6 × 4in). Spread a little of the leek mixture along the length of each piece and place a whole leek on top. Damp the edges of the pastry, bring together at the top and crimp. Place on greased baking sheets and brush with egg or milk. Bake in a fairly hot oven (200°C/400°F, Gas Mark 6) for 20–25 minutes until golden brown. Serve hot or cold.

Serves 3–6

Venison Pasties

Venison used to be very popular but because of the difficulty in obtaining it and the increasing price, it more or less disappeared for most people. However, there is now a limited supply available again and should you obtain or be given some, it makes a delicious meal. A small amount of venison can be used to make these simple pasties to serve hot or cold.

450g (1lb) venison (from the haunch or saddle, if possible)

2 onions, peeled and chopped

450ml ($\frac{3}{4}$pt) stock

150ml ($\frac{1}{4}$pt) port or red wine

salt and pepper

1 bouquet garni

2 tablespoons redcurrant or rowan jelly

1 level teaspoon cornflour

1 recipe quantity shortcrust pastry (see page 122)

1 level tablespoon freshly chopped mixed herbs or parsley

beaten egg or milk to glaze

Cut the venison into small dice and put into a saucepan with the onions, stock, wine, seasoning, bouquet garni and jelly. Bring to the boil, cover and simmer gently until the meat is tender – about 45 minutes. Strain off the liquor, return to the pan and boil until reduced to about 200ml ($\frac{1}{3}$pt), then thicken with the cornflour blended in a little cold water and bring back to the boil. Roll out the pastry and cut into four 20cm (8in) circles. Place the meat and onion on one side of each pastry circle and sprinkle with herbs; damp the edges and fold the other side over to enclose the filling. Press well together and crimp. Place on greased baking sheets and brush with egg or milk. Make a slit in the top and bake in a fairly hot oven (200°C/400°F, Gas Mark 6) for about 30 minutes. Reheat the sauce and pour a little into each pasty through the slit in the pastry.

Serves 4

Note This can be made into a pie if preferred, by putting the cooked venison and stock (without reducing or thickening it) into a pie dish with a pie funnel, sprinkling with herbs and then covering with a pastry lid. Bake at the same temperature as pasties for 30–40 minutes.

Ham and Mushroom Envelopes

Pasties and individual pies were created for packed lunches, as they were easy to carry and eat and did not take up too much space.

25g (1oz) butter or margarine
1 small onion, peeled and chopped
50g (2oz) mushrooms, chopped
1 tablespoon flour
150ml ($\frac{1}{4}$pt) milk
$\frac{1}{2}$ level teaspoon made mustard
salt and pepper
50g (2oz) Cheddar cheese, grated

175g (6oz) cooked ham, diced
2 cooked sausages, diced
1 recipe quantity shortcrust pastry (see page 122)
beaten egg or milk to glaze

Melt the fat and fry the onion and mushrooms until soft, then stir in the flour and cook for 1 minute. Gradually add the milk and bring up to the boil. Stir in the mustard, seasoning, cheese, ham and sausages, and cook for 1 minute. Leave to cool. Roll out the pastry fairly thinly and cut into four 15cm (6in) squares. Divide the filling into four and place 1 portion in the centre of each piece of pastry. Brush the pastry edges with water and bring all 4 corners together in the centre. Press the edges together to seal and make the envelope shape, and then crimp. Place on a greased baking sheet and brush with beaten egg or milk. Bake in a hot oven (220°C/425°F, Gas Mark 7) for 20–25 minutes until golden brown. Serve hot or cold.

Serves 4

Plaited Fish Puff

This is my version of the famous Russian dish called Koulibiac. Here the fishy filling is enclosed in a plaited puff pastry crust, but it can also be baked in yeasted pastry. Serve it hot or cold; it is ideal for picnics and outdoor eating. The filling can also be based on cooked chicken, eggs or vegetables in place of the fish, and some people prefer to use three or four thin pancakes cut into strips instead of the layer of cooked rice.

$\frac{1}{2}$ recipe quantity puff pastry (see page 123)
350–450g ($\frac{3}{4}$–1lb) white fish fillets, skinned (cod, haddock or plaice)
150ml ($\frac{1}{4}$pt) milk

salt and pepper

1 bayleaf

25g (1oz) butter or margarine

1 small onion, peeled and chopped

75g (3oz) mushrooms, sliced

1 level tablespoon flour

1 level tablespoon freshly chopped parsley

2 teaspoons capers, chopped (optional)

99g (3½oz) can tunafish, drained and flaked

25–40g (1–1½oz) long grain rice, cooked

2 hard-boiled eggs, thinly sliced

beaten egg to glaze

Prepare the pastry, wrap in polythene or foil and chill in the refrigerator. Put the fish into a saucepan with the milk, seasoning and bay leaf. Bring to the boil, cover and simmer for 10 minutes or until tender. Drain off the liquor and reserve 150ml (¼pt). Discard the bayleaf, then flake the fish. Melt the fat and fry the onion until soft, then add the mushrooms and continue for 1–2 minutes. Stir in the flour and cook gently for 1 minute, then gradually add the cooking liquor and bring up to the boil for 2 minutes, stirring continuously. Remove from the heat, stir in the parsley, capers, tunafish and flaked fish, then season to taste and leave to cool. Roll out the pastry and trim to a square about 30cm (12in). Spread half the fish mixture down the centre third of the pastry, leaving a 2·5cm (1in) margin at each end. Cover with the cooked rice, then the sliced eggs and finally the remaining fish mixture. To make the plaited topping, cut the pastry at each side into strips about 2·5cm (1in) wide to within 4cm (1½in) of the filling. Turn the plain pastry margins up and over the ends of the filling and brush with beaten egg. Then take a strip first from one side and then the other and lay them over the filling, brushing each piece with egg once it is in position. Continue until the plait is complete and the filling enclosed. Transfer carefully to a lightly greased baking sheet and brush all

over with beaten egg. Cook in a hot oven (220°C/425°F, Gas Mark 7) for about 30 minutes, then reduce to moderately hot (190°C/375°F, Gas Mark 5) and continue for a further 10–15 minutes until golden brown. Cover with a sheet of greaseproof paper if overbrowning. Serve hot or cold.

Serves 4–5

Suitable to freeze for 6–8 weeks.

Poacher's Roll

Not, as it may sound, a game pie, but a very good substitute, consisting of sausagemeat and bacon, flavoured with sage, onion and mushrooms, and baked in a puff pastry crust. Serve cold in slices with salads or for picnics.

450g (1lb) pork sausagemeat

225g (8oz) lean bacon rashers, rinded and chopped

1 small onion, peeled and finely chopped

100g (4oz) mushrooms, chopped

salt and pepper

1 level teaspoon dried sage

½ recipe quantity puff pastry (see page 123)

beaten egg to glaze

Combine the sausagemeat, bacon, onion, mushrooms, seasoning and sage, and form into a brick shape. Roll out the pastry and trim to a square about 30cm (12in). Lay the sausagemeat down the centre of the pastry, fold one side over, brush with egg and cover with the other side of the pastry to enclose the filling. Trim off any surplus pastry from the ends, brush with egg and fold up to enclose the filling completely. Turn the roll over and place on a greased baking sheet with the seam underneath. Brush all over with beaten egg, make 2 slits in the top and decorate around them with leaves made

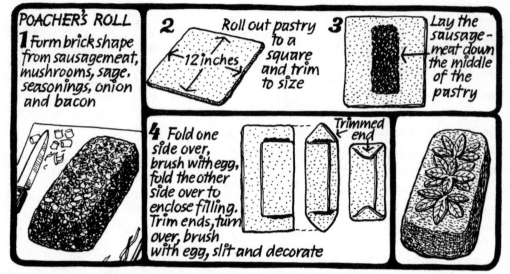

POACHER'S ROLL
1 Form brick shape from sausagemeat, mushrooms, sage, seasonings, onion and bacon

2 Roll out pastry to a square and trim to size 12 inches

3 Lay the sausage-meat down the middle of the pastry

4 Fold one side over, brush with egg, fold the other side over to enclose filling. Trim ends, turn over, brush with egg, slit and decorate

Trimmed end

from the pastry trimmings. Glaze again and bake in a hot oven (220°C/425°F, Gas Mark 7) for 20 minutes. Reduce to moderately hot (190°C/375°F, Gas Mark 5) and continue for 30–40 minutes until well browned. Lay a piece of greaseproof paper over the roll if the decoration is over-browning. Leave to get cold and serve in slices.

Serves 6–8

Suitable to freeze for up to 3 months.

Artichoke Pie

Both globe and Jerusalem artichokes can be used for this pie, which is served as an accompaniment to roast meats. The globe variety were originally used when it was a popular West Country pie – now of course canned artichoke hearts make the preparation much easier. Later on Jerusalem artichokes were preferred for they were much simpler to prepare even though they altered the flavour. Dates, grapes and hard-boiled eggs were an addition in Elizabethan times and they do in fact turn this into a delicious main-course dish.

2 × 425g (15oz) can artichoke hearts, drained, or about 10 freshly cooked artichoke hearts, or 675g (1½lb) Jerusalem artichokes

1 small onion, peeled and finely chopped

25g (1oz) butter or margarine

1 recipe quantity shortcrust pastry (see page 122)

salt and pepper

freshly grated nutmeg or ground mace

1 level teaspoon mixed herbs (optional)

beaten egg or milk to glaze

4–6 tablespoons cream

Prepare the artichokes; either cut the globe hearts in half, or for the Jerusalem variety, peel carefully, plunging them immediately into cold salted water, then cook gently until tender-crisp and drain well. Fry the onion gently in the fat until soft. Roll out two-thirds of the pastry and use to line a 20cm (8in) pie dish or flan tin. Arrange the artichokes in it and sprinkle with the onion, seasoning, nutmeg or mace and herbs, if used. Cover with a lid made from the remaining pastry, trim the edges, then crimp. Make a fairly large slit in the top and decorate around it with pastry leaves. Brush with egg or milk and bake in a fairly hot oven (200°C/400°F, Gas Mark 6) for about

35–40 minutes or until golden brown. Heat the cream gently and pour it into the pie through the slit in the top, using a small funnel. Serve hot or cold.

Serves 4–6

Elizabethan Artichoke Pie

Replace half the artichokes with 2 sliced hard-boiled eggs, 100g (4oz) halved and pipped white grapes and a few roughly chopped stoned dates. Continue as above.

The basic pie is suitable to freeze for 2–3 months, adding the cream after reheating.

Eel Pie

The jellied eel stalls and Eel and Pie shops are a fast disappearing sight of old London, but there are still a few remaining dotted around the city. The old shops used to sell jellied eels, stewed eels, eel pie and also a selection of meat pies, all of which could be eaten on the premises or be taken away; the live eels lived in tanks at the back of the shop. The stalls are a Cockney reminder of Victorian London, when it was quite normal to see plates of jellied eels or shellfish being eaten at the stall, with the bones spat out on to the pavements! These stalls are found nowadays at some seaside resorts and at large race meetings, fairgrounds and other places of amusement. The eel pie was famous in London and even gave its name to an island in the Thames near Richmond, for excellent eels used to be taken from that part of the river.

900g (2lb) eels, skinned, cleaned and cut into 5cm (2in) pieces
2 onions, peeled
2 bay leaves
sprig of parsley
slice of lemon
50g (2oz) butter or margarine
25g (1oz) flour
salt and pepper
1 tablespoon freshly chopped parsley
1 tablespoon lemon juice
½ recipe quantity puff, flaky or rough puff pastry (see pages 125, 126, 128)
beaten egg or milk to glaze

Put the eels in a saucepan with 1 chopped onion, the bay leaves, parsley, lemon and sufficient water to just cover them. Bring to the boil, cover and simmer for 20–30 minutes until the eels are firm. Remove eels, cool a little, then remove as much bone as possible and place the flesh in a pie dish. Strain the stock and reserve 450ml (¾pt) for the sauce. Slice the remaining onion and fry gently in the fat for 1 minute. Stir in the flour. Gradually add the reserved stock and bring up to the boil, season well and add the parsley and lemon juice, and simmer for 2 minutes. Pour over the eels and leave to cool. Roll out the pastry and use to cover the pie as for Steak and Kidney Pie (see page 149). Decorate with pastry trimmings, brush with egg or milk and bake in a very hot oven (230°C/450°F, Gas Mark 8) for 20 minutes, then reduce to moderately hot (190°C/375°F, Gas Mark 5) and continue for 25–30 minutes until the top is golden brown. Serve hot.

Serves 4–6

Note For another version of this pie add 2 or 3 quartered hard-boiled eggs to the eels before pouring on the sauce.

Cockle Pie

The Welsh produce lots of cockles from their famous cockle beds and consequently they have a recipe for making this tasty shellfish pie. As with eels, cockles are an acquired taste but many people are firm addicts. Clams, mussels, scallops or a mixture of these can also be used for this pie.

about 1·75 litres (3pt) cockles

salt and pepper

1 recipe quantity shortcrust pastry (see page 122)

6–8 spring onions, chopped or 2 tablespoons chives, chopped

6–8 rashers lean bacon, rinded and chopped

milk to glaze

To prepare the cockles, first wash and scrub them thoroughly in several changes of clean water to remove sand and grit, then place in a saucepan and barely cover with salted water. Bring up to the boil and simmer for 2–3 minutes or until the shells open. Strain, reserving the liquor, and carefully remove the cockles from their shells with a sharp knife. Roll out two-thirds of the pastry and use to line a shallow 20–21cm (8–8½in) pie dish or flan tin. Arrange layers of cockles, onion (or chives) and bacon in the pastry case until all are used up, seasoning each layer with pepper. Pour on the cockle liquor to half fill the pie, then cover with a lid made from the remaining pastry. Trim and crimp the edge, decorate the top with trimmings and make a hole in the centre. Brush with milk and bake in a fairly hot oven (200°C/400°F, Gas Mark 6) for 30–40 minutes until golden brown. Serve hot or cold.

Serves 4

Note Once prepared, the cockles can be eaten cold as they are with lemon juice or vinegar and brown bread and butter instead of being baked in a pie. If fresh cockles are unavailable, use the canned or bottled variety, but if preserved in vinegar, rinse them thoroughly in water before use and add milk to the pie in place of the cooking liquor.

Stargazey Pie

This pie belongs to Cornwall and is rather strange, having whole pilchards or herrings baked in a double-crust pie with their heads left on and protruding from the pastry. By leaving the heads on, the oil from the fish runs back into the flesh during cooking, instead of being lost when the heads are, as is usual, removed. The fish can be arranged with the heads around the edge of the pie or gathered together in the centre where they are pulled up through a hole in the pastry; whichever way is chosen, they are baked gazing upwards. A round pie dish is usual but in the markets long ago, the pies used to be baked in long strips so the fish could be easily cut off singly or in groups.

1½ recipe quantity shortcrust pastry (see page 122)

4–6 pilchards or small herrings

1 onion, peeled and finely chopped (optional)

1 level teaspoon mixed herbs (optional)

salt and pepper

beaten egg to glaze

Roll out just over half the pastry and use to line a fairly large round pie dish or cake tin about 2·5cm (1in) deep. Remove the guts from the fish, keeping the heads on, and trim off the fins and scales. Combine the onion, herbs and seasoning and spoon a little into each fish. Lay the fish in the pastry-lined dish with the heads protruding over the edge and the tails overlapping each other a little in the middle. Season lightly. Roll out the remaining pastry for a lid and position it carefully over the fish. Trim round each fish head sealing the pastry

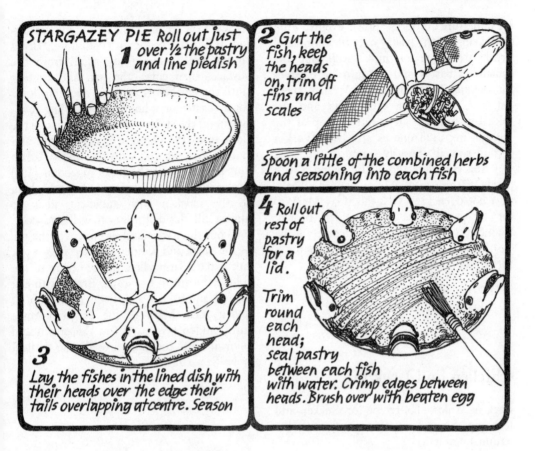

1 **STARGAZEY PIE** Roll out just over ½ the pastry and line piedish

2 Gut the fish, keep the heads on, trim off fins and scales

Spoon a little of the combined herbs and seasoning into each fish

3 Lay the fishes in the lined dish with their heads over the edge their tails overlapping at centre. Season

4 Roll out rest of pastry for a lid.

Trim round each head; seal pastry between each fish with water. Crimp edges between heads. Brush over with beaten egg

between the fish with water. Crimp the edges between the heads and brush all over the pie with beaten egg. Bake in a moderate oven (180°C/350°F, Gas Mark 4) for about 40 minutes or until the pastry is golden brown. Serve hot or cold.

⸻⸻ 4–6 (one fish per portion)

350–450g (¾–1lb) pork fillet or lean pork, diced

25g (1oz) butter or margarine

2 onions, peeled and sliced

2 eating apples, peeled, cored and sliced

salt and pepper

1 recipe quantity shortcrust pastry (see page 122)

beaten egg or milk to glaze

ickly in the melted fat until :move to a bowl. Fry the .me fat until lightly browned, the pork, together with the enty of seasoning. Roll out the pastry and use to line a (8in) square tin. Spoon in the pork mixture and press down evenly. Fold in the edge of the pastry over the filling and brush with egg or milk. Roll out the remaining pastry and cut into large leaves for the petal-patterned lid. Arrange these petals – overlapping each other and the folded-in pastry – all round the top of the pie, glazing each one as attached. Work a second row all the way round in the same way and complete the lid by laying 2 or 3 petals in the centre. Glaze again and bake in a hot oven (220°C/425°F, Gas Mark 7) for 25–30 minutes until golden brown. Reduce the temperature to moderate (180°C/350°F, Gas Mark 4) and continue for a further 15–20 minutes. Serve hot.

Serves 4

Chicken and Leek Pie

Back in Wales, this recipe for chicken and leek pie shows another way of using the national emblem.

1·4kg (3lb) oven-ready chicken or 4 chicken portions

1 onion, peeled and sliced

2 sticks celery, sliced

1 carrot, peeled and sliced

1 bay leaf

salt and pepper

2 rashers streaky bacon, rinded and chopped (optional)

1 level tablespoon freshly chopped parsley

4 large leeks, trimmed and thickly sliced

½ recipe quantity puff or rough puff pastry (see pages 123, 126)

beaten egg or milk to glaze

3–4 tablespoons double cream

Put the chicken (a roaster or a boiling fowl will do) in a saucepan with all the vegetables

– except the leeks – the bay leaf and seasoning, and barely cover with cold water. Bring to the boil, remove any scum from the surface, then cover the pan and simmer until the chicken is tender – about an hour for a roaster or 2 hours for a boiling fowl. Strain off the stock and reserve. Remove the flesh from the chicken, chop roughly and put it into a pie dish with the streaky bacon and parsley. Boil the leeks in 300ml (½pt) of the stock for 3–4 minutes, then add them to the chicken with sufficient stock to almost fill the dish; season well and cool. Roll out the pastry and use to cover the pie as for Steak and Kidney Pie (see page 149), but make a larger hole in the centre of the lid for the steam to escape. Brush with egg or milk and bake in a fairly hot oven (200°C/400°F, Gas Mark 6) for 45–50 minutes until golden brown. Warm the cream and pour it into the pie through the central hole. Serve at once.

Serves 4–6

Bacon and Egg Pie

There are many recipes for this very traditional British pie which dates far back into the eighteenth century. Many are made with a rich egg custard and chopped or sliced bacon or ham, resembling the Quiche Lorraine we know today. This version, however, uses chopped bacon and hard-boiled eggs in a white sauce.

40g (1½oz) butter or margarine

1 onion, peeled and chopped

25g (1oz) flour

275ml (scant ½pt) milk

salt and pepper

¼ level teaspoon made mustard

175g (6oz) cooked bacon or ham, chopped

1 recipe quantity shortcrust pastry (see page 122)

2–3 hard-boiled eggs, sliced

beaten egg or milk to glaze

Melt the fat in a pan and fry the onion gently until soft but not coloured. Stir in the flour, cook for 1 minute, then gradually add the milk and bring up to the boil for 2 minutes. Remove from the heat, season lightly with salt and well with pepper, then stir in the mustard and bacon or ham. Leave to cool. Roll out two-thirds of the pastry and use to line a 20cm (8in) pie plate or tin. Spread half the filling in this, cover with the sliced eggs and then the remaining filling. Damp the pastry rim and cover with a lid made from the rest of the pastry, pressing the edges well together. Trim off excess pastry, crimp the edges and decorate the top with pastry trimmings. Make a hole in the centre, brush with egg and bake in a fairly hot oven (200°C/400°F, Gas Mark 6) for 30–40 minutes until golden brown. Serve hot or cold.

Serves 4

Scotch Mutton Pies

Mutton pies are the Scottish equivalent in popularity of our pork or veal and ham pies, being sold as a snack with a pint of beer, or served with vegetables and gravy for a hot meal. They have been popular for a very long time and are eaten hot for preference but can be eaten cold. The Scottish pies are usually made with hot water crust pastry, but the English version, which were said to be a favourite of George V and were widely eaten until World War I, were more often made with shortcrust or puff pastry.

350g (12oz) fairly lean raw lamb

1 small onion, peeled

1 tablespoon oil or dripping

about 150ml (¼pt) stock

salt and pepper

2 level teaspoons freshly chopped parsley

1 teaspoon Worcestershire sauce

25g (1oz) fresh breadcrumbs (optional)

50g (2oz) mushrooms, chopped (optional)

¾ recipe quantity hot water crust pastry (see page 127)

beaten egg or milk to glaze

Mince the lamb and onion, and fry them gently in the oil or dripping until well sealed. Add sufficient stock to moisten, season well and cook gently for about 5 minutes. Stir in the parsley, Worcestershire sauce, breadcrumbs and mushrooms, if used, and leave to cool. Make up the pastry, divide it into 6 portions and keep in a bowl covered with a cloth. Take two-thirds of each piece of pastry and either roll out to fit a 7·5cm (3in) patty tin or ring mould, or roll out and mould round the base of a tumbler. Fill with the meat mixture and cover with a lid made from the remaining pieces of pastry, damping the edges and pressing them well together. Trim edges, make a hole in the centre of each pie for the steam to escape and stand them on greased baking sheets, if necessary. Glaze with beaten egg or milk and bake in a fairly hot oven (200°C/400°F, Gas Mark 6) for about 20 minutes. Glaze again and return to a moderate oven (180°C/350°F, Gas Mark 4) for about 30 minutes or until cooked through and well browned. Remove from the tins and add a tablespoon of hot stock to each pie through the central hole, if liked. Serve hot or warm if possible.

Serves 6

Note If hand-moulded pies become misshapen, tie a piece of greased double foil around each one for most of the cooking time.

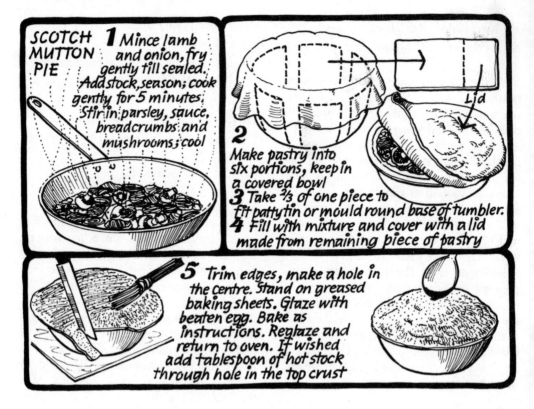

SCOTCH MUTTON PIE

1 Mince lamb and onion, fry gently till sealed. Add stock, season; cook gently for 5 minutes. Stir in parsley, sauce, breadcrumbs and mushrooms; cool

2 Make pastry into six portions, keep in a covered bowl

3 Take ⅔ of one piece to fit patty tin or mould round base of tumbler.

4 Fill with mixture and cover with a lid made from remaining piece of pastry

Lid

5 Trim edges, make a hole in the centre. Stand on greased baking sheets. Glaze with beaten egg. Bake as instructions. Reglaze and return to oven. If wished add tablespoon of hot stock through hole in the top crust

English Mutton Pies

The filling is much the same but a chopped lamb's kidney can be added. Use the same quantity of puff, rough puff or shortcrust pastry and make the pies in individual Yorkshire pudding tins. Bake as on page 143.

Raised Game Pie

Game pies are often included in elegant picnic hampers as well as being part of a traditional shooting lunch or hunt breakfast. They formed part of Elizabethan banquets along with all the elaborate food of that time and still make a good display on any buffet table. They are made with hot water crust pastry which is filled with chopped game of some type; this recipe also has a layer of veal and ham in it. The baked pie is filled up with a good stock which jellies as the pie cools. It is always served cold, cut into slices so the layers of meat and jelly are clearly visible, accompanied by salads and, when possible, a glass or two of wine!

225g (8oz) pie veal

225g (8oz) cooked ham

1 small onion, peeled

salt and pepper

good pinch of ground mace or nutmeg

1 recipe quantity hot water crust pastry (see page 127)

about 350g (12oz) cooked game, diced (see opposite)

beaten egg to glaze

2 level teaspoons powdered gelatine

300ml (½pt) game stock

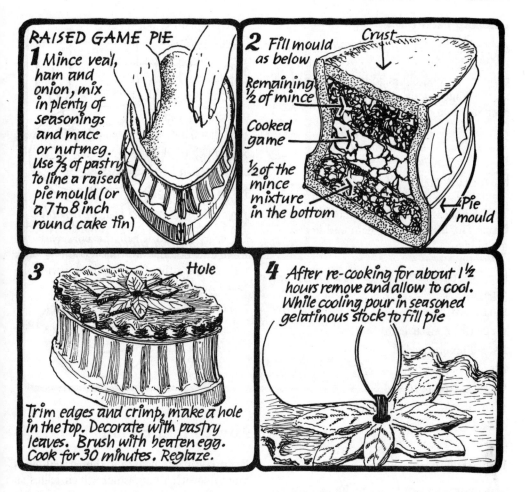

RAISED GAME PIE

1 Mince veal, ham and onion, mix in plenty of seasonings and mace or nutmeg. Use ⅔ of pastry to line a raised pie mould (or a 7 to 8 inch round cake tin)

2 Fill mould as below

Crust

Remaining ½ of mince

Cooked game

½ of the mince mixture in the bottom

Pie mould

3 Hole

Trim edges and crimp, make a hole in the top. Decorate with pastry leaves. Brush with beaten egg. Cook for 30 minutes. Reglaze.

4 After re-cooking for about 1½ hours remove and allow to cool. While cooling pour in seasoned gelatinous stock to fill pie

Mince the veal, ham and onion, and mix in plenty of seasoning and mace or nutmeg. Make up the pastry and use two-thirds to line a raised pie mould or an 18–20cm (7–8in) round cake tin, preferably with a loose bottom, or raise the pie by hand (see method page 128). Put half the minced mixture in the bottom, cover with the game and then add the remaining mince, pressing down evenly but not too firmly. Roll out the remaining pastry (kept in a covered bowl) for a lid; damp the edges, position and press well together. Trim the edges and crimp, then make a hole in the centre of the lid and decorate the top with pastry leaves. Brush with beaten egg and cook in a fairly hot oven (200°C/400°F, Gas Mark 6) for 30 minutes. Reduce the temperature to moder-

ate (170°C/325°F, Gas Mark 3), glaze the pie again and continue to cook for 1¼–1½ hours, covering with greaseproof paper when sufficiently browned. Dissolve the gelatine in the stock, season well and, as the pie cools, fill it up with the stock through the central hole. Chill thoroughly until firm and serve in slices with salads.

Note The game used must be stripped from the bones before weighing, with all sinews and gristle removed. It can be of any type – pheasant, partridge or any other game bird, hare or venison – and can be used on its own or as part of a mixture of several types of game.

Serves 8–10

145

Chicken Picnic Pie

As Raised Game Pie; use cooked chicken or turkey meat in place of the game, with 6–8 chopped stuffed olives added to the minced meats. Chicken or white stock should be used in place of game stock.

Raised Veal and Ham Pie

This is made in the same way as the Raised Game Pie, but has veal, ham and herbs for the filling.

1 recipe quantity hot water crust pastry (see page 127)
350g (12oz) pie veal
450g (1lb) cooked ham
1 small onion, peeled
salt and pepper
1 level teaspoon mixed herbs
4 hard-boiled eggs (optional)
beaten egg to glaze
2 level teaspoons powdered gelatine
300ml (½pt) stock

Make as for Raised Game Pie (see page 144) but coarsely mince the veal with only half the ham and the onion. Chop the remaining ham, mix it with the minced meats and add the seasoning and herbs. If using the hard-boiled eggs, put half the meat in the pastry case, lay the eggs on top and cover with the remaining meat.

Raised Pork Pie

Another traditional pie, which is made with pork and a variety of flavourings. Sometimes the meat is chopped, sometimes minced; I prefer a combination of the two with a touch of apple and onion.

1 recipe quantity hot water crust pastry (see page 127)
675g (1½lb) lean pork
1 apple, peeled and cored
1 onion, peeled
salt and pepper
good pinch each of sage and thyme (optional)
beaten egg to glaze
2 level teaspoons powdered gelatine
300ml (½pt) stock

Make as for Raised Game Pie (see page 144) but coarsely mince half the pork with the apple and onion, chop the remaining pork and add it to the minced mixture with the seasoning and herbs, if used.

Note This mixture can also be made into individual pies (see Scotch Mutton Pies page 145).

Minted Lamb Flan

Roast lamb is traditionally served with mint sauce, so why not a mint-flavoured flan containing diced lamb, peas and onions.

¾ recipe quantity shortcrust pastry (see page 122)
40g (1½oz) butter or margarine
1 large onion, peeled and thinly sliced
1 level tablespoon flour
200ml (8fl oz) milk
salt and pepper
2 teaspoons freshly chopped mint and 1 teaspoon vinegar or 2 teaspoons mint sauce
225g (8oz) cooked lamb, diced
100g (4oz) cooked peas

Roll out the pastry and use to line a 21cm (8½in) flan tin or pie plate. Prick the base, lay a sheet of greaseproof paper inside and cover the surface with baking beans or rice. Bake blind (as this process is called) in a hot oven (220°C/425°F, Gas Mark 7) for 15 minutes, then remove the baking beans or rice and paper, and return the pastry case to the oven for 5–10 minutes until dried out and cooked. Meanwhile, melt the fat in a pan and fry the onion gently until soft but only lightly coloured. Stir in the flour and cook for 1 minute, then gradually add the milk and bring up to the boil, stirring continuously. Season well, add the mint and vinegar (or the mint sauce) and the lamb, and simmer for 2–3 minutes. Stir in the peas and pour the mixture into the pastry case. Reduce the oven temperature to moderate (180°C/350°F, Gas Mark 4) and return the flan to the oven for 10–15 minutes. Serve hot.

Serves 4

Crab Flan

In Scotland this is called Partan flan, but whatever its name, it is worth making when crab is available.

¾ recipe quantity shortcrust pastry (see page 122)

150g (6oz) crab meat, flaked (fresh, frozen or canned)

2 level tablespoons onion, finely grated

2 eggs

salt and pepper

pinch of cayenne pepper

300ml (½pt) single cream or milk

2 level tablespoons chopped parsley

sliced cucumber and parsley sprigs to garnish

Roll out the pastry and use to line a 20cm (8in) flan ring, dish or tin, either plain or fluted. Lay the crab meat in the bottom and sprinkle with grated onion. Beat the eggs, seasonings and cream or milk together, then stir in the parsley. Pour carefully into the pastry case, placed on a baking sheet, and bake in a hot oven (220°C/425°F, Gas Mark 7) for 20 minutes. Reduce the temperature to moderate (180°C/350°F, Gas Mark 4) and continue for about 25 minutes or until set firm and golden brown. Serve hot or cold, garnished with slices of cucumber and parsley sprigs around the edge.

Serves 4–6

Note Smoked salmon pieces can be used in place of crab for this flan. It can also be made into individual flans using four 10cm (4in) deep patty tins or rings, or Yorkshire pudding tins; they will take about 10 minutes less cooking.

Suitable to freeze for up to 2 months.

Spider Pie

The name does not describe the filling of this open pie, but the decorative 'wheel' of pastry strips – the filling is onion and cheese.

1 recipe quantity shortcrust pastry (see page 122)

450g (1lb) onions, peeled and sliced

1–2 tablespoons oil

1–2 teaspoons Worcestershire sauce

salt and pepper

175g (6oz) mature Cheddar cheese, grated

Roll out three-quarters of the pastry to line a deep 20–21cm (8–8½in) pie plate or tin. Trim the edge and roll out the trimmings and reserved pastry to a strip long enough to stretch over the top of the pie. Cut into 10 strips about 2cm (¾in) wide. Fry the onions very gently in the oil until soft but not coloured – 10–15 minutes. Cool a little, drain well and spoon into the pastry case. Sprinkle with Worcestershire sauce, season well and cover with the cheese. Put 8 twisted strips of pastry over the cheese to represent a wheel, or in fact the spider, damping the ends to attach. Brush the pastry rim with water and lay the remaining strips all round the edge to enclose the ends of the spider. Trim and crimp the edge and bake in a hot oven (220°C/425°F, Gas Mark 7) for 25–30 minutes until the pastry is browned and the cheese firm. Serve hot or cold.

Serves 4–5

Suitable to freeze for up to 2 months.

Leek Tart

Another Welsh recipe using the leek, this is similar to a French dish served in the northern part of France and Brittany, and in other forms all over France, and shows that the past link between these countries still exists in some ways.

6 leeks, trimmed, thickly sliced and washed

25g (1oz) butter or margarine

¾ recipe quantity shortcrust pastry (see page 122)

50–75g (2–3oz) cooked ham or bacon, diced

2 eggs

salt and pepper

300ml (½pt) single cream

Sweat the leeks in melted fat in a covered pan for about 5 minutes, shaking the pan frequently to prevent sticking; do not allow the leeks to brown. Leave to cool. Roll out the pastry and use to line a 20cm (8in) flan tin or ring. Lay the leeks in the bottom and sprinkle with the ham or bacon. Beat the

eggs, seasoning and cream together and pour into the tart. Bake in a hot oven (220°C/425°F, Gas Mark 7) for 15 minutes; reduce to moderate (180°C/350°F, Gas Mark 4) and continue for 25–30 minutes or until golden brown and set. Serve hot or cold.

Serves 4–5

Note A little grated cheese may be sprinkled over the tart before baking or can be used in place of the ham or bacon.

Bacon and Egg Tart

This filling resembles that of the old fashioned Bacon and Egg Pie and can be made into a double-crust pie, if preferred. I think the added chives help considerably, but they are not essential.

¾ recipe quantity shortcrust pastry (see page 122)

175–225g (6–8oz) streaky bacon rashers, rinded and chopped

2–3 teaspoons chopped chives

2 large eggs

salt and pepper

150ml (¼pt) double cream

150ml (¼pt) milk

Roll out the pastry and use to line a 20cm (8in) flan ring or tin. Fry the bacon gently in its own fat until lightly browned, stirring frequently. Drain well and place in the pastry case, then sprinkle with chives. Beat the eggs, seasoning, cream and milk together and pour into the flan. Bake in a hot oven (220°C/425°F, Gas Mark 7) for 15–20 minutes. Reduce to moderate (180°C/350°F, Gas Mark 4) and continue for 20–25 minutes until golden brown and set. Serve hot or cold.

Serves 4

STEAK AND KIDNEY PIE

1 Pour into a 2 pint dish – with a pie-funnel – the pre-cooked onion, steak, kidney, and other ingredients

2 Roll out pastry to an oval about 3 inches larger than dish. Cut off narrow strip all round. Place on dampened rim of dish. Brush with water, put on lid and press edges

3 Flake the edge, flute with knife and thumb. Make a hole for steam to escape, decorate top with trimmings from pastry. Brush with beaten egg

Steak and Kidney Pie

For the best results, the filling for this traditional British dish is cooked and cooled before the pastry lid is added. They can be baked together, but the length of time required to cook the meat tends to over-harden the pastry. Oysters or mushrooms can be added after the initial cooking period – indeed oysters used to be a necessary ingredient but their cost has more or less ruled them out nowadays. Although puff or rough puff pastry is usual, shortcrust pastry can be used, if preferred.

2 tablespoons dripping

1 large onion, peeled and sliced

450g (1lb) stewing steak, cut into 2cm (¾in) cubes

100g (4oz) ox kidney, chopped

1 level tablespoon flour

1 meat extract cube (optional)

1 teaspoon Worcestershire sauce

1 level tablespoon tomato paste

salt and pepper

600ml (1pt) water

a few oysters, fresh or canned (optional)

½ recipe quantity puff or rough puff pastry

(see pages 123, 126)

beaten egg to glaze

Melt the dripping in a pan and fry the onion until soft. Add the steak and kidney, and continue until well sealed. Stir in the flour and cook for 1 minute. Blend the extract cube, Worcestershire sauce, tomato paste and seasonings in the water, then add to the pan. Bring to the boil, cover and simmer gently for about 1½ hours or until tender, stirring occasionally. Adjust the seasoning, pour into a 1 litre (1½–2pt) pie dish with a pie funnel in the centre and leave to cool. (The meat can be cooled completely and refrigerated overnight at this stage.) Stir in the oysters, if used. Roll out the pastry to about 7·5cm (3in) larger than the top of the dish, cut off a narrow strip all round and place it on the dampened rim of the dish. Brush this with water and position the lid. Press the edges well together and trim. Flake the edge by making horizontal cuts into the cut edge of the pastry and then use the back of the knife and your thumb to flute the edge. Make a hole in the centre of the pie for the steam to escape and decorate the top with leaves made from the pastry trimmings. Brush with beaten egg and bake in a hot oven (220°C/425°F, Gas Mark 7) for 20 minutes or until beginning to brown. Reduce the temperature to moderately hot (190°C/375°F, Gas Mark 5) and continue for about 20–30 minutes or until the filling is piping hot and the crust well risen and browned. Serve hot.

Serves 4

Note This type of pie can have numerous fillings – chicken, game, beef, lamb, pork or a combination of ingredients.

Beef and Chestnut Pie

This beef pie filling is flavoured with chestnuts; they can be freshly roasted or, when out of season, dried ones can be utilised. Chestnuts have been popular for a very long time and nowadays the antique chestnut roasters are hard to find and a shovel or special roasting spoon needs to be used on an open fire. The advantage of the roaster, which was a perforated metal box on a long handle, was that the chestnuts 'popped' when ready and the box caught any flying bits and pieces of shell and skin; with modern methods of roasting the skins must be 'nicked' to prevent an explosion!

550g (1¼lb) chuck or braising steak
40g (1½oz) dripping or margarine
1 large onion, peeled and sliced
2 level tablespoons flour
450ml (¾pt) beef stock
150ml (¼pt) red wine or cider
salt and pepper
175g (6oz) chestnuts, lightly roasted and peeled or 50g (2oz) dried chestnuts, re-constituted
½ recipe quantity puff or rough puff pastry (see pages 123, 126)
beaten egg or milk to glaze

Trim the meat and cut into 2·5cm (1in) cubes. Fry in the fat until browned then transfer to a casserole. Fry the onion in the same fat until lightly browned, then stir in the flour and cook for 1 minute. Gradually add the stock and wine or cider, and season well. Bring up to the boil, add the chestnuts and pour into the casserole. Cover and cook in a moderate oven (180°C/350°F, Gas Mark 4) for about 1¼ hours or until tender. Pour into a pie dish with a pie funnel in the centre and leave to cool. Roll out the pastry and use to cover the pie, then decorate, brush with egg or milk and bake as for Steak and Kidney Pie, until the pastry is golden brown. Serve hot.

Serves 4

Note If you dislike chestnuts, add one diced aubergine in their place at the same stage.

Huntingdon Fidget Pie

This combination of streaky bacon, apples and onions, baked under a flaky pastry crust, turns into a thick sauce during cooking and has an interesting and unusual flavour. The farmers' wives of Huntingdon-shire made it as a cheap dish, perhaps adding pieces of chopped rabbit or other meat if it was available and sometimes oddments of vegetables which needed to be used up.

675g (1½lb) cooking apples, peeled, cored and sliced
2–3 large onions, peeled and sliced
450g (1lb) streaky bacon, rinded and diced
salt and pepper
2–3 tablespoons water
½ recipe quantity puff or flaky pastry (see pages 123, 124)
beaten egg or milk to glaze

Layer the apples, onions, bacon and seasoning in a pie dish with a pie funnel in the centre. Press down evenly and add the water. Roll out the pastry to about 7·5cm (3in) larger than the top of the pie dish; cut off a strip all round about 2·5cm (1in) wide and place on the dampened rim of the dish. Brush this with water and position the lid. Trim off the surplus pastry, knock up the edges and crimp, and make a hole in the centre of the lid. Decorate the top with pastry trimmings and brush well with egg or milk. Bake in a hot oven (220°C/425°F, Gas Mark 7) for 15 minutes, then reduce to moderate (180°C/350°F, Gas Mark 4) and continue for 1½ hours, covering the pastry with foil or greaseproof paper when sufficiently browned.

Serves 5–6

Note If the apples are very tart, add 1–2 tablespoons sugar to the pie.

Pigeon Pie

A true pigeon pie (as distinct from a Squab Pie) can have a wide variety of flavourings – some have a high proportion of vegetables, others sweeter ingredients such as sultanas, raisins, dates or prunes, whilst many are cooked in a rich wine sauce – all of which are to enhance the rather gamey flavour of these plump-breasted birds. Both wild and tame pigeons are suitable to eat.

4 plump pigeons, prepared
grated rind and juice of 1 small orange
8 rashers streaky bacon, rinded and chopped
1 tablespoon oil
25g (1oz) butter
1 large onion, peeled and chopped
1 tablespoon flour
150ml (¼pt) Marsala or red wine
300–450ml (½–¾pt) stock

50g (2oz) sultanas (optional)
salt and pepper
3–4 tablespoons cream (optional)
1 recipe quantity shortcrust pastry (see page 122)
beaten egg or milk to glaze

Cut each pigeon in half, sprinkle with orange rind and wind a rasher of bacon around each piece, securing with wooden cocktail sticks. Fry in a mixture of oil and butter until well browned, then remove from the pan. Fry the onion in the same fat until beginning to brown, then stir in the flour and cook for 1 minute. Add the Marsala or wine, orange juice, stock and sultanas (if used) and bring up to the boil. Replace the pieces of pigeon, season well, cover the pan and simmer for about an hour or until tender. Stir the cream into the sauce, adjust seasoning and pour into a pie dish with a funnel in the centre; leave to cool. Cover with a pastry lid as for Steak and Kidney Pie (see page 149), decorate with pastry trimmings, and brush with egg or milk. Bake in a hot oven (220°C/425°F, Gas Mark 7) for 20 minutes, then reduce to moderately hot (190°C/375°F, Gas Mark 5) and continue for about 30 minutes. Serve hot.

Serves 4

Squab Pie

A squab is a young pigeon and a squab pie is a West Country dish made sometimes with young pigeons but more often from neck of lamb chops of about the same size as a squab, with apples and onions added. Apples, or sometimes oranges, were often cooked with lamb until the nineteenth century for they were said to help balance the fattiness of lamb or mutton. Devon and Cornwall both had their versions of this pie with the Cornish variety often adding raisins, which could make it rather sweet unless the apples used were particularly tart.

900g (2lb) neck of lamb or mutton chops

900g (2lb) cooking apples, peeled, cored and sliced

3 onions, peeled and sliced

salt and pepper

good pinch of thyme

good pinch of ground allspice

good pinch of ground cinnamon

1 recipe quantity shortcrust pastry (see page 122)

beaten egg or milk to glaze

Cut the lamb into small pieces and layer in a pie dish with the apples and onions, seasoning each layer and adding the thyme and spices. Add about 6 tablespoons water and cover with a pastry lid. Decorate with pastry trimmings and make a hole in the centre for the steam to escape. Glaze with egg or milk and bake in a moderate oven (180°C/350°F, Gas Mark 4) for about 2 hours, covering the pastry with foil or greaseproof paper when sufficiently browned.

Serves 4–6

Note Another method of making this pie is to brown the lamb and onions in 25g (1oz) butter or margarine, then add 600ml (1pt) water and all the ingredients except the apples, and simmer for 1 hour. Add the apples and continue for a few minutes then pour into a pie dish with sufficient stock barely to cover and leave to cool before adding the pastry lid. Bake in a fairly hot oven (200°C/400°F, Gas Mark 6) for about 40 minutes.

If squabs are used then 6–8 will be sufficient and they should be browned in fat before adding the other ingredients.

Pheasant Pie

A traditional game pie is probably recognised as a raised pie served as part of a cold buffet or with salads. However, hot game pies are also famed and have remained an exclusive favourite through the years; the main problem now is the expense and difficulty in obtaining game birds, unless you are perhaps the member of a shoot. Pies are an ideal way to serve mature birds, some of which are now appearing in supermarkets, fresh in season or in frozen form. Although pheasant is stated here, any other game bird or a combination of game may be used for this creamy pie filling.

1 large mature pheasant, prepared

salt and pepper

40g (1½oz) butter or margarine

2 onions, peeled and sliced

450ml (¾pt) stock

1 bay leaf

1 level tablespoon cornflour

150ml (¼pt) single cream

100g (4oz) mushrooms, sliced

2–4 tablespoons port or sherry

½ recipe quantity puff, flaky or rough puff pastry (see pages 125, 126, 128) or 1 recipe quantity shortcrust pastry (see page 124)

beaten egg or milk to glaze

Cut the pheasant into 4 or 8 portions and season well. Fry in the melted fat until browned all over. Remove from the pan and fry the onions until soft. Return the pheasant to the pan with the stock, bay leaf and seasoning and bring up to the boil. Cover and simmer gently for about an hour or until tender, adding a little extra stock if necessary during cooking. Discard the bay leaf and thicken the sauce with sufficient cornflour blended with the cream. Bring back to the boil, stir in the mushrooms, port or sherry and adjust seasoning. Pour into a pie dish with a funnel in the centre and leave to cool. Cover with a pastry lid as for Steak and Kidney Pie (see page 149), decorate with pastry trimming and glaze. Bake flaked pastry in a very hot oven (230°C/450°F, Gas Mark 8) and shortcrust pastry in a hot oven (220°C/425°F, Gas Mark 7) for 15–20 minutes, then reduce to moderately hot (190°C/375°F, Gas Mark 5) and continue for about 30 minutes or until golden brown. Serve hot.

Serves 4

Game Pie

Another recipe for a hot game pie, this time using steak to stretch out the amount of flesh on smaller birds; if venison or hare is used the steak is not necessary.

1 small pheasant or 2 grouse or partridge and 225g (8oz) braising steak or 1 hare, jointed or 675g (1½lb) venison, cubed
a little seasoned flour
50g (2oz) dripping
12 baby onions, peeled or 2 large onions, peeled and sliced
2 sticks celery, sliced
25g (1oz) flour
300ml (½pt) red wine or dry cider
300ml (½pt) stock
1 level tablespoon tomato paste
1 teaspoon Worcestershire sauce
salt and pepper
100g (4oz) mushrooms, sliced (optional)
½ recipe quantity puff, rough puff or flaky pastry (see pages 123, 124, 126)
beaten egg or milk to glaze

Portion the game and cut the steak into neat cubes. Coat in seasoned flour. Fry in melted dripping until browned all over, then remove from the pan. Fry the onions and celery in the same fat until soft, then stir in the flour and cook for 1 minute. Gradually add the wine (or cider) and stock, and bring up to the boil, then stir in the tomato paste, Worcestershire sauce and seasoning. Return the game to the pan, cover and simmer for about 1¼ hours or until tender, adding a little more stock if necessary during cooking. Stir in the mushrooms (if used), adjust the seasoning and pour into a pie dish with a funnel in the centre; leave to cool. Cover with a pastry lid as for Steak and Kidney Pie (see page 149), decorate with pastry trimmings, glaze and bake in a very hot oven (230°C/450°F, Gas Mark 8) for 20 minutes. Reduce to moderately hot (190°C/375°F, Gas Mark 5) and continue for about 30 minutes until well risen and golden brown. Serve hot.

Serves 4

Rabbit Pie

The use of rabbit in pies has been popular for centuries and this is one of our oldest traditional pies. However, as with everything, flavours change and many rabbit pie fillings now have rather unusual additions. Juniper has always been a traditional flavouring but I like the combination of rabbit and prunes.

1 young rabbit, about 900g (2lb), jointed
225g (8oz) lean bacon, rinded and diced
1 onion, peeled and sliced
2 carrots, peeled and sliced
1 bay leaf
450ml (¾pt) stock or water
salt and pepper
1 level tablespoon cornflour
1 level tablespoon chopped parsley
8–12 prunes, soaked

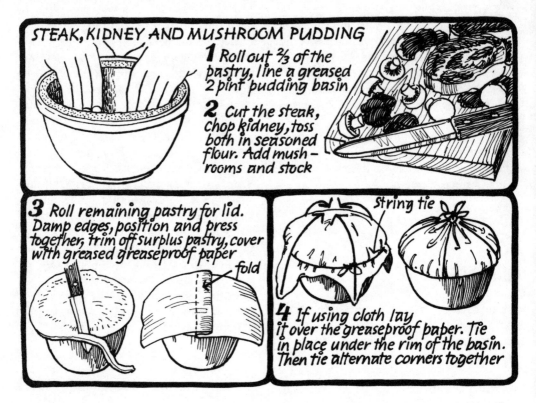

STEAK, KIDNEY AND MUSHROOM PUDDING

1 Roll out ⅔ of the pastry, line a greased 2 pint pudding basin

2 Cut the steak, chop kidney, toss both in seasoned flour. Add mushrooms and stock

3 Roll remaining pastry for lid. Damp edges, position and press together, trim off surplus pastry, cover with greased greaseproof paper

fold

String tie

4 If using cloth lay it over the greaseproof paper. Tie in place under the rim of the basin. Then tie alternate corners together

1 tablespoon lemon juice or sherry

1 recipe quantity shortcrust pastry (see page 122)

beaten egg or milk to glaze

Soak the rabbit in salted water for 2 hours if time allows, then drain well. Place in a saucepan with the bacon, onion, carrots, bay leaf, stock or water and seasonings. Bring up to the boil, cover and simmer gently for ¾–1 hour until tender. Remove the rabbit and cool slightly, then strip the meat from the bones and return it to the cooking liquor and vegetables; discard the bayleaf. Blend the cornflour with a little cold water, add it to the saucepan and bring up to the boil again, stirring until thickened. Adjust seasoning, stir in the parsley, prunes and lemon juice or sherry, and pour into a pie dish with a funnel in the centre. Leave to cool. Roll out the pastry to about 5cm (2in) larger than the top of the dish and cut

a 2·5cm (1in) strip all round to place on the dampened rim of the dish. Brush the pastry rim with water and position the lid. Press the edges well together, trim and crimp, then decorate the top with pastry leaves. Make a hole in the centre, brush with egg or milk and bake in a hot oven (220°C/425°F, Gas Mark 7) for 20 minutes. Reduce to moderately hot (190°C/375°F, Gas Mark 5) and continue for 25–30 minutes. Serve hot or cold.

Serves 4–6

Steak, Kidney and Mushroom Pudding

Steak and kidney pudding was thought to have originated in Sussex, but has moved around the country so much that it is now a well loved traditional British pudding.

Oysters were often added but they were not improved by the long cooking necessary to tenderise the meat. I think it better to add oysters to a steak and kidney pie, if you like the flavour, and use mushrooms in their place in the pudding.

1 recipe quantity suet crust pastry (see page 122)
450g (1lb) best chuck steak
about 175g (6oz) ox kidney
2 level tablespoons well seasoned flour
100g (4oz) mushrooms, sliced (optional)
about 4 tablespoons beef stock or water

Roll out two-thirds of the pastry and use to line a lightly greased 1 litre (2pt) pudding basin. Cut the steak into cubes, discarding any fat or gristle and chop the skinned and cored kidney then toss the meat in seasoned flour. Spoon meat into the lined pudding basin, alternating with mushrooms, until it is almost full. Add 3–4 tablespoons stock or water. Roll out the remaining pastry for a lid, place lid in position, pressing the edges well together, damp the edges, trim off the surplus pastry. Cover with greased greaseproof paper with a fold across the centre for expansion, then add either a pudding cloth or foil lid, tying or folding it very securely under the rim of the basin. When using a pudding cloth, lay it over the greaseproof paper, tie in place with string under the rim of the basin, then pull up alternate corners of the cloth over the pudding and tie or pin first two and then the other two corners together. Stand it either in a saucepan with boiling water coming two-thirds of the way up the side of the basin, or in the top of a steamer. Cover and simmer gently for about 4 hours, adding more boiling water to the pan as necessary. To serve, remove the cloth or foil and paper, and either serve from the basin with a cloth tied round it or turn the pudding out very carefully on to a warmed dish, hoping it will not split open or collapse before it is cut.

Serves 4

Note In place of the kidney, 2 chopped sticks celery and 1 chopped onion may be used.

Bacon and Onion Pudding

Add 1 level teaspoon dried mixed herbs or sage to the dry suet crust mix and continue as above, using 675g (1½lb) diced lean bacon, 2 large sliced onions, 4 tablespoons stock or water and black pepper only to season, for the filling. Boil for 3–3½ hours.

Chicken and Herb Pudding

Make the crust as for Steak and Kidney Pudding. For the filling use: 550g (1¼lb) cubed raw chicken or turkey meat (boneless), 100g (4oz) diced lean bacon, 1–2 sliced onions, 2 peeled and quartered tomatoes, 1 level teaspoon dried herbs and 3–4 tablespoons stock or water. Boil for 3–3½ hours.

Quorn Bacon Roll

This bacon and onion roly-poly is a substantial, cheap dish which was often served to the huntsmen and farmers to satisfy their huge appetites after a busy day. Although named after the Quorn Hunt in Leicestershire, similar recipes appear all over the country, particularly in farming areas.

1 recipe quantity suet crust pastry (see page 128)
225g (8oz) lean bacon rashers, rinded
1 large onion, peeled and chopped
1 level teaspoon dried sage
salt and pepper

Make up the suet crust pastry and roll out to a thickness of 0·5cm (¼in) on a floured surface. Lay the bacon over the pastry and sprinkle with onion, sage and seasoning. Roll up the pastry carefully and place on a well floured cloth or a piece of greased foil. Wrap the cloth tightly round the roll and secure the ends with string. If using foil make a pleat along the length, then fold up, securing the join and ends tightly. Place in a saucepan of boiling water for 2 hours, making sure it does not go off the boil at all. Serve hot with vegetables and a gravy or savoury white sauce.

Sweet Pastries

A sweet tooth is a failing of many of us, so when pastry is combined with one of the many sweet fillings, it is easy to understand how these particular foods have become firm favourites. Some of the recipes here have been passed down through families for generations, while others are relatively modern creations. Most types of pastry can be used with sweet ingredients, the exception being perhaps hot water crust; some, such as rich flan pastry and choux pastry, were obviously created especially to blend with sweetness.

Pies and open tarts date back a long time but became very popular in the seventeenth century when all manner of fillings were used, both sweet and savoury, with the pastry more often flaky than shortcrust. As time passed, some of these fillings and pies were forgotten, but many still remain today or at least the basic ideas are the same. Cakes made with pastry also continued in popularity; many completely enclosed a fruit or dried fruit mixture, helping to keep it fresh longer. Several areas produced similar cakes with different names: for instance, the Eccles and Banbury Cakes which, although the towns are over a hundred miles apart, appear to really differ only in shape, Eccles preferring round and Banbury oval cakes. Coventry Godcakes are similar but have a solid mincemeat filling and are shaped into triangles; these crisp delicacies were baked as a gift from godparents to godchildren on New Year's Day and bear a close resemblance to Mince Pies. Mincemeat once really did include raw minced meat with plenty of spice and dried fruit added to overcome its steady decomposition; and today, although the meat has disappeared from it, shredded suet is still an important ingredient. Treacle Tarts have remained strong favourites and were originally made with brown treacle and spices, hence the name; now it is common to use golden syrup and breadcrumbs.

One recipe that is disappearing is Flead Cake. At the beginning of the century it was a teatime favourite, being a sweet and spicy cake of a flaked pastry; now flead is more difficult to obtain as the old family butchers' shops slowly continue to disappear and supermarkets spring up in their place. The Lemon Pie has largely died out too, but has been replaced with the much more interesting Lemon Meringue Pie. Still around are the Richmond Maids of Honour – little pastry tarts filled with a curd cheese, almond and brandy mixture, said to date from the days of Henry VIII at Hampton Court – and also Black Bun – the Scottish rich fruit cake baked in a pastry case to serve at Hogmanay.

Whatever your favourite – be it an open tart, a double-crust Apple Pie or a teatime pastry oozing with cream – somewhere amongst these recipes there is sure to be something to tempt you, or for which you have a secret longing.

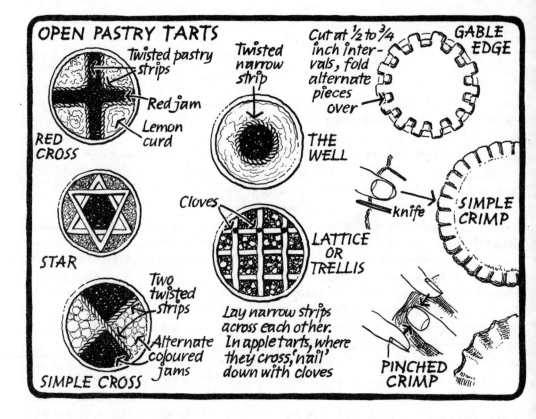

OPEN PASTRY TARTS

Twisted pastry strips

Red jam

Lemon curd

RED CROSS

Twisted narrow strip

THE WELL

Cut at ½ to ¾ inch intervals, fold alternate pieces over

GABLE EDGE

STAR

Cloves

knife

SIMPLE CRIMP

SIMPLE CROSS

Two twisted strips

Alternate coloured jams

LATTICE OR TRELLIS

Lay narrow strips across each other. In apple tarts, where they cross, 'nail' down with cloves

PINCHED CRIMP

Open Pastry Tarts

There were many ways to decorate the edges and surfaces of open tarts or pies in England, using up the pastry trimmings. Some were always associated with a certain filling, others were interchangeable. The fillings could be jam, lemon curd, mincemeat, fruit purée, treacle etc, and it was said that the better the cook, the better she judged the quantity of pastry required and therefore the smaller the decoration on top of the tart! These are just a few of the decorations which are still used and no doubt there are very many more; the first four show how divisions made by strips of pastry can be filled with various coloured jams to give very spectacular results. The tarts with only one filling were often decorated just around the edge, or covered with a simple lattice.

Red Cross

Cut 4 narrow strips of pastry, twist and place on the tart to divide it into 4 sections with a plain cross in the centre. Fill the cross with red jam and the remaining parts with lemon curd or a green jam.

Star

Cut 6 narrow strips of pastry; arrange three in a triangle in the tart to touch the edges, then the other three in a second triangle to lie alternately on top of the first one. Fill the centre with 1 colour of jam and the other portions with alternating colours or, for a really spectacular tart, each one with a different jam!

Simple Cross

Cut 2 long strips of pastry, twist and arrange

in a cross over the tart. Fill with 2 or 4 types of jam.

The Well

Cut a narrow strip of pastry, twist it and shape to form a small circle; place in the centre of the tart. Fill the centre with a dark jam and the outer part with a contrasting colour.

Lattice or Trellis

Use for tarts with 1 filling. Cut narrow strips of pastry and lay either straight or twisted across the filled tart, leaving an even gap between each one. Then lay a second layer of strips at right-angles to the first, to complete the design. For apple tarts, the strips were usually laid straight and where they crossed could be 'nailed' down with whole cloves.

Gable Edge

Again used for a tart or pie with 1 filling. The pastry edging on the rim of the plate or tin is cut at 1–2cm ($\frac{1}{2}$–$\frac{3}{4}$in) intervals with every alternate piece folded inwards to lay over the filling.

Simple Crimp

Put your thumb on the pastry edge on the rim of the plate and pull the pastry next to it towards the centre with the back of a knife to make an indentation. Move your thumb to the other side of the knife mark and repeat all the way round.

Pinched Crimp

Place the first finger of your right hand on the pastry edge on the rim of the plate, facing out from the filling; with thumb and first finger of the left hand, pinch the pastry around the finger into a point. Repeat all the way round.

Treacle Tart

This tart has been well known for a very long time. Although called treacle tart, it does in fact use golden syrup; however, in the nineteenth century it was made with brown treacle, dried fruit, mixed peel and spices which must be how the name originated. Nowadays it is often made with just syrup and breadcrumbs in a pastry case, although lemon rind, ginger and other flavourings can be added.

$\frac{1}{2}$ recipe quantity shortcrust pastry (see page 122)
6–8 tablespoons golden syrup
finely grated rind of $\frac{1}{2}$ lemon
50g (2oz) fresh white breadcrumbs

Make up the pastry and use to line a pie plate or tin about 21cm ($8\frac{1}{2}$in). Trim and crimp the edge and lightly prick the base. Warm the syrup slightly and pour it into the pastry case. Sprinkle first with lemon rind and then with breadcrumbs, and leave to stand for 5 minutes. Bake in a fairly hot oven (200°C/400°F, Gas Mark 6) for about 25 minutes or until the pastry is a light golden brown and the filling firm and golden. Serve hot or cold.

Serves 4–5

Note To measure syrup easily, brush the spoon all over with oil before dipping into the syrup and it will simply slide off.

Rich flan pastry can be used in place of shortcrust.

Suitable to freeze for up to 3 months.

Custard Tarts

Baked custard is a favourite of many and can be made into delicious pastry tarts. Care must be taken to prevent the pastry base rising during cooking and the custard sinking into it – a thin coating of egg white on the uncooked pastry seems to be one answer.

1 recipe quantity rich flan pastry (see page 123)
2 eggs
1 egg yolk
25g (1oz) caster sugar
275ml (scant ½pt) milk
grated nutmeg (optional)

Roll out the pastry and use to line about 15 fairly deep patty tins, using a fluted cutter. Brush the pastry inside with the white of one egg. Beat the remainder of the egg white with the other egg, egg yolks and sugar until fluffy, then whisk in the milk. Strain into a jug and pour into the pastry cases. Sprinkle each with a little grated nutmeg (fresh if possible) and bake in a fairly hot oven (200°C/400°F, Gas Mark 6) for 15 minutes. Reduce the temperature to moderate (170°C/325°F, Gas Mark 3) and continue for a further 15–20 minutes until the custard is set and lightly coloured. Cool slightly then remove carefully from the tins. Serve warm or cold.

Makes about 15

Note For a large tart, use the pastry to line a deep 20–21cm (8–8½in) pie plate or flan tin and bake as above, but increase the lower cooking time to about 30 minutes or until set.

Bakewell Tarts

Said to be named after the town of Bakewell, these tarts are really more of a pudding than a teatime fancy, but can be served equally well at both times. There are many versions of the almond filling, some of which are very rich and extravagant and can be very soggy.

½ recipe quantity shortcrust pastry (see page 122)
50g (2oz) margarine
50g (2oz) caster sugar
1 large egg
a few drops of almond essence
15g (½oz) self-raising flour
40g (1½oz) ground almonds
raspberry jam
icing sugar to decorate (optional)

Roll out the pastry and use to line 12–15 patty tins or a deep 18–20cm (7–8in) pie plate. Cream the margarine and sugar together until light and fluffy, then beat in the egg and almond essence. Fold in the flour and ground almonds. Put a small teaspoon of jam in each pastry case, then add a tablespoon of almond mixture and spread to cover the jam completely. For the large tart, spread a thin layer of jam over the base, then spread all the almond mixture over the jam. Bake in a moderately hot oven (190°C/375°F, Gas Mark 5) for about 20 minutes for the small tarts and 30–35 minutes for the large one, or until the sponge is well risen, golden brown and firm. Cool on a wire rack or in the pie plate and dredge lightly with icing sugar before serving.

Makes 12–15 small tarts or 1 large tart

Suitable to freeze for up to 4 months.

Lemon Meringue Pie

This open pie with a lemony filling and meringue topping is a favourite with all. Rich flan pastry is best but shortcrust is also acceptable. The flavouring can also be orange or grapefruit for a change, and the pie can be served warm or cold.

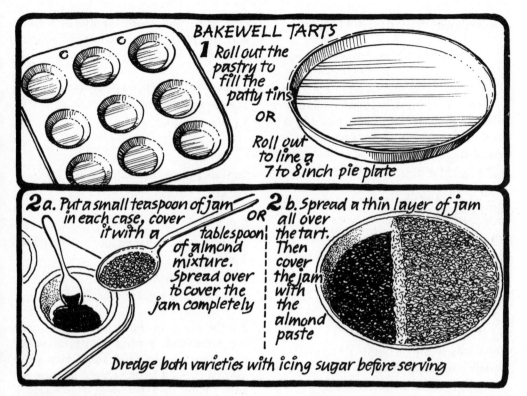

BAKEWELL TARTS

1 Roll out the pastry to fill the patty tins

OR

Roll out to line a 7 to 8 inch pie plate

2 a. Put a small teaspoon of jam in each case, cover it with a tablespoon of almond mixture. Spread over to cover the jam completely

OR

2 b. Spread a thin layer of jam all over the tart. Then cover the jam with the almond paste

Dredge both varieties with icing sugar before serving

---

1 recipe quantity rich flan pastry (see page 123)

finely grated rind and juice of 2 lemons

3 level tablespoons cornflour

150ml ($\frac{1}{4}$pt) water

50–75g (2–3oz) caster sugar

2 egg yolks

knob of butter (optional)

Meringue

2 egg whites

50g (2oz) granulated sugar

50g (2oz) caster sugar

Roll out the pastry and use to line a 19–20cm (7$\frac{1}{2}$–8in) shallow pie tin or flan case. Prick the base, lay a sheet of greaseproof paper inside and cover the surface with baking beans or rice. Bake blind (as this process is called) in a moderately hot oven (190°C/375°F, Gas Mark 5) for 15 minutes; remove the beans and paper carefully and return the pastry case to the oven for about 5 minutes or until cooked through. Leave to cool. For the filling, make the fruit rind and juice up to 125ml (scant $\frac{1}{4}$pt) with water if necessary, then blend with the cornflour and 150ml ($\frac{1}{4}$pt) water in a saucepan. Bring slowly up to the boil, stirring continuously, until thickened and clear. Stir in the sugar, then beat in the egg yolks and butter. Pour quickly into the pastry case. For the meringue, whisk the egg whites until stiff, beat in the granulated sugar a little at a time and then fold in the caster sugar. Pipe or spread over the lemon filling so it is completely covered; bake in a moderate oven (170°C/325°F, Gas Mark 3) for 15–20 minutes until lightly browned.

Serves 4–6

Note For Orange Meringue Pie, use the grated rind of 2 oranges and juice of 1 orange and 1 lemon; for Grapefruit Meringue Pie, use the rind and juice of 1 grapefruit.

Richmond Maids of Honour

These tartlets became popular in the reign of Henry VIII with the Queen's maids of honour at Hampton Court. The exact recipe was kept a closely guarded secret and for many years they were only made by one shop in Richmond. Nowadays there are several versions – they should contain curd cheese, ground almonds and brandy.

¼ recipe quantity puff pastry (see page 123)
100g (4oz) curd cheese
75g (3oz) butter, softened
2 egg yolks
1 tablespoon brandy
75g (3oz) caster sugar
40g (1½oz) cold mashed potato
40g (1½oz) ground almonds
grated rind of ½ lemon
1 tablespoon lemon juice
good pinch of freshly grated nutmeg

Lightly grease 16–18 patty tins. Roll out the pastry, cut into 16–18 rounds and line the tins. Beat the cheese and butter together until smooth, then gradually beat in the egg yolks and brandy. Add the sugar, potato, almonds, lemon rind and juice and nutmeg, then beat until smooth. Spoon into the pastry cases and cook in a moderately hot oven (190°C/375°F, Gas Mark 5) for about 30 minutes or until well risen and golden brown. Cool on a wire rack.

Makes 16–18

Note As they cool, the tarts tend to sink a little – this is correct.

Chocolate Eclairs

Choux pastry has a very special taste and texture, and éclairs are probably one of the best loved and more traditional ways to bake it. As well as a chocolate topping, coffee glacé icing can also be used.

1 recipe quantity choux pastry (see page 129)
150ml (¼pt) double cream
2 tablespoons top of the milk

Chocolate Icing
50g (2oz) plain chocolate, broken up
25g (1oz) butter

Coffee Icing
1–2 teaspoons coffee essence or strong black coffee
a little warm water
100g (4oz) icing sugar, sifted

Put the made-up choux paste into a piping bag fitted with a plain 1cm (½in) nozzle. Pipe into straight lines about 6cm (2½in) long on greased baking sheets, keeping well apart. Bake in a hot oven (220°C/425°F, Gas Mark 7) for 20–25 minutes until well risen, firm and a light golden brown. Make a slit in the side of each one for the steam to escape and return them to the oven for 1–2 minutes. Cool on a wire rack. Whip the cream and milk together until stiff and use to fill the éclairs, after carefully slitting them open with a sharp knife. First make up the chocolate icing by melting the chocolate and butter in a basin over a pan of gently simmering water and mixing until smooth; spread this over half the éclairs. Then make up the coffee glacé icing: add the coffee essence or black coffee and sufficient water to the icing sugar to give a thick smooth spreading consistency, and use to spread over the tops of the remaining éclairs. Leave to set.

Makes about 20

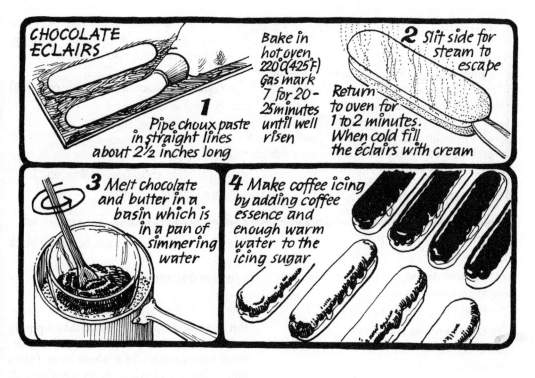

CHOCOLATE ECLAIRS

1 Pipe choux paste in straight lines about 2½ inches long

Bake in hot oven 220°C (425°F) Gas mark 7 for 20-25 minutes until well risen

2 Slit side for steam to escape

Return to oven for 1 to 2 minutes. When cold fill the éclairs with cream

3 Melt chocolate and butter in a basin which is in a pan of simmering water

4 Make coffee icing by adding coffee essence and enough warm water to the icing sugar

PROFITEROLES

Pipe mixture into small bun shapes about the size of a walnut. Bake; fill and ice tops as for éclairs. For a dessert, pile buns on serving dish, dredge with icing sugar, serve chocolate sauce to pour over

Profiteroles

Pipe the choux pastry into small bun shapes about the size of walnuts. Bake, fill and ice the tops as for éclairs, or, for a dessert, pile the cream-filled buns into a pyramid shape on a serving dish, dredge with icing sugar and serve with a chocolate sauce to pour over.

For the sauce, melt 100g (4oz) plain chocolate and 25g (1oz) butter in a basin over a pan of simmering water. When smooth, gradually beat in 150ml (¼pt) single cream or evaporated milk and 1 tablespoon rum, if liked. Serve warm or cold.

Cream Buns

These are choux pastry buns puffed up to several times their original size during baking by inverting large tins over them; this traps the steam and makes them expand. If disturbed during baking the buns promptly sink!

165

CREAM BUNS

1 Put dessertspoons of mixture on to greased baking sheet, cover tightly with baking tins

2 Split buns in half, add whipped cream and jam

3 Brush tops with jam and sprinkle with toasted nuts or dredge with icing sugar

1 recipe quantity choux pastry (see page 129)

300ml (½pt) double or whipping cream, whipped

a little apricot jam

50g (2oz) flaked or chopped almonds, toasted

icing sugar

It is essential to have a deep, covered roasting tin, or baking sheets with a deep roasting tin or loaf tins to invert over the buns and keep in all the steam. Spoon dessertspoons of the choux pastry on to well greased baking sheets leaving plenty of space around each one, then cover tightly with the inverted tins. Bake in a fairly hot oven (200°C/400°F, Gas Mark 6) for 40–50 minutes until the buns move when the tin is gently shaken. Do not touch or remove the tins during baking or the steam will escape and the buns sink sadly. When ready, cool on a wire rack. Just before serving either split the buns in half and add a little whipped cream and jam, if liked, or make a hole in the side of each bun and pipe in some cream. Brush the tops with a little jam and sprinkle with toasted nuts; for a plainer bun, simply dredge with icing sugar.

Makes 12–16

Cream Horns

These are favourite pastry confections which, when baked, are filled with whipped cream and jam. A sugar coating may be added before baking (if preferred to an egg glaze) which is dredged with icing sugar before serving. Savoury horns are obviously baked without the sugar and can be filled with any type of savoury filling, preferably with a thick sauce base.

½ recipe quantity puff or flaky pastry (see pages 123, 124)

1 egg, beaten or 1 egg white, lightly beaten

caster sugar (optional)

lemon curd or jam

whipped cream

icing sugar

Lightly grease 8–10 cream horn tins and a baking sheet. Roll out the pastry thinly to a long strip about 60 × 13cm (25 × 5in) and cut into narrow strips 1cm (½in) wide. Brush all over the pastry with beaten egg for a shiny glaze, or egg white for a sugar-crusted glaze. Wind one strip carefully around each tin, beginning at the tip and with the glazed side outwards, overlapping slightly each time. Cut off the pastry when the metal is covered. Place on the baking sheets with the join underneath. Glaze again and sprinkle the egg white with caster sugar. Bake in a hot oven (220°C/425°F, Gas Mark 7) for 8–10 minutes until well puffed up and golden brown. Cool slightly to allow the pastry to shrink a little, then ease out the metal tins and cool the pastry horns on a wire rack. When cold put a good spoonful of the lemon curd or jam in the tip and fill the rest of the horn with whipped cream, using a piping bag fitted with a large star nozzle, if possible. Dredge the egg-glazed horns with a little icing sugar before serving.

Makes 8–10

Note The unfilled horns can be stored in an airtight container for 2–3 days before filling to serve. Stale unfilled horns can be refreshed in a moderate oven for a few minutes.

Cream Crisps

These are also known as Palmiers and are made from puff or flaky pastry, which is dredged with sugar, then folded in a special way and sliced to give the traditional curved pastry that opens out during baking. Although they can be left plain, they are more usually filled with cream or jam or a combination of the two.

½ recipe quantity puff or flaky pastry (see pages 123, 124)
caster sugar
mixed spice (optional)
whipped cream (sweetened, if liked)
raspberry jam
icing sugar (optional)

Roll out the pastry thinly and evenly to a rectangle about 30×23cm (12×10in). Sprinkle well with caster sugar and a little

spice, if liked. Fold the long sides halfway to the centre, dredge with sugar, then fold the folded edges right to the centre. Dredge again with sugar and fold in half lengthwise to hide all the other folds. Press together lightly and then cut into 12–16 even-sized slices. Place, with a cut side downwards, on greased baking sheets, open out a little and press gently with a round-bladed knife. Dredge with sugar and bake in a hot oven (220°C/425°F, Gas Mark 7) for about 7–10 minutes until golden brown and puffed up. Turn over carefully and continue for 4–5 minutes. Cool on a wire rack. To assemble, spread 1 pastry crisp with cream and/or jam and top with another one.

Makes 6–8 pairs or 12–16 plain pastry crisps

Note Unfilled pastry crisps may be stored in an airtight container for up to a week, and can be refreshed in a moderate oven if they appear a little stale.

Sacristans

These were invented as a means to use up left-over scraps of puff or flaky pastry. They do not need the extra rise found in the first rollings of these pastries, for once cut, the strips are tied into knots, circles and twists, etc. They are flavoured with nuts and spice.

about ¼ recipe quantity puff or flaky pastry (see pages 123, 124) or the equivalent in pastry trimmings
1 egg white, lightly beaten
25g (1oz) blanched almonds or hazelnuts, finely chopped
25g (1oz) caster or soft brown sugar
1–1½ level teaspoons ground cinnamon or mixed spice

CREAM SLICES **1** Roll out pastry on floured surface, trim to 16 by 10 inches. Cut in half lengthwise; then into strips 5 by 2 inches

Prick lightly. Bake in very hot oven

2 To make the pastry cream. Cream egg and sugar together; add flour, cornflour and a little milk. Blend to smooth paste

3 Heat remainder of milk to just below boiling and whisk into egg mixture

Return to pan. Bring slowly to boil. Remove from heat, add essence

Stir

4 Make the glacé icing and add enough water to make a smooth coating. Spread over the best 8 pieces, leave to set

5 Spread remaining pieces with jam and then a thick layer of pastry cream

6 Finally carefully put the iced pastry lids in position on top

If using pastry trimmings, knead them lightly together first. Roll out the pastry thinly to an oblong about 35 × 10cm (14 × 4in), trimming the edges. Brush all over with egg white, then sprinkle first with the nuts and then with the sugar mixed with the spice. Cut into strips about 1cm ($\frac{1}{2}$in) wide from the narrow edge. Either place these strips as they are on greased baking sheets or twist them, tie them into knots or shape them into circles, etc, before placing them on the baking sheets. Bake in a hot oven (220°C/425°F, Gas Mark 7) for about 10 minutes or until well browned and puffy.

Cool on a wire rack and store in an airtight container.

Makes about 24

Cream Slices

Layers of puff pastry, sandwiched together with pastry cream or fresh cream and raspberry jam, and topped with glacé icing – fit to grace any table be it teatime or a lavish dinner party.

½ recipe quantity puff pastry (see page 123)
6–8 tablespoons raspberry jam

Pastry Cream
1 egg
50g (2oz) caster sugar
15g (½oz) flour
15g (½oz) cornflour
200ml (8fl oz) milk
vanilla essence

Glacé Icing
100g (4oz) icing sugar, sifted
1–2 tablespoons warm water

Roll out the pastry on a floured surface and trim to a rectangle 40×25cm (16×10in). Cut in half lengthwise and then cut each strip into pieces 13×5cm (5×2in). Place these 16 pieces on greased or dampened baking sheets and prick lightly. Leave to stand in a cool place for 10 minutes then bake in a very hot oven (230°C/450°F, Gas Mark 8) for about 10 minutes or until well risen and golden brown. Leave to cool on a wire rack. Make the pastry cream: cream the egg and sugar together, then add the flour, cornflour and a little milk, and blend to a smooth paste. Heat the remainder of the milk to just below boiling and whisk it into the egg mixture. Return to the pan and bring slowly up to the boil, stirring continuously; continue for 1–2 minutes until thick. Remove from the heat, add the vanilla essence to taste and leave to cool with a plate over the pan. Make up the glacé icing: add sufficient water to the icing sugar to obtain a thick, smooth, coating consistency and spread a little over the best 8 pieces of pastry. Leave to set. Spread the remaining pieces of pastry with jam, then with a thick layer of pastry cream. Arrange on a serving plate and put the iced pastry lids carefully in position.

Makes 8

Note   300ml (½pt) stiffly whipped double cream can be used in place of the pastry cream.

Flead Cakes

These are remembered by various friends of mine whose grandmothers often baked Flead cakes as specialities for Sunday tea. They are a type of semi-flaked pastry, flavoured with sugar and spice, and baked in squares. Flead used to be widely available from the pork butcher for it is the inner membrane of the pig's inside, being a thin skin dotted with little pieces of pure lard. It also makes an excellent pastry for savoury pies if you use a good pinch of salt in place of the sugar and spice. The pastry requires the same proportion of flead (cleaned from the membranes) to flour as shortcrust, but has a much shorter texture. Flead cakes were best known in Kent and the south-east of England.

200g (8oz) plain flour
100g (4oz) flead, cleaned from the membranes
50g (2oz) caster sugar
1–2 level teaspoons mixed spice
cold water to mix
egg white to glaze
granulated sugar for dredging

Sift the flour into a bowl. Add the flead cut into small pieces and the sugar and spice. Mix to a firm dough with water and turn on to a floured surface. Roll out the pastry, banging it hard with the rolling pin to break up the flead, then fold up and reroll as for puff pastry; repeat the banging, folding and rolling until the hard pieces of flead are well blended with the flour. This cannot be done quickly. Then roll out the pastry to about 1cm (⅓–½in) thick and cut into 4–5cm (1½–2in) squares. Lightly score the tops, place on greased baking sheets and brush with egg white. Sprinkle with granulated sugar and bake in a fairly hot oven (200°C/400°F, Gas Mark 6) for about 20 minutes or until puffed up and golden brown. Cool on a wire rack.

Makes 12–16

Note Some butchers will still be able to find the necessary flead for these cakes. Pure lard which has been melted down is not the same.

Mince Pies

As the name implies, mincemeat was once made from minced beef which was mixed with dried fruits and other spicy ingredients. It was a method of preserving the meat throughout the winter months, for of course there was no refrigeration, and it made a change from salting or smoking. Nowadays we only use shredded beef suet, not beef, when making our mincemeat, although the other ingredients are much the same. With the cost of dried fruit constantly rising, a higher proportion of apple can be used to make a special mincemeat to keep in the freezer. Mince Pies are traditional Christmas fare and can be made from any type of pastry – these have a special rich, melt-in-the-mouth texture.

225g (8oz) self-raising flour
pinch of salt
50g (2oz) butter
50g (2oz) block margarine
25g (1oz) lard
1 egg yolk
about 3 tablespoons milk
about 350g (12oz) mincemeat
a little egg white, lightly beaten
caster sugar for dredging

Sift the flour and salt into a bowl. Add the fats and rub in until the mixture resembles fine breadcrumbs. Add the egg yolk and sufficient milk to mix to a fairly firm dough, then knead lightly. Chill for 20 minutes if possible, wrapped in polythene or foil. Roll out the pastry on a lightly floured surface and cut into about eighteen 7·5cm (3in) plain rounds and the same number of 6cm (2½in) fluted rounds. Place the large circles in dampened or lightly greased patty tins and fill each with about 2 teaspoons mincemeat. Damp the edges of the tops and place in position, pressing the edges together. Brush the tops with egg white and dredge with sugar. Bake in a fairly hot oven (200°C/400°F, Gas Mark 6) for 20–25 minutes until golden brown. Cool on a wire rack. Serve hot or cold.

Makes about 18

Suitable to freeze for up to 4 months.

Apple Pie

A good apple pie is superb, a poor one is a misery. The pastry must be good and light, and there should be ample filling whether raw or precooked apples are used. The old manuscripts stated that puff pastry was used for fruit pies, but now shortcrust is probably used more often, especially with a double-crust pie as this one is. Traditionally, sweet pastry pies were not decorated with the pastry trimmings, but simply brushed with milk and dredged with sugar – this is definitely not always followed now. Some fruit pies are indeed highly decorated, especially those with just a top crust of a flaked pastry.

1 recipe quantity shortcrust pastry (see page 122)
675g (1½lb) cooking apples
about 100g (4oz) caster sugar

½ teaspoon mixed spice or ground cinnamon or a few whole cloves or the finely grated rind of ½ lemon or orange

milk to glaze

sugar

Roll out the pastry and use just over half to line a deep 20–21cm (8–8½in) pie plate or shallow tin. Peel, core and slice the apples, mix with the sugar and spice (or other flavouring), then spoon into the pastry case. Dampen the edge of the pastry with water. Roll out the remaining pastry for a lid, position it carefully and press the edges well together. Trim off the surplus pastry and crimp the edges. Make a small slit in the top and if liked, decorate with a few pastry leaves. Brush the pie with milk, stand it on a baking sheet and bake in a hot oven (220°C/425°F, Gas Mark 7) for 20 minutes. Reduce the temperature to moderate (180°C/350°F, Gas Mark 4) and continue for about 35 minutes or until the pastry is lightly browned. Remove from the oven and sprinkle with sugar. Serve hot or cold with cream, custard or ice cream.

Serves 4–6

Note For a single-crust pie, slice 675–900g (1½–2lb) apples into a pie dish, adding about 100g (4oz) sugar, spice if liked, and 2 tablespoons water. Cover with puff, flaky, rough puff or shortcrust pastry as for Steak and Kidney Pie (see page 149). Bake the flaked pastries in a very hot oven (230°C/450°F, Gas Mark 8) and the short-crust in a hot oven (220°C/425°F, Gas Mark 7) for 15–20 minutes, then reduce to moderate (180°C/350°F, Gas Mark 4) and continue for 30–40 minutes until the pastry is golden brown and the fruit tender.

Variations
Plums, rhubarb, blackcurrants, blackberries, etc, or a combination of fruits may also be used to fill this pie.

Mincemeat and Apple Jalousie

This recipe is borrowed from the French and becomes English with a filling of mincemeat and apples. It is a semi-open rectangular puff pastry tart with a sugar-crusted topping. The 'lid' is cut into narrow strips which open out during baking to give the traditional lines of pastry and filling. The filling can be varied widely.

½ recipe quantity puff pastry (see page 123)

225g (8oz) mincemeat

450g (1lb) cooking apples, peeled, cored and sliced

milk to glaze

a little caster sugar

Roll out the pastry and trim to a 30cm (12in) square. Cut in half and place 1 piece on a dampened baking sheet. Roll the remaining piece out further until it measures 33 × 20cm (13 × 8in), then fold it in half lengthwise and using a sharp knife, cut into the fold at 1cm (½in) intervals to within 2·5cm (1in) of the edges and ends. Spread the mincemeat over the pastry on the baking sheet, leaving a 2·5cm (1in) margin all round, then lay the sliced apples on top. Brush the pastry margin with milk, position the lid carefully on top, unfolding it to completely enclose the filling, and press the plain margins well together. Flake the edges with a sharp knife and crimp. Brush all over with milk and dredge with sugar. Bake in a hot oven (220°C/425°F, Gas Mark 7) for 25–30 minutes until well risen and golden brown. Serve hot or cold in slices with cream or ice cream.

Serves 4–6

Suitable to freeze for up to 3 months.

See diagrams overleaf.

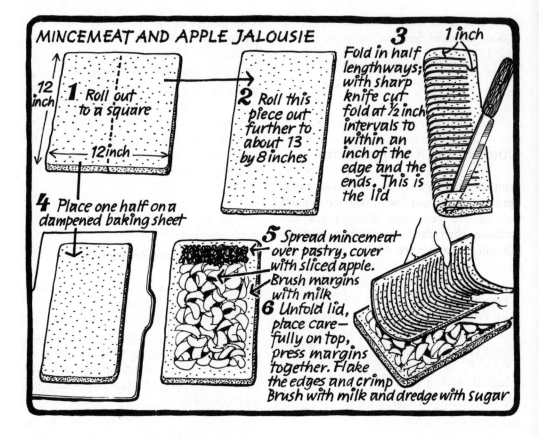

MINCEMEAT AND APPLE JALOUSIE

1 Roll out to a square

12 inch

12 inch

2 Roll this piece out further to about 13 by 8 inches

3 1 inch
Fold in half lengthways; with sharp knife cut fold at ½ inch intervals to within an inch of the edge and the ends. This is the lid

4 Place one half on a dampened baking sheet

5 Spread mincemeat over pastry, cover with sliced apple. Brush margins with milk

6 Unfold lid, place carefully on top, press margins together. Flake the edges and crimp. Brush with milk and dredge with sugar

Fruit Turnovers

Turnovers have been popular for a long time but they vary almost from family to family, for everyone has their own special method of making them. The pastry can be shortcrust, flaky, puff or rough puff and the fillings are unlimited. Apart from apple, which is probably the most often used, I like blackcurrant and apple or gooseberry turnovers. The fruit used can be raw, semi-cooked or completely cooked.

100g (4oz) blackcurrants or blackberries
1 medium-sized cooking apple, peeled, cored and chopped
about 1 level tablespoon caster sugar
¼ recipe quantity puff or flaky pastry (see pages 123, 124)

beaten egg or milk to glaze

Mix together the blackcurrants (or blackberries), apple and sugar. Roll out the pastry thinly and cut into four 15cm (6in) squares. Divide the mixture between the squares, placing it on one triangular side. Damp the edges with water, fold the plain pastry over to enclose the filling and press the edges firmly together. Press together again, flake and flute the edges, then place the triangular turnovers on greased baking sheets. Brush with egg or milk and cut 2 or 3 slits in the top of each one. Bake in a fairly hot oven (200°C/400°F, Gas Mark 6) for 20–25 minutes until golden brown. (Do not worry if they split open a little.) Cool on a wire rack. Serve hot or cold.

Makes 4

Note For other fruits use about 175–225g (6–8oz) prepared fruit.

Suitable to freeze for up to 6 months.

Cherry and Almond Flan

Another sweet pastry flan suitable for a dessert or the tea-table. Fresh or canned cherries are best, but if these are not available, then glacé cherries may be used but will give a sweeter result.

1 recipe quantity rich flan pastry (see page 123)

450g (1lb) fresh cherries (red or black), stoned and 1 level tablespoon sugar, or a 425g (15oz) can cherries, stoned and well drained, or 225g (8oz) glacé cherries, halved, washed and dried

50g (2oz) butter or margarine

50g (2oz) caster sugar

1 large egg, beaten

few drops almond essence

50g (2oz) ground almonds or 25g (1oz) each ground almonds and self-raising flour, mixed

a few flaked almonds

icing sugar (optional)

Roll out the pastry and use to line a 20cm (8in) flan ring or case. Bake blind as for Lemon Meringue Pie (see page 164) in a moderately hot oven (190°C/375°F, Gas Mark 5) for 10 minutes. Remove the beans and paper and lay the cherries over the pastry. Cream the fat and sugar together until light and fluffy, then beat in the egg and almond essence to taste. Fold in the ground almonds (or ground almond and flour mixture) and spread carefully over the cherries. Sprinkle with flaked almonds and return to a moderate oven (180°C/350°F,

Gas Mark 4) for 30–40 minutes until golden brown and firm to the touch. Serve hot or cold. The flan may be lightly dredged with icing sugar before serving.

Serves 4–6

Variations
In place of cherries, use 450g (1lb) peeled and sliced apples or 3 sliced fresh peaches or 450g (1lb) sliced fresh apricots.

Apple Strudel Slices

Strudel paste is not at all British but comes from Austria and surrounding countries. It is, however, quite delicious when made properly, with thin layers of flaking pastry mixed with apples, ground almonds and dried fruit, but is rather difficult and time-consuming to prepare. It is worth the effort when tasted!

225g (8oz) plain flour

good pinch of salt

1 egg, beaten

2 tablespoons oil

4 tablespoons warm water

40g (1½oz) currants

40g (1½oz) raisins

75g (3oz) caster sugar

½ level teaspoon ground cinnamon or mixed spice

1·1kg (2½lb) cooking apples, peeled, cored and very thinly sliced

40g (1½oz) melted butter

100g (4oz) ground almonds

a little icing sugar

Sift the flour and salt into a bowl, make a well in the centre, then add the egg, oil and water; mix to form a soft, sticky dough. Turn on to a floured surface and knead by

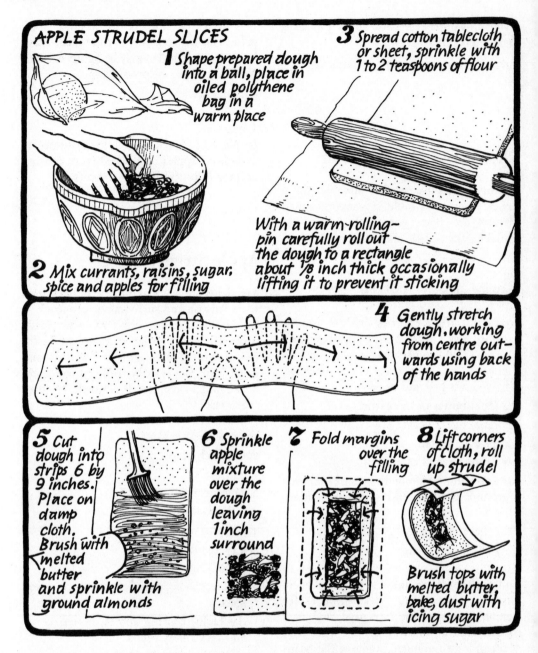

APPLE STRUDEL SLICES

1 Shape prepared dough into a ball, place in oiled polythene bag in a warm place

2 Mix currants, raisins, sugar, spice and apples for filling

3 Spread cotton tablecloth or sheet, sprinkle with 1 to 2 teaspoons of flour

With a warm rolling-pin carefully roll out the dough to a rectangle about ⅛ inch thick occasionally lifting it to prevent it sticking

4 Gently stretch dough, working from centre outwards using back of the hands

5 Cut dough into strips 6 by 9 inches. Place on damp cloth. Brush with melted butter and sprinkle with ground almonds

6 Sprinkle apple mixture over the dough leaving 1 inch surround

7 Fold margins over the filling

8 Lift corners of cloth, roll up strudel

Brush tops with melted butter, bake, dust with icing sugar

hand for about 15 minutes, or in a large electric mixer fitted with a dough hook for about 5 minutes, until smooth and even. Shape into a ball, place in an oiled polythene bag and leave to rest in a warm place for about an hour. Combine the currants, raisins, sugar, spice and apples for the filling. Spread a clean old cotton tablecloth or sheet on the table and sprinkle it with 1–2 tablespoons flour. Place the dough in the centre and, using a warmed rolling pin, roll it out carefully to a rectangle about 0·25cm (⅛in) thick, lifting it up occasionally to prevent it sticking. Now gently stretch the

PANJOTTERY

1 Roll out ⅔ of the pastry to line shallow 8 inch square tin (or 8 inch sandwich tin) Mix all the ingredients thoroughly and place in tin. Press down well and spread evenly

2 Roll remaining ⅓ of pastry and cut into 10-12 long narrow strips

3 Arrange strips in a lattice over the filling; damp edges to stick to pastry edge. Trim, crimp, brush with beaten egg

dough, using the backs of the hands underneath it and working from the centre outwards, until it is thin enough to read through! Take care not to tear it. Leave to rest for 15 minutes. Cut the dough into strips 15×23cm (6×9in), then place each piece on a damp cloth, brush with melted butter and sprinkle evenly with ground almonds. Sprinkle the apple mixtuie over the dough, leaving a 2·5cm (1in) plain margin all round. Fold these margins over the filling, then lift the corners of the cloth carefully and roll up the strudel, beginning at a narrow end and using the cloth to help. Place on greased baking sheets, brush the tops with melted butter and bake in a moderately hot oven (190°C/375°F, Gas Mark 5) for about 30 minutes or until golden brown. Dust with icing sugar and serve warm or cold with cream.

Makes 8-10

Panjottery

A Scottish friend of mine introduced me to this delicious concoction of dried fruits, apples and lemon baked in a lattice pastry case, after telling me it had been in his family for as long as he could remembei. It is equally good served hot or cold as a pudding or cut into slices for the tea-table.

1 recipe quantity shortcrust pastry (see page 122)

175g (6oz) sultanas

50g (2oz) currants

50g (2oz) mixed peel

50g (2oz) soft brown sugar

grated rind of 1 lemon

50g (2oz) glacé cherries, chopped (optional)

350-450g (¾-1lb) cooking apples, peeled, cored and thinly sliced

beaten egg to glaze

Roll out two-thirds of the pastry and use to line a shallow tin about 20cm (8in) square or a deep, round 20cm (8in) sandwich tin. Mix all the other ingredients together thoroughly and place in the pastry case, pressing down well and evenly. Roll out the remaining pastry and cut into 10–12 narrow strips which are long enough to lay over the top of the tin. Arrange these strips in a lattice pattern over the filling, dampening the ends with water and sticking them to the pastry edge. Trim the edges and crimp all round carefully. Brush with beaten egg and bake in a hot oven (220°C/425F, Gas Mark 7) for 15 minutes, reduce the temperature to moderate (180°C/350°F, Gas Mark 4) and continue for 25–30 minutes. Serve hot or cold, cut into squares or slices, on its own or with cream or custard.

Serves 6

Suitable to freeze for up to 4 months.

Rhubarb and Apple Cobbler

A 'cobbler' or scone topping to both sweet and savoury dishes appears to be a modern way of making an attractive and tasty pie. Sugar and spices can be added to complement the fruit used, whilst savoury cobblers can be flavoured with cheese, herbs, onion, etc. The dough is cut into rounds which are placed in an overlapping circle around the edge of the dish, leaving the centre uncovered – a change from a conventional pie crust.

450g (1lb) rhubarb, trimmed
225g (8oz) cooking apples
6–8 tablespoons water
sugar to taste

Scone Topping
150g (6oz) self-raising flour

40g (1½oz) butter or margarine
40g (1½oz) caster or soft brown sugar
about 5–6 tablespoons milk
1 level tablespoon demerara sugar (optional)

Cut the rhubarb into 2·5cm (1in) lengths. Peel, core and slice the apples and put them into a saucepan with the rhubarb and 6 tablespoons water. Bring to the boil, cover and simmer for about 5 minutes until beginning to soften, adding a little more water if too dry. Add sugar to taste and pour into an ovenproof dish so it is not more than two-thirds full. For the topping, sift the flour into a bowl, rub in the fat, then stir in the sugar. Add sufficient milk to mix to a fairly soft dough. On a floured surface, flatten out to 1cm (½in) thick and cut into 4cm (1½in) rounds – plain or fluted. Arrange in an overlapping circle around the edge of the dish over the fruit, leaving the centre uncovered. Brush the scones with milk, sprinkle with demerara sugar and bake in a fairly hot oven (200°C/400°F, Gas Mark 6) for about 30 minutes or until well risen and golden brown. Serve hot.

Serves 4–6

Note Any fruit or combination of fruits can be used for the base of a cobbler but it is better to lightly stew the fruit first.

Coventry Godcakes

These are a cross between the Eccles or Banbury Cake and a Mince Pie, which used to have a solid fruit filling similar to today's mincemeat. They are made into triangles and were said to have been presented to godchildren by their godparents as a gift on New Year's Day.

½ recipe quantity puff or flaky pastry (see pages 123, 124)

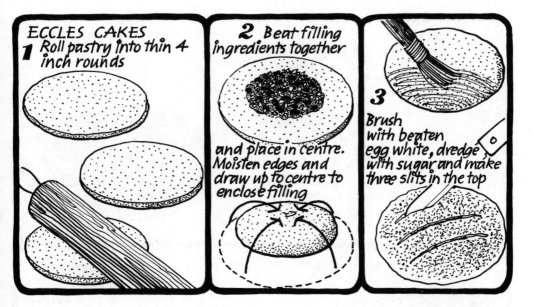

1 ECCLES CAKES Roll pastry into thin 4 inch rounds

2 Beat filling ingredients together and place in centre. Moisten edges and draw up to centre to enclose filling

3 Brush with beaten egg white, dredge with sugar and make three slits in the top

about 450g (1lb) mincemeat
1 egg white, lightly whisked
caster sugar for dredging

Roll out the pastry fairly thinly and cut it into triangles with a base of about 20cm (8in). Place a good spoonful of mincemeat on 1 side of the pastry, damp the edges with water and fold over the other side to enclose the filling and make a smaller triangle. Press the edges firmly together and flatten the triangle a little. Place on a lightly greased baking sheet, brush with egg white and dredge with caster sugar. Cut 2 or 3 small slits in the top and bake in a hot oven (220°C/425°F, Gas Mark 7) for about 20 minutes or until golden brown. Serve warm or cold.

Makes about 12

Eccles Cakes

The Eccles and Banbury Cakes we know today are very similar, both having a filling of spiced dried fruit in a puff pastry envelope which is rolled out thinly so the fruit just shows through. Eccles Cakes are traditionally round whilst Banbury Cakes are oval. They were known as far back as the eighteenth century, although they were then made with a yeast dough and more often baked as a large cake similar to a Black Bun. It is not known exactly when or why they became individual cakes or why the outer casing changed to flaky pastry. However, they were very light and flaky with a sugar crust and were sometimes sold by a street seller who wrapped them in a cloth in a wicker basket to keep them warm and fresh.

¼ quantity puff or flaky pastry recipe (see pages 123, 124)
beaten egg white
caster sugar

Filling
25g (1oz) butter, softened
25g (1oz) soft brown sugar
25g (1oz) mixed peel
50g (2oz) currants
¼–½ level teaspoon mixed spice

BLACK BUN

Fruits, peel, almonds, sugar

1 Line 8 inch cake tin with pastry. For the filling; sift flour, spices, cream of tartar and soda. Mix evenly through the fruit. Add egg, whisky and sufficient milk

2 Pack all together into pastry case

3 Roll out remaining pastry to make a lid. Brush edges with beaten egg and position on fruit. Trim edges and crimp

4 Brush with the beaten egg, make 6 to 8 holes right through the cake with a skewer, prick all over with a fork and then reglaze

Roll out the pastry thinly and cut into 10cm (4in) plain rounds. Beat all the filling ingredients together, then place a spoonful in the centre of each pastry round. Moisten the edges of the rounds with water and draw them up to meet in the centre. Press well together to completely enclose the filling. Turn over so that the join is underneath and roll out carefully until the currants just show through the pastry, to a circle about 1cm ($\frac{1}{3}$in) thick. Place on greased baking sheets and stand them in a cool place for 10 minutes. Brush each cake with beaten egg white, dredge with sugar and then make 3 slits in the top. Bake in a very hot oven (230°C/450°F, Gas Mark 8) for about 15 minutes or until golden brown and crisp.

Cool on a wire rack.

Makes 8–10

Suitable to freeze for up to 2 months.

Black Bun

This pastry-covered fruit cake is baked well in advance to serve at Hogmanay in Scotland to the 'first footer' who calls to wish the family a Happy New Year. It goes particularly well with a glass of sherry or port. Often the cake is kept for 6 months before cutting as it mellows and matures slowly. Although shortcrust pastry is stated here, sometimes a much plainer pastry is used.

1 recipe quantity shortcrust pastry (see page 122)

450g (1lb) currants

450g (1lb) raisins

50g (2oz) chopped mixed peel

100g (4oz) blanched almonds, chopped

100g (4oz) soft brown sugar

200g (8oz) plain flour

1 level teaspoon ground cinnamon

1 level teaspoon ground ginger

1 level teaspoon ground allspice

1 level teaspoon cream of tartar

1 level teaspoon bicarbonate of soda

1 egg, beaten

150ml ($\frac{1}{4}$pt) whisky, brandy or sherry

about 4 tablespoons milk

beaten egg to glaze

Grease a 20cm (8in) round cake tin and line the base with greased greaseproof paper. Roll out two-thirds of the pastry to a circle about 35cm (14in) in diameter and use to line the tin carefully. For the filling, mix together the fruits, peel, almonds and sugar in a bowl. Sift the flour with the spices, cream of tartar and soda, and mix evenly through the fruit. Add the egg, whisky, brandy or sherry and sufficient milk to just moisten the mixture and then carefully pack it into the pastry case. Roll out the remaining pastry to make a lid, brush the edges with beaten egg and position over the fruit, pressing it down evenly. Trim edges and crimp lightly. Brush with beaten egg and then make 6–8 holes right through the cake to the base, using a skewer; prick all over the lid with a fork. Glaze again and bake in a moderate oven (180°C/350°F, Gas Mark 4) for 2$\frac{1}{2}$–3 hours, covering the top with foil or double greaseproof paper when sufficiently brown. Cool in the tin for at least 30 minutes before turning on to a wire rack. Store in an airtight container or a tin, or wrap in foil and store in a cool place.

CHAPTER 9

What Could Go Wrong?

Sometimes, even though you feel you have followed a recipe correctly, the result is not quite what you had hoped for. It may be that something small has been forgotten or possibly that metric and imperial measures have been mixed – remember to use either one or the other, never both. But if this is not so, then here the causes of some common faults are identified.

Yeasted Doughs

1. *Insufficient volume and a pale crust* Flour used too soft or self-raising; try a strong bread flour. Dough either too wet or too dry. Not enough salt or yeast, or stale yeast. Put to rise in too warm a place or for too long. Not kneaded sufficiently.
2. *Uneven texture and/or holes* Too much liquid or salt. Insufficient or too much proving. Insufficient kneading after first rise. Dough put to rise uncovered, causing a skin to form and streak in the dough when it is kneaded for the second time.
3. *Coarse-textured crumb* Flour used not strong enough. Insufficient salt. Too much liquid. Insufficient or too much proving. Dough left uncovered during rising.
4. *Close texture* Insufficient or stale yeast. Too much salt. Too much or too little water. Insufficient kneading. Put to rise in too warm a place.
5. *Cracked crust* Tin too small or too shallow. Proving too short.
6. *Wrinkled top* Proving too long. Dough not covered during rising.
7. *Bread stales quickly and crumbles* Too much yeast. Put to rise in too warm a place, causing much too speedy a rise. Flour not strong enough.

Pastries

Shortcrust Pastry

1. *Hard and tough* Not enough fat or rubbing in. Too much water. Too much

handling. Cooked too long or oven too cool.
2. *Soft and crumbly* Not enough liquid. Too much fat. Overmixing.
3. *Soggy* Too much water in the pastry or the filling. Oven too cool. Not cooked sufficiently.
4. *Shrunk* Pastry over-stretched during rolling or shaping process.

Flaky, Puff and Rough Puff Pastry

1. *Hard and tough* Same possible causes as with shortcrust. Or too much flour used during rolling out. Pastry not kept cool during rolling.
2. *Hard outside, soft inside* Oven too hot or position in oven too high. Insufficient cooking.
3. *Uneven rise* Fat unevenly distributed. Rolling and folding uneven and sides and corners not kept straight and square during rolling. Edges not cut with a sharp knife before use.
4. *Insufficiently flaky* Fat used too warm. Rolled out too heavily. Insufficient chilling between rolling.
5. *Soggy* Too short a baking time or oven too cool.
6. *Shrunk* Rolled too harshly, causing over-stretching. Insufficient chilling.

Choux Pastry

1. *Cracked surface* Oven too hot.
2. *Soft or soggy* Insufficient beating of mixture or cooling before adding eggs. Oven too cool or insufficient baking.
3. *Uncooked* Usually incorrect proportions or too little or too much egg added.

Hot Water Crust Pastry

1. *Difficult to mould or handle* Too little fat or water. Water not boiling. Too much water or flour. Pastry cooled too much before moulding.
2. *Cracked surface* Too little water or water too cool. Insufficient kneading.
3. *Hard and tough* Too little water or too much handling.

Suet Crust Pastry

1. *Lumpy pieces of suet in pastry* Suet too coarse – grate very finely or use a commercially shredded suet.
2. *Tough* Overhandled or cooked too quickly.
3. *Soggy* Water not kept boiling during cooking process. Pastry not covered tightly enough to prevent water getting in.

Index

A

ascorbic acid *see* vitamins: C

B

bannocks *see* scones
bread, 7, 8, 13, 16, 21–64
  baking, 16, 23
  freezing, 16; *see also* individual recipes
  glazing, 16, 23
  shaping, 23
    batch tin, 26
    bloomer, 25
    cob, 24
    coburg, 23–4
    college, 24–5
    cottage, 25
    crescent, 26
    crinkled, 27
    farmhouse, 26–7
    jointed baton, 27
    loaves and fishes loaf, 61
    London bloomer *see* bloomer
    pan coburg *see* coburg
    plait, 25–6
    porcupine *see* college
    pulled, 52
    ribbed *see* crinkled
    split tin, 26
    wheatsheaf loaf, 61
  recipes:
    basic white bread, 22–3
    bran bread, 58
    brown country bread, 32–3
    crown loaf, 30–1
    farmhouse brown bread, 30
    flowerpot bread, 28–9
    granary bread, 45
    harvest bread, 60
    milk bread, 31–2
    oatmeal twists, 42
    quick rye bread, 49
    rice bread, 54–5
    rye bread, 45–6
    rye crispbread, 49
    short-time enriched white bread, 34
    short-time white bread, 33–4
    short-time wholemeal bread, 34
    soda bread, 105–6
      coarse brown soda bread, 106
      white soda bread, 106
    Vienna loaves, 57

wholemeal bread, 27, 30
wholewheat bread, 27
see also savoury breads, teabreads
buns, 13, 67
  recipes:
    Banbury cakes *see* Eccles cakes
    Bath buns, 90–1
    Chelsea buns, 76–7
    Cornish splits, 75
    Coventry godcakes, 176–7
    cream buns, 165
    Devonshire splits *see* Cornish splits
    doughnuts, 82–4
      cream, 84
      ring, 84
    Easter buns *see* hot cross buns
    Eccles cakes, 177–8
    fruit finger buns, 77–8
    Good Friday buns *see* hot cross buns
    hot cross buns, 80
    London buns, 75–6
    saffron buns, 82
    Sussex plum heavies, 79
    teacakes, 72–4
      ginger teacakes, 73
      lemon teacakes, 73
      nutty teacakes, 73
      orange teacakes, 73
      plain teacakes, 73
      Sally Lunn, 73–4
      Yorkshire teacakes, 72
    'Thunder and Lightning' *see* Cornish splits
    Wigs, 81–2

C

cakes,
  recipes:
    black bun, 178–9
    dough cake, 79
    lardy cake, 78–9
    parkin, 112
    saffron cake, 82
    singing hinny *see* scones: singing hinny
crumpets, 67, 70–1

D

Danish pastries *see* yeasted pastries
dough, 15–17
  baking, 16